LINCOLN'S DAUGHTERS OF MERCY

Marjorie Barstow Greenbie

LINCOLN'S
DAUGHTERS
OF MERCY

G·P·PUTNAM'S SONS
NEW YORK

Copyright, 1944,

by Marjorie Barstow Greenbie

CONTENTS

PREFACE

This is the story of the United States Sanitary Commission, the great relief organization of the Civil War, which was the ancestor of the American Red Cross. From it are derived most of our techniques for mitigating the horrors of war and binding up the wounds of battle. The U.S.O., the American Women's Voluntary Services, the United Seamen's Services, and most other War Relief agencies present modern variations of its over-all structure and specific ministrations. The WACS, the WAVES, the SPARS, and other women's military services find in it the first great example of the enlistment of women for war. And, in the present conflict, the armies of all civilized nations pattern their ambulance and hospital services, and their arrangements for the welfare and recreation of the armed services, after the models first set by the United States Sanitary Commission.

The story has many heroines, and some heroes. All of them deserve to be remembered now, with gratitude, both on the battle front and the home front. On the battle front, the life of the soldier would be much less tolerable than it is today, if it were not for the many arrangements for the care and comfort of men under arms, first worked out by the Sanitary Commission for the Union Army.

The Union Army was the first great popular army of the modern type. It was the first army to include more than a million men under a single national command, and the first large army composed almost entirely of men who had been civilians before the outbreak of war. Small volunteer armies have sprung up and fought for the people's rights, under rude conditions, since the beginning of history. But never before had there been such enormous masses of men to be conditioned and trained quickly for

vii

military operations that, compared with anything that had preceded them, were highly mechanized.

The way this army was assembled and organized explains to the soldier many of the routines he is required to follow today. These routines may sometimes seem rather tiresome. But when a man realizes what military life was like before the heroines of this book first taught the army to keep house, he may feel reconciled even to Kitchen Police.

To the home front the story of the Sanitary Commission demonstrates the kind of spirit, and the kind of citizen co-operation that not only wins a war but keeps it won. The victors in the American Civil War did what the victors in the First World War never did. They kept their victory after they got it. During the long struggle the northern states attained such interior social organization, such unity and articulateness in formulating the ideals for which they were fighting, that their triumphant industrial democracy maintained its supremacy, without serious challenge, through all the years that followed.

This achievement, which the victors in the present war have yet to equal, was due largely to the ingenuity and heroic self-devotion of the home front behind the army. The behavior of these women of the Civil War shows what a genuine democracy is. They were members of a society which, though crude and primitive in many respects, was vital in all its parts. The individual person had enterprise and courage. And in the family and the neighborhood there was a habit of unselfishness heartening to record. Here is the ultimate and unfailing source of democracy, both political and social, in the warm, just, and merciful heart of the average citizen and his wife. And that is something for us to study and remember at this time, for never will justice and mercy and simple ingenuity in good works be more needed than in the days that lie just ahead in this tormented world.

The documentation for this story is enormous, much of it in the form of letters or personal reports by women who liked to write. Though many passages in the book read like fiction, I have taken no liberties in the way of putting words into people's mouths or thoughts into their heads. Words quoted as conversation are either in the record or are only direct discourse for material given in indirect discourse in the sources.

After the publication of the condensation of this book in

Reader's Digest (August, 1943), several persons wrote me protesting because my reference to the founding of the International Red Cross seemed to differ from the story they had learned in Red Cross classes. Others made similar protests to the *Reader's Digest*. The *Digest* story was a condensation, and, as such, omitted some details that appear in the book. I hope that that those who were troubled by the brief magazine story will feel better when they read the whole book. For there is nothing in my story that contradicts what is taught by the Red Cross. There is, however, a great deal that supplements it. It was partly because I felt that the official Red Cross history was incomplete that I wanted to write this book.

One or two people jumped to the hasty conclusion that I was somehow detracting from the great and well-earned glory of Henri Dunant, the founder of the International Red Cross, and they rather belligerently challenged me to show my sources. This I have done at the end of this volume. As for the relation between Henri Dunant's Committee in Geneva and the United States Sanitary Commission, no one needs to quarrel about that, because the magnanimous leaders of each group themselves worked together in perfect harmony. About the time that Henri Dunant published his *Souvenir de Solférino,* which all Red Cross workers are taught to regard as the beginning of their great endeavor, the United States Sanitary Commission appointed a European representative, Mr. Charles Bowles. One of his duties was to confer with Henri Dunant's Committee, which was just forming, and to give it the advantages of the American experience in initiating, for the first time in history, general care of the wounded, on an adequate scale, under skilled professional auspices, and with the support of the military authorities. The reports of Mr. Bowles on the progress of the Committee in Geneva were published from time to time in the *Bulletin of the United States Sanitary Commission* which may be found in most large libraries. No honest telling of the great story of the United States Sanitary Commission and of the International Red Cross and the American Red Cross diminishes the stature of anyone whom the Red Cross worker is taught to revere. There is, on this field of battle, more than enough glory to go around.

The protests, however, were very few compared with the many letters from generous persons who offered me interesting material from family archives. Many of these letters made me feel rather melancholy because they reminded me again that the heroes and heroines of the Sanitary Commission were so numerous, and their work so many-sided, that it is impossible to do justice to them all. I want particularly to say to Mrs. Katherine Baren of Dayton, Ohio, that I wish I could have given some pages to her grandmother, Mrs. E. L. Miller, for whom the E. L. Miller Home For Nurses in Dayton is named. No doubt many in Dayton remember the military funeral of queenly little "Major Miller," in 1914. And I want to tell Lieutenant Charles Van Ravenswaay (U.S. N.R.) I quite agree with him that the Western Sanitary Commission of St. Louis deserved a place in the book. Since he has done so much research on this subject, he will have to write that story himself, if ever he gets off his rolling ship. To Mrs. Ethelwyn Cleveland Rice of Larchmont, New York, I should like to say that I wish I had been able to speak particularly of her grandmother, Dr. Emeline Horton Cleveland, who later became the first resident woman physician of the Woman's Hospital of Philadelphia, and who was one of the sanitary corps sent to the battlefield of Gettysburg.

And to all others who wrote me rich and interesting letters I wish to say "thank you." It is a great satisfaction to hear a chorus of living voices thus greeting the revival of this old, heroic story.

LINCOLN'S DAUGHTERS OF MERCY

1.   *Mrs. Anderson's Re-enforcement*

All that rainy Saturday, April 13, 1861, old Mr. Rice, from his sickbed in his comfortable Boston home, kept sending his daughter, Mary, down into the street to get the telegraph news chalked up hourly on the bulletin board near the Old North Church. When she returned, he would scan her firm, comely face, and ask tensely, "Is our flag still there?"

"Yes, Father," she would answer quietly.

"Thank God," he would say, falling back on his pillow.

Since two o'clock of the previous afternoon, volunteers from the six Southern states that had recently seceded had been trying to shoot down the flag of the United States flying above Fort Sumter, at the entrance to the harbor of Charleston, South Carolina. Gentlemen in Charleston looked on the performance as a sort of sporting event, and were betting on the time it would take to bring the flag down. Ladies were watching from the shore, laughing and cheering every time there was a close shot, as if this were all a gigantic game of target practice.

The terrible sport these Southerners were so enjoying was recorded, play by play, on telegraph boards set up, at intervals, in most towns and cities of the North. Surging around these boards, the people of the North could see the firing on the flag in imagination, almost as vividly as if it were taking place before their very eyes. So intense was the excitement that almost every family had a watcher on the streets, tuned to the telegraph board for the latest flash.

In the intervals between news reports, Mary, as a daughter at the bedside of a sick father, had certain routines to go through. In those days there were no trained nurses. But under the influence of a great and glamorous Englishwoman, Miss Florence Nightingale, intelligent housewives were perfecting a system of home nursing. This they worked out by fusing whatever they were able to learn from the doctor or from medical books with their own notions of dainty and efficient housekeeping.

Mary, for example, had learned from Miss Nightingale that the first requisite in the care of the sick is a "moving current of fresh air," so managed that a direct draft does not strike the patient. So, whenever she came in from outside, she would critically sniff the atmosphere of the sickroom. Always it seemed a mite less fresh than the odor of spring rain on the small, neat dooryard gardens outside, all up and down the street. While her father kept pressing her for more and more details about Fort Sumter, she was setting a screen to shield him from sudden light and wind. Then she drew back the heavy curtains which swathed the windows, and lifted the sash.

Next to fresh air, Mary knew that perfect cleanliness was necessary in the care of the sick. Hence while she was airing the room, she also cast a housewifely eye on all the details of its thick and padded comfort. She adjusted the immaculate tidies on the backs and arms of the easy chairs. She inspected the small scatter-rugs which covered the carpet at all points of heavy traffic, and spirited them outside to be cleaned if there was a suspicion of mud or dust on them. And she scrutinized the washbowl and huge white pitcher on the washstand, and the rows and rows of hemstitched towels above it. Of prophylaxis in the modern sense she knew nothing. But she was well acquainted with the virtues of elbow grease.

Not only must the patient be kept clean. He must also be kept warm and tranquil. After she had aired the room, Mary carefully mended the fire. Then she served notice on her father that there was to be no more excited discussion of Fort Sumter by seating herself before the fire, with her back to him.

While she was drying out the velveteen hem of her wide and fashionable hoop-skirt, which no "waterproof" could quite protect from damage on a rainy day, she became visibly absorbed in correcting a small sheaf of manuscript with a pencil. This manuscript was a kind of "Log" she had been keeping of her hourly voyage through mud and rain and impassioned crowds to the corner where the telegraph board stood. She intended to send it to her husband, Doctor Daniel Parker Livermore, to be published in the *New Covenant* of Chicago, Illinois, of which he was the owner and

4

editor. The *New Covenant* was a prosperous weekly paper, widely read in the Northwest.

For a time there was no sound in that comfortable upper room, except the occasional faint thud or clink of the coals in the grate, collapsing in ash. Then wave after wave of shouting in the streets below began to break against the tranquillity Mary had so carefully created. Mr. Rice raised himself on one elbow and listened intently. "Hear that, Mary?" he said. "There's another dispatch. Please, be a good girl, and go and see."

Mary laid down her pencil, and donned her "waterproof" and her "gumshoes," and sallied forth once more into the rain.

This, or something like it, had been happening regularly every hour since two o'clock of the previous day, when the news of the firing on Fort Sumter had first appeared on the telegraph board.

2

Mary A. Livermore, born Mary Ashton Rice, was at that time only an attractive housewife with some talent for writing. Today, if you look up her name in the card catalogue of a public library, you will very likely come upon a card which refers to her as one of the "women who have ennobled life." She was to ennoble life, in the bitter days that following the firing on the flag at Sumter, by taking to the battlefield and the devastated areas the meticulous housewifery that women like her had been developing for the sick and helpless in their own homes. In this way, amid the horrors and misery of a terrible war, Mary A. Livermore and thousands of other housewives initiated the two great professions of trained nursing and of social service. They provided fighting men with such unheard-of and blessed institutions as mobile canteens, ambulances, and hospital ships. And they invented the many services now performed by the home service agents, the Gray Ladies, the recreation leaders, the field agents, and the nurses of the Red Cross.

In her later years, when all these innovations had become part of the very fabric of modern society, a publisher persuaded Mary Livermore to write her own story of the war. This story she began by describing her vigil by the bedside of her sick father, and her hourly descent into the streets for the latest news of Fort Sumter. There seems no better way of understanding what Mary and other women were finally to accomplish than to begin where she began, and to review the news that was coming over the telegraph wires to hundreds of thousands of anxious households.

3

The shooting at Fort Sumter was the climax of a drama that had opened the day after Christmas, 1860. At that time the governors of the six Southern states that seceded after the election of Lincoln seized the forts of the United States within their borders, in the name of a new collective government headed by Senator Jefferson Davis of Mississippi. Some Federal forts were surrendered without serious resistance because President Buchanan, who was still in power in Washington, was not willing to guarantee re-enforcements. Pending the inauguration of President Lincoln, it was deemed best to yield a little to these rebellious states, rather than to start a conflict whose end no man could foresee.

This was the official opinion. But there was another, a popular opinion, gradually crystallizing in the crowds who waited for the telegraph news. It was now sixteen years since news had first been reported to a nation-wide audience by telegraph. The discovery of a method of reaching everyone at the same time, at the moment when vital news was in the making, introduced a great change in the workings of democracy. It meant that thenceforth popular opinion was to be molded less by political leaders than by enterprising newsgatherers who were always on the lookout for a striking situation or a human interest story. By 1861 reporters had already begun that momentous process of dramatizing the People's story to itself, from hour to hour, which is the distinctive feature of the modern democracy. To this end they were making the most of the behavior of one officer in the United States army and of his wife.

This officer was Major Robert Anderson, in command of the forts in Charleston Harbor. Major Anderson was a tall, grave, smooth-shaven Kentuckian who had married Elizabeth Clinch, daughter of General D. L. Clinch of Georgia, and had owned a plantation and slaves. Through his own connections, and those of his wife, Major Anderson was socially allied to many of the political and military leaders of the newly formed Confederate

6

States of America, and on the best visiting terms with them. His personal opinion was that secession was inevitable. All the Federal Union could do was to hope, by patience and conciliation, to draw these states back into the national fold at some future date. If his own state of Kentucky should secede, he intended to ask his government for permission to resign, and to go to Europe. In this way he hoped to avoid the necessity of fighting either his own state or that great union of states which he still called his country.

Nevertheless, when Major Anderson was called on to surrender the forts in Charleston Harbor, he figured that, as an officer in the United States army, he could not haul down the flag of his country on the mere say-so of Jefferson Davis. The forts under his command were on territory properly and legally leased by the Federal government from the state of South Carolina. They had been built up and equipped by the Federal government, with money paid in taxes by all the people of the United States, in order to protect the people of Charleston from an outside invader. If the Southern authorities wanted to change the lease, they'd have to talk to the government of the United States. But so far as he, as an officer of the United States Army was concerned, he didn't see what he could do but to stay where he had been stationed and to keep his flag flying.

While Major Anderson was coming to this conclusion, he was at Fort Moultrie, on Sullivan's Island in Charleston Harbor. His garrison consisted of ten officers, fifteen musicians, and fifty-five artillerists. Near the entrance to the harbor, rising sheer out of the water, on an artificial island, was a magnificent new fort —Fort Sumter. It was still unfinished, and had no garrison. There were only some workmen there. During a scrupulously polite exchange of notes between Anderson and his ex-friends of the seceded state of South Carolina, it occurred to Anderson that these courteous South Carolinians were not going to disturb him at Fort Moultrie. They were going to seize Sumter, and raise the new flag of the Confederacy over its ramparts. With their banner flying high, at the entrance to the harbor, they could command his position at Moultrie with their guns, and impudently out-brave his flag. So on the night of December 26, Anderson and his men quietly spiked the guns at Moultrie, and burned the installations there. Then, in three small boats, they moved over to Fort Sumter.

At noon the next day, in the face of the seceded population

7

of Charleston, Major Anderson solemnly raised the flag of the United States over Sumter. It was in his mind a symbolic and religious act, and as such he and his garrison performed it. For holding in his hand the cord of the flag, Major Anderson knelt with his chaplain, and all his garrison knelt with him. The chaplain prayed for the support of God in what they were about to do, and for mercy in Heaven if they should have to give their lives for it. "Amen," said all the kneeling men. With these words, the flag mounted and flew out in the face of Charleston, announcing that here at Sumter were officers and soldiers of the United States who intended to do their duty.

When this news was carried to the North by telegraph, there was a cheer which began around the bulletin boards of Boston and continued in a steady roar across the country till it lost itself somewhere in the empty spaces beyond Nebraska. The legislature of Nebraska sent Anderson a telegram of commendation. Massachusetts mustered its best regiment, the Massachusetts Sixth, and New York its famous Seventh regiment, recruited among the rich and the great, provided with handsome uniforms, the best arms, and a regimental band that was a whole show in itself. These military ornaments to two great states were put into training, that they might be ready to go and fight with Anderson at a moment's notice. But President Buchanan's government in Washington was still unwilling to make any move that might precipitate civil war.

Jefferson Davis gave the job of handling Anderson and his flag to Major Beauregard, who had resigned his position as Superintendent of West Point to secede with his own state, Louisiana. Pierre Beauregard was a talented army engineer—a lively, inventive, gallant little French creole from Louisiana. He forthwith put his engineering talents to work to fix Anderson. He rebuilt the fortifications on Fort Moultrie which Anderson had burned and destroyed, and set up there some new batteries masked from view by shrubs and plantings. He stationed companies of the troops the Confederacy was rapidly recruiting on the various points of land around Sumter. And then he produced his masterpiece. This was a "floating battery"—a large, strong raft, one hundred feet long and twenty-five feet wide on which, behind armor made of railroad ties and boiler plate, were mounted four guns so powerful that it took sixty men to man them properly. This contraption

8

was towed into position right off Sumter, and its guns turned on Anderson there. Anderson was now surrounded and besieged. Beauregard dared any one to send him re-enforcements!

Only one person in the North took that dare. This was Anderson's wife, Elizabeth. When news of her husband's situation began to come in by telegraph, Mrs. Anderson was very ill, in New York City. Lying on her sickbed, she could hear the crowds surging up and down the streets, calling for re-enforcements to be sent to Anderson. No doubt Mrs. Anderson's first reaction was a purely wifely impulse to go to her husband, or at least to make sure that, in a position of isolation and danger, he had as much comfort and help as possible. But under the stress of the clamor for re-enforcements, her personal concern began to merge with the general sense of public obligation. She understood that her husband was maintaining a token occupation of Federal property in the South until a genuine occupation of all the threatened points could be effected. Why couldn't she send him a token re-enforcement pending the dispatch of adequate military aid?

This was the question Mrs. Anderson was turning over in her mind as she tossed on her bed. Suddenly she remembered a former military companion of her husband—Peter Hart. Hart had been Anderson's sergeant in the Mexican war, and had been so faithful and competent that Anderson was very devoted to him. Mrs. Anderson had an idea! If only she could find Hart, she would take him to her husband, to act as his personal aide in this emergency. She felt sure that her own social influence and personal connections in Charleston would enable her to take Hart through the Confederate lines.

The last time Mrs. Anderson had seen Hart had been seven years ago. At that time he had been living in New York City. If only he were there still! She sent for the City directory, and, propping herself up in bed, she looked up the name Hart. Alas! Every other citizen of New York City seemed to be named Hart. There were Harts and Harts and Harts. Which of them, if any, was the family of their Peter? She got up and dressed, against the protests of her physician, who said that she would kill herself, and ordered a cab, and proceeded to drive from door to door calling on every Hart listed in the directory. After a day and a half she actually located Peter, and told him what she wanted.

The next day Peter and Mrs. Hart got on the train, and traveling continually, arrived at Charleston in forty-eight hours. During the last stage of the journey the train was crowded with Confederate recruits hastening to join the forces around Sumter, spitting tobacco juice, and loudly boasting of what they were going to do to Anderson. Most of them thought hanging would be too good for a man that had dared to defy the sovereign power of the state of South Carolina.

In Charleston Mrs. Anderson easily obtained an interview with Governor Pickens, because the governor was an old friend of her father's, and she had herself known him from childhood. In her conversation with him she seems to have put on a nice womanly act, in the best Southern style. She said that she was so worried about Bob that she just couldn't stand it. She had got right up out of her sickbed and had come down to see how he was. Oh no, she hadn't come alone. She had brought Peter Hart who was an old friend and acted as a sort of servant, and was such a help. She didn't know what she would do without Peter, or what Bob would do either. Bob was so devoted to him. If only Peter could stay out there on Sumter with her husband, and look after him personally, and send her word how Bob was—because Bob was not young—he was fifty-six—and he'd never tell her anything himself to worry her—if only she could have Peter out there with Bob, she would feel so much better about it all.

"My dear girl," said Governor Pickens kindly, "I will gladly send you out under an escort to see your husband for a few minutes. But I can't send this man. It is out of the question."

"But why?" protested Mrs. Anderson. "You'd let him have a black body-servant, I am sure you would if I asked. And if we'd rather do the way the Yankees do, and have a white man to look after him, who is a sort of personal friend? I'm so worried, so far from him, alone up there in the North with the children."

"But the man is a trained soldier," said Governor Pickens. "I cannot let the garrison out there be increased by one man able to bear arms."

"The idea!" said Mrs. Anderson. "You have thousands mobilized, and do you mean to say that you're afraid several thousand soldiers of the great and sovereign nation of South Carolina can't whip eighty Yankees—and fifteen of them musicians—if you add one man to them and make them eighty-one?"

Finally because she was her father's daughter, and because

10

she was behaving just the way a man liked to see a Georgia girl behave, even if her husband was on the wrong side, Governor Pickens yielded. He said he would let her take Hart out to Sumter and leave him there if Major Anderson would give his word of honor not to employ him as a soldier.

This word of honor was duly negotiatied, and Governor Pickens had Mrs. Anderson and Hart rowed out to the fort. As they passed through the harbor, Mrs. Anderson looked on boats and barges flying new standards and strange flags, but there was no sign anywhere of the Stars and Stripes until she came to Sumter. There over its ramparts, alone in all that concourse of new banners, was the old red, white, and blue. When she raised her eyes, and saw it there, flying out so bravely, she burst into tears. "Oh Bob," she said, falling on her husband's shoulder at the sally port, "I c-can't help crying to see it up there—the dear banner of our country."

"My glorious wife!" he said, folding her in his arms.

This is the story and these are the very words that were reported by telegraph and enlarged on in the newspapers and talked about in all the families of the North.

Leaving Peter Hart with Anderson, Mrs. Anderson was rowed back to Charleston that night. The report was that she had said to her husband on leaving. "Of course your duty is here, and you have to do it. Don't worry about us. The children are well and I can take care of them."

But, her mission over, she collapsed. A bed was placed for her on the train, and she was carried north to Washington. There she was taken off the train unconscious and carried in a coach to Willard's Hotel. The slow progress of the coach, bearing within it what seemed the dead form of a woman, through the streets of the nation's capital, made a profound impression on a nation to which every detail of this story had been communicated by telegraph. It seemed terribly like the appearance of the first casualty from the battlefront. Hundreds of thousands were hanging breathlessly on the latest bulletin concerning the health of Mrs. Anderson. "She did what the Government failed to do," commented *Leslie's Weekly,* afterwards. "She did not wait to *send* re-enforcements. She *took* them."

Slowly Mrs. Anderson recovered, and the attention of the people turned to Peter Hart, who was usually referred to in the newspaper items as "Mrs. Anderson's re-enforcement." Major Anderson held scrupulously to his promise that Hart would not be used as a soldier. But the Confederates allowed him to be used in lieu of a body servant, as a mailman and marketman and general help to the Major personally. As such he was useful and ingenious in putting the whole establishment in the way of making itself as comfortable as possible under the circumstances, in stretching the rations, and in slipping out personal reports to Mrs. Anderson.

The people never tired of hearing what Peter Hart was doing, for "Mrs. Anderson's re-enforcement" had become, in their minds, their own re-enforcement. She had done what they wanted to do. And they liked to be sure that what she had done was of real assistance.

Around supper-tables at night they used to discuss what Hart could do, if he couldn't bear arms. He could be, they thought, the man behind the man behind the gun. He could release a man to fight. He could be the lookout, and, to some extent, the scout and spy for the whole garrison. If there was fighting, he could see to food and water supply, and nurse the wounded, and even rebuild or repair what was destroyed in the United States. In those days people in the United States didn't know much about war. There hadn't been a really first-class war on a grand scale in the world since the defeat of Napoleon at Waterloo nearly a half century before. And that was before there were telegraphs or railroads or steam navigation—before anyone was really civilized, as the man of 1861 considered himself civilized.

In those comfortable but romantic days of 1861, most people's notions of what it would be like to be shut up in a fortress on the water and besieged were derived from Sir Walter Scott. It was not something that happened to ordinary people like you and me. It belonged only to history and romance. But now it had happened to a good honest fellow like Major Anderson. And bringing their imaginations down to humble details like food and water and daily routines of cleanliness and comfort, people liked to think that Peter Hart was doing everything possible to make life tolerable at Sumter. They did not know that in figuring out what Hart could do if he could not bear arms, they were inventing something new in the history of warfare, a complete non-combatant service. But so it was. In the years to come there were to be many thousand Mrs. Andersons, bringing up re-enforcements by the hundred thousand.

4

When Lincoln was inaugurated on March 4, Major Anderson had already been besieged within Sumter for two months. The first question that faced Lincoln was whether to re-enforce him there. The Confederates were tightening their ring, and had cut Anderson off from access to the Charleston markets. It was only a question of time before he would be starved out. But a re-enforcement of sufficient power to break through the Confederate lines would amount to a military and naval invasion of the South and be the first move in a war. Lincoln was unwilling to make that first move. So he finally announced that he was sending Anderson "bread not guns," by some small ships which would endeavor to provision him peaceably. These ships were fired on as they approached Charleston Harbor, and stopped outside the sand bar. They did not try to break through.

By April 11 Anderson and his garrison were reduced to pork and cold water, in full sight of their own ships laden with food for them, and of the negro boatmen rowing fat chickens, and sides of beef, and oranges, and fresh vegetables out to the Southern troops and ships all around them. But when Anderson was asked by the Confederates whether he was ready to haul down his flag, he replied. "I will evacuate this fort, in my own time and in my own way, and, if in the course of a normal movement, under the orders of my own government, I haul down this flag, I will do it with appropriate ceremonies, when and as I please, and will give the flag a salute of fifty guns and march out taking my flag with me. I will leave on transports which I will order up, as I choose, from among those your troops are now using. And these transports will then take me to any part of the United States to which I may order them to proceed. Under no other circumstances will I take down this flag."

At twenty minutes after three o'clock on the morning of April 12, Anderson received the following note: "Major Anderson: Sir: By authority of Brigadier-General Beauregard, commanding the provisional forces of the Confederate States, we have the honor to notify you that he will open the fire of his batteries on Fort Sumter in an hour from this time."

Exactly at 4:20, just as the faint glow of a particularly red sun-

13

rise was lighting the horizon, Beauregard opened up with fire from masked batteries on Sullivan's Island. These were batteries he had constructed since he bottled up Anderson in the fort, and had so camouflaged with trees and brush that Anderson had no idea that they were there. This was far worse than Anderson had anticipated. By the time the sun rolled up, Fort Sumter was blazing with fires started by the shells. These were put out as rapidly as they flared up by Peter Hart, who figured that his promise not to fight as a soldier did not bind him not to act as a one-man fire-brigade. As such "Mrs. Anderson's re-enforcement" did the work of a whole fire company.

All day the firing continued, aimed primarily at the flagpole, while the excitement of the crowds around telegraph boards in cities all over the country mounted with every bulletin. Hour after hour the reports came in. "Flagpole hit, but flag still flying." "Fort Sumter ablaze, but flag still discernible above the flames." "Flag hit and burned through one of the white stripes, Flag still flying." "Flag hit and apparently torn or burned through the blue field of stars, but flag still flying."

When evening fell, the flag was still there. By this time a storm had come up. It was a wild night, surf running high in Charleston Harbor, sea beating on all the shores of the Atlantic north to Maine, streets of northern towns whipped by rain. But all night long lights shone in Northern homes and crowds marching dripping up and down the streets, whiling away the time between news bulletins by singing alternately "The Star-Spangled Banner" and a new song-hit, "Bob Anderson, my Bo."

Next morning, in the fog and rain street bands were playing the song whose familiar words were on every one's lips. "Oh say, can you see, by the dawn's early light, what so proudly we hailed at the twilight's last gleaming." The answer was that they could see it. "The rockets' red glare and bombs bursting in air" had given "proof through the night that our flag was still there."

All morning and into the afternoon, the firing continued. Once there was great excitement. The report came that the flag had finally been shot down. In the harbor of Charleston, Confederate emissaries, seeing that the flag had disappeared, started toward the fort, thinking that Anderson was ready to surrender. They sent in word to him, "Your flag has been shot down, and you are on fire. Let us quit."

"My flag is not down," replied Major Anderson.

The Confederate emissaries raised their eyes. There, above the smoke, were the Stars and Stripes. Peter Hart had climbed out through the blaze and had raised the flag again on a jury mast.

Till late in the afternoon of Saturday, the watchers in the North hung on the reports. "Fort a smoking ruin. Flag still visible." "Flag shot down." "Flag up again." Somehow an impression got abroad that it was Mrs. Anderson's re-enforcement who kept climbing out and raising the flag again. This was what the people wanted to believe, and it happened that it was true.

But there came at last the inevitable end. After thirty-four hours of continual bombardment, Fort Sumter, its quarters entirely burned out, its main gates destroyed, its outer walls seriously injured, and its powder magazine surrounded by flames—Fort Sumter at last surrendered.

5

Mr. Rice read the news in Mary's face when she came in that evening, carrying a lamp, and followed by the maid with a tray. He knew it by the way she said nothing—she only set out the tea-things with especial care and ceremony, and then seated herself, and, spearing a slice of bread on the prongs of a long fork, composedly began toasting it over the coals. It was Mary's way to steady herself against big shocks by going through all the little domestic routines more carefully and elaborately.

"Mary!" said Mr. Rice, in a trembling voice.

"Yes, Father," she replied quietly, "They have had to give up. The flag has come down."

He turned his face to the wall with what Mary described afterwards as an "exceedingly bitter cry."

"My God," he groaned. "Now let me die, for I cannot survive the ruin of my country."

All that night Mary's father moaned and talked fitfully about his childhood and youth. His father had fought in the Revolution. He himself had fought in the War of 1812. All his family kin had fought in one war or the other. They had all had such high hopes of their new country. And in the half century that followed that spirited beginning, through all the active years of Mr. Rice's life, everything had been wonderful in this new land. Every year

15

Americans had invented new or better machines to relieve human toil. Every year they had opened new frontiers and new homes for people in the West. Every year the miserable and downtrodden of Europe had poured in, and had begun to take hope and to prosper. It was all because we had started free from the old feudal restrictions and snobberies of Europe, and its wretched tyrannies and border squabbles, giving every man, no matter who he was, a chance to work up by his own efforts from the very bottom to the very top.

"We had conquered everything," said Mr. Rice, "except poverty, and we were going to conquer that. And now it is all done for! Smashed. One state fighting another! Oh Mary, the best life your children will ever have known is the life that they have already had, in a country that was still whole."

The history of Mary's country was so short that it was all bound up like that in the span of one man's memories and hopes and ambitions for his family. Listening to him, Mary realized that this illness, which had brought her flying to his bedside from the West, was due entirely to his worry about the future of his country. For months his people had appeared to him to lie under the "paralysis of death," as Mary called it, with no clear and simple resolution anywhere, except in the man at Fort Sumter. And even that man had been forced to surrender. "The dreary winter of secession," wrote Mary later, "when the nation seemed slowly disintegrating, had brought low my father's pride, and consumed both life and hope, and it seemed doubtful if he would survive the fall of Fort Sumter."

But with what seemed his dying breath he was endeavoring to fire his daughter with a sense of the preciousness of what, as an American, she had had, and to show her the utter abyss that opened ahead if she should lose it.

Mary listened quietly, and endeavored to soothe her patient with careful tendance, according to the precepts of Miss Nightingale. But when he was quiet at last, and she sat alone by the fire, in the somber solitude of a sickroom at night, she could not but face the fact that the fall of Fort Sumter was the collapse of the security on which her happy life had been built.

Up to this time, Mary Livermore had done nothing to distinguish herself. She was only the typical American woman in the contented bloom of her early middle years. She had no remarkable gifts—unless to be perfectly normal is itself a gift as rare as genius. A devoted mother, a happy wife, and an enthusiastic mother of young children, she had always enjoyed companionship and co-operation with the men she loved—first with her father, and then with her husband—and had found her own life completely fulfilled in sharing theirs.

Her happiness and good fortune shone in her appearance. Though she was forty, she looked thirty. Her face, under the brown braid of hair which was wound like a halo above it, was fresh and serene. Her figure, snugly encased in a modestly fashionable bodice above the enormous circumference of her hoop-skirt, was firm, rounded, womanly, but slender, too, in accordance with the contemporary standard of "elegance" in woman's "shape."

Though she was, in type, the generic woman, the kind of human being poets and artists have picked from the beginning of time to represent the idea of daughterhood, wifehood, and motherhood, there was something enterprising and untrammeled about her. It was implicit in herself, and implicit also in the attitude of her men-folk to her. For example, as a girl she had quickly exhausted the limited curriculum of the Charlestown Female Academy, which offered all the education considered necessary for young ladies in those days. When her mind began to beat about restlessly, wanting something to occupy it, her father engaged tutors for her from Harvard who taught her anything she wanted to study, in serene disregard of the natural limitations of the female mind.

Then she took a little fling at seeing life for herself by going to Virginia to teach a "family school" on a big plantation where there were five hundred slaves. After three years she returned to her father's house, quite sure that she did not approve of slavery as an institution, and married a young Universalist preacher, named Daniel Livermore. With him she tried some experiments in running a modern sort of church in Fall River, with forums, and discussion circles, and study groups. Then she and her husband moved to Chicago, and he started a weekly newspaper which quickly prospered. She worked with him, helping him to get out each edition. Meanwhile she had three children, and established a charming home in the suburbs of Chicago, which she delighted to equip with every new domestic labor-saving device that came along. She had always done pretty much what she wanted to do, but she had usually contrived to please while doing it. Her father talked to her like a man and an equal; her husband was inordinately proud of her; and her children chattered like magpies the minute she appeared, in an effort to tell her all about everything.

She was only the standard American housewife, of the more up-and-coming type, as found in the more privileged business and professional circles from that day to this. But that Saturday night after the fall of Sumter, as she sat with her father in the snug, dim-lighted comfort of that Victorian upper room, and heard the crowds restlessly tramping in the fog outside, the walls of her home seemed to collapse around her. And she found herself looking, with horrified eyes, upon a prospect of universal suffering and devastation. What, as a woman, she would be able to do about it she did not know. But she and many other women like her were to be taught what to do by the inexorable events now swiftly moving to their climax in the greatest and bloodiest war that had ever been fought on this earth.

2. *The Great Uprising*

After the despair of that night, the waking next day was glorious. For Major Anderson had not hauled down the flag. It was still flying above the smoking ramparts of Fort Sumter.

What had happened was this: On Saturday afternoon Beauregard noticed that the Confederate troops were cheering every time the guns of Sumter fired back at them, and jeering meanwhile at the relief ships from Washington because they did not come to Anderson's aid. The whole situation was getting out of hand. If those men out there on Sumter should be allowed to martyr themselves, it might be hard to persuade any more Americans to join the Confederate cause. So the Confederates sent a conciliatory mission to Anderson, under a flag of truce, to talk over the means of bringing it all to a halt.

Anderson was very stiff. "General Beauregard knows the terms on which I leave Fort Sumter," he said. "I will not discuss any other."

"Good," said the Confederate emissary. "Then the flag is yours and the fort is ours."

Major Anderson was surprised. "Understand me," he said. "I said that I have the permission of my government to leave this fort, and that I will do so only in my own time and my own way, acting under the authority of my government only. And I said I will order up transports from among those your troops are now using to carry my men and my flag to any part of the United States that I may designate."

"We understand this, and we agree," said the Confederate emissary, and he added handsomely, "You have defended your flag nobly, Sir. You have done all that it is possible for man to do."

Next morning Major Anderson had the personal and company

19

baggage of his garrison transferred to the transports which he called for and which the Confederates furnished. His men marched out with their side-arms and other arms, with the honors of war. The men who had been told off as gunners fired fifty salutes to their flag, and then slowly lowered it, to the cheers of the rest of the company already on the transport. Then they formed and marched down, carrying their flag, while the band played "Yankee Doodle" and "Hail to the Chief." The transport Major Anderson had asked for to carry them away from Sumter was *The Clinch*. Clinch was the maiden name of his wife. The vessel had been named for "that gallant soldier," her father.

Major Anderson boarded one of the ships of the relief expedition waiting for him, and, with his burned and tattered flag, set sail for New York City.

2

To this news the response of the people of the North was such an unfurling of flags as was never seen in this country before or since. By church time every flag in every town was out on display.

Father Rafina of the Montrose Catholic Church of Williamsburg, New York, was raising the flag on his steeple with his own hands. Father Creadon at Auburn, from a flag-draped pulpit, was calling on "every Irishman who hears me to be ready to fight for the flag of this country, which is the only country an Irishman ever had that he could call his own." A rigger by trade, Mr. Thomas Davidson, offered to raise the flag on any spire in New York City, no matter how high. At the risk of his life he climbed to the pinnacles of Trinity and St. Paul's, and flung out the Stars and Stripes. Two painters clambered up the Grace Church lightning rod, fastened a flagpole to the cross, raised the flag, and then swept off their hats to the crowds below. In Cincinnati Archbishop Purcell unfurled a flag ninety feet long from the spire of his church. In New York City Archbishop Hughes, standing under the folds of a great flag, said, "This has been my flag and shall be to the end. May it wave for a thousand years and afterwards, as long as Heaven permits, without limit of duration."

Protestant congregations entered churches between stands of flags, while the organ played "The Star-Spangled Banner." Not only did they fill the pews. They stood massed at the doors, and

20

out into the streets. And when the preacher said something that pleased the audience, they forgot the decorum of the sacred edifice and cheered and clapped. "We are ready to fight for this flag," said Parson Brownlow, in Knoxville, Tennessee, "till Hell freezes over, and then we'll fight on the ice."

Out of doors the people, having commandeered all flags and bunting, were raiding the dry goods stores, and stringing bolts of red, white or blue dress-goods across the streets. Anything that could serve for the national colors was dragged out. Men wore red flannel shirts with white and blue trimmings. Women who were fortunate enough to possess a red dress, hastened to put white collars and cuffs on it, and to pin on a blue ribbon bow. Florists' shops were cleaned out of red flowers, white flowers, and blue flowers. During the next few days the American people spent a million dollars for flags and bunting and half a million more for anything else that was colored red, white, or blue. They were ready to spend more. But the cloth and the dyestuffs gave out.

On Monday morning President Lincoln called out the state militia, to the number of 75,000, to assist in retaking property of the United States seized by the Confederate forces. These volunteers were called for three months. According to law the militia could not be held for a longer period without an act of Congress. Congress was called to meet on July 4.

Each state governor received a telegram from the War Department fixing the number of regiments he was to furnish. The Governor of Iowa was working in his cornfield when a man on horseback dashed up with the telegram asking for one regiment from Iowa. The Governor looked out on the empty land, lying peaceful under the spring sunshine. Some crows flew cawing across the sky. Nearby some cattle were grazing. But there was not a man in sight. "A regiment is 1,000 men," said the Governor doubtfully. "Where are we going to find 1,000 men?" Within a few days ten regiments from Iowa had volunteered.

It was like that everywhere. No one knew where so many men came from, but they came, converging on the villages in wagons, on horseback, and on foot, pouring into the cities on trains. Every village green was a recruiting station, and every city an armed camp. Mary Livermore said they could have raised 750,000 as easily as 75,000.

There was normally considerable jealousy and rivalry between the states of the North, as of the South, and every state was inclined to be a law unto itself and to believe itself the center around which the rest of the Americans, if any, revolved. But now the heat of this enthusiasm for their flag was fast forging a national sentiment. So when the telegraph began to flash the news that the first regiment was ready to go to the defense of the national capital —that the Sixth of Massachusetts was ready to march within twenty-four hours of Lincoln's call—the people everywhere looked on this regiment as a national institution. "The Bunker Hill Boys," they called them, and heard in the mustering of Massachusetts the old drum-beat of the American Revolution, and the tread of the men of Lexington and Concord.

The first soldiers uniformed, armed, and ready to go, began coming into Boston from the outlying villages early Tuesday morning. Each trainful was met by the people of Boston who walked beside them, and in front of them, and behind them, a passionate, surging throng. As the soldiers and the escorting people passed, the omnibuses and horsecars stopped and the passengers waved flags. Clerks in stores ran out bareheaded and shouted greetings. Women leaned far out of the windows, waving handkerchiefs, throwing down kisses, and scattering the red, white, and blue faded remnants of the raids on the florists' shops. So, with drums and fifes and singing, and waving of flags, the people swarmed toward Faneuil Hall, the time-honored center of Boston oratory and symbol of New England freedom, which had been turned over to be used as a barracks.

Ever since the people started rising, old Mr. Rice had been getting better by the minute. Every time the fife and drum corps played "The Star-Spangled Banner" under his window, it was like a draught of medicine. By Tuesday morning he declared that he was well enough to go to Faneuil Hall, too. So Mary got him into a carriage, and forth they went, through the rain—for it was raining again—carrying their own dripping flag. Suddenly the mass of people seethed with fervid excitement. Mr. Rice, his trembling hands clasped over the top of his cane, leaned far out and lifted his eyes to the gray sky. "God bless it," he said, in tender and reverent tones.

Mary's eyes followed his, and those of the thousands all around. They were running up the flag over Faneuil Hall! "I saw," said Mary, "the dear banner of my country, rising higher and higher

22

to the top of the flag staff, fling out fold after fold to the damp air, and float proudly over that hallowed edifice. Oh, the roar that rang from ten thousand throats! Old men with white hair and tearful faces lifted their hats to the national ensign, and reverently saluted it. Young men greeted it with fierce and wild hurrahs."

And Mary who, in all her happy girlhood and wifehood, had never thought of the flag save as a decoration, and had taken her country for granted, the way one takes the earth and the sky, felt all the thoughts which had been going through her mind since the fall of Sumter, crystallizing in one idea, and one resolve. "If it be the question of supremacy of freedom or slavery underlying this war," she thought, "then I pray God that it be settled now by us, and not by our children. Oh that I may have a hand or a foot or an eye or a voice, an influence on the side of freedom and my country!"

"I was weak," she said afterwards, "with the new tides of feeling coursing through my body."

3

The Sixth Massachusetts left for Washington Wednesday afternoon, April 17. Its leaving, as reported by telegraph to every town and city, was a national event. From Faneuil Hall the regiment, 1,000 strong, was escorted to the railroad station by the citizenry of Boston, while all along its route to Washington the citizens of other towns were making ready to welcome it and speed it on its way.

The Boston escort of the soldiers was a solid, earnest crowd. The songs and bravado of the previous days had died down. Many people had crammed rather fiercely under their arms a copy of the afternoon paper which told of the secession of Virginia. The news made them look pretty grim.

The regiment was not, for the most part, composed of young men. They were bearded men, substantial men, fathers of families, farmers, blacksmiths, schoolteachers, storekeepers, lawyers. Up to the siege of Fort Sumter, when they had begun to train in earnest, their state militia had been almost wholly a social organization. It had never done much except parade on Fourth of July. And now here they were, good, peaceable citizens of Salem and Marblehead, of Lexington and Concord, called from

23

that military play-acting, in which men naturally delight, to the business of blood and bullets with which they had had no experience whatever, and for which they had no taste.

But the people of Massachuetts were proud that the foresight of their governor had enabled them to turn out a regiment that was actually uniformed and armed. This was a good deal more than could be said of regiments preparing elsewhere. However, each company in the regiment had uniformed itself according to its own notions of military splendor. Some tramped along in high boots and wore tall helmet-like headgear. Some wore civilian hats above blue suits that endeavored, not too successfully, to look martial. But most of them wore a kind of military blue overcoat, a handsome, substantial garment with a cape, that gave a certain uniformity to an otherwise motley display.

They marched to the station not in military formation, but walking with their wives and families. Middle-aged wives walked arm in arm with uniformed husbands. Little girls clung to the hands of their soldier fathers. Sweethearts walked with their arms around each other's waists. Sons in blue walked with an old father and mother on each arm.

At the station the crowd closed together and listened quietly while a clergyman mounted a platform and offered a prayer. Then came the unfamiliar command, "Fall in line." The soldiers released themselves from their families, and men stooped and kissed again and again the faces of women and children turned up to them. Then they formed into long lines, company by company, and marched into the cars. The two locomotives which drew the long train whistled. Every whistle and bell in Boston answered, and from the crowds that packed streets and roofs, there rose a roar of cheers. The first regiment was off for Washington.

All night, there were crowds at New London, at New Haven, and at Bridgeport, waiting to see that soldier-train go by. Arriving in New York, early in the morning, the troops were met by 5,000 citizens, the police, and all the brass bands of the city, and escorted to the various hotels for breakfast. Then they had to march down Broadway under canopies of flags, while the populace shouted itself hoarse. Down that long, wide, winding Broadway, bordered with neat, new-looking brick buildings, four and five stories high, the soldiers marched, and with bands and flags and much ceremony, 100,000 persons saw them off on the ferryboat for Jersey

City. In Jersey City companies of ladies carrying flags so filled the docks that for twenty minutes the troops could not make their way through. And all the while the bands played "The Star-Spangled Banner" and the flags waved and the people, massed on every roof, and all along the streets, and on boats on the river, all shouted, "God bless you!" "Three Cheers for the Bunker Hill Boys!" Finally they were off for Trenton, the state capital of New Jersey, escorted by the New Jersey militia on their way to their own camps.

So they went on till they came to Baltimore, where the crowd had been worked up by telegraph to a different point of view. "It is not to be endured," said the *Richmond Examiner,* "that this flight of abolition harpies shall come down from the black North to their roosts in the heart of the South, to defile and brutalize the land." And so, on the nineteenth of April, which was their own great Massachusetts holiday, the anniversary of the Battle of Lexington, the "Bunker Hill Boys" were set upon by the angry mobs of Baltimore, and had to fight their way through to the train for Washington.

When they arrived in Washington, they were carrying seventeen wounded men on stretchers made by fastening their blankets over their muskets. Their dead, who numbered four, they had left behind in Baltimore.

4

For the next week, from April 19 to April 24, Washington was isolated from the outer world. Virginia and Maryland were in arms, Confederate troops were rushing to capture the capital city before further Northern regiments could break through. A Southern railroad superintendent telegraphed Jefferson Davis that he could carry from 5,000 to 7,000 Confederate troops 350 miles daily. "One dash," he wired, "and Lincoln is taken, the country saved, and the leader who does it will be immortalized." The *Richmond Examiner* said, "There is one wild shout to capture Washington City, at all and every human hazard. The filthy cage of unclean birds must and will be purified by fire. The just indignation of an outraged and deeply injured people will teach the Illinois ape to retrace his journey across the borders of the free negro states more rapidly than he came."

Washington was besieged on all sides. The railroad bridges north of Baltimore had been blown up. The railroad between Annapolis and Washington had been destroyed. The two great arsenals of Norfolk and Harper's Ferry had been seized by the Confederates. The Potomac was blockaded. General Scott, Lincoln's commander-in-chief, said that Fort Washington, which guarded the Potomac below Washington, could be taken by the Confederates with a bottle of whisky. The last he had heard, he said, was that it was guarded by one old soldier, who was a good enough fighter if he didn't make contact with liquor. But for a bottle of whisky he would give away anything he had.

In this situation all the military protection the capital city had consisted of the green regiment from Massachusetts, and volunteer companies of local citizens and office-seekers. The Bunker Hill Boys were barracked in the Senate Chamber. On the lower floor of the White House were barracked the "frontier guards," a company of gun-toting abolitionists, recruited from among strangers in Washington who had fought against the "Missouri Ruffians" in Kansas. In the ballroom of Willard's Hotel, Cassius Clay, famous Kentucky abolitionist, armed with "three pistols and an Arkansas toothpick," was drilling volunteers from among the office-seekers in Washington who said they could shoot.

The telegraph messages telling of the imminent danger of Washington kept coming through to the North till Sunday night. Then all communication stopped. The people were left to mobilize themselves with no military or political guidance whatsoever. With passionate determination, they sent off regiments in the direction of Washington, and expected them to get there somehow.

There was no longer a question of raising 75,000 men. They were mobilizing everybody, in one tremendous turmoil of activity. At the moment when they lost the guidance of President Lincoln, they found another figure in whom to center their enthusiasm, in the person of Major Anderson, actually present among them now in the flesh, For on April 19, while the Bunker Hill Boys were fighting their way through Baltimore, Major Anderson and some of his garrison arrived in New York, carrying their tattered flag. Major Anderson appeared on Broadway on Friday afternoon, April 19, and reviewed the magnificent New York Seventh regiment, the pride of the city, in all its superfluity of up-to-date and martial decoration, bought out of the pocketbooks of its own

26

wealthy members. The New York Seventh set off with cheers and hurrahs, heard of the trouble in Baltimore en route, found that it could not get through to Washington by train, seized a steamer, set sail for Annapolis, and discovered there that the railroad from Annapolis to Washington was destroyed.

Next day, with garbled reports of bloodshed all around Washington coming in, 50,000 people gathered in Union Square and reared over the equestrian statue of George Washington the flag Major Anderson had brought from Sumter, and started to raise sixty-six regiments. The different foreign-born groups in the city volunteered their quotas. The Irish raised four regiments; the Germans four; the Italians two; and the British recruited the "British volunteers" from among the British subjects in the city.

Everywhere the rugged individualism and advertising genius of the American people ran wild in competitive military whoopee. Any man who could muster some friends and a financial backer could form a company, with himself as captain. The state government would be responsible for shelter, food, and training only as the men were mustered in companies of eighty-four, under the command of a captain and his lieutenants. Until he could get eighty-four men together, the captain was responsible for the food and lodging of his men. Hence he had to be either a man of means, ready to spend all for his country, or an enterprising person who could get backers. Usually the captains were not philanthropists but go-getters. And such was the eagerness of the people that a reasonably persuasive fellow, ready to lead warriors to fight below the Potomac, could go out any day and get not only a guarantee of all necessities for his men until the state took them over, but a large assortment of luxuries and special favors as well.

For example, one captain might be able to offer an arrangement whereby the Insurance Company would insure the life of every man who enlisted, the premium to be paid for him while in service by interested fellow citizens. Another captain could offer allowances for the man's family, to be contributed by sympathetic friends. Colonels could go even further. They could offer—or thought they could—a few choice advantages in the way of military procedure. One colonel advertised: "Lynch law for guerillas, and no rebel property guarded!"

Recruiting posters were contests in advertising, and the rallies to stimulate enlistments that went on almost constantly in every

27

town were a cross between a circus and a revival meeting. There were flags and streamers of red, white, and blue. There were pretty girls handing out pink lemonade and cookies, and a saloon around the corner doing a roaring business selling something stronger. There were bands playing "Hail, Columbia." There was a fife and drum corps marching around the town, drumming up trade, followed by all the urchins in the place.

The program featured an old soldier of the War of 1812, several Mexican War veterans in their antiquated uniforms, a sentimental lady of uncertain years who said she wanted to shoulder a gun herself, and the town's oldest inhabitant who, in a quavering voice, wished that he were young again and could go straight away and whip the rebels. Betweentimes the band played not only patriotic songs but familiar hymns, and the Methodist minister made his best revivalist appeal, substituting country for God. Whenever a high moment was reached, a paper was passed around on which all who were ready to join Captain So and So's glorious company, or Colonel What's His Name's gallant regiment, would please sign their names.

When a company was filled, it was frequently treated to a big feast by the local hotel-keeper, or by a prosperous citizen, or more often by the women relatives and friends of the men. The ladies of Augusta, Maine, promised to make the Third Maine regiment fifty bushels of doughnuts. "The soldiers drew up in a hollow square—how apt is the word hollow when applied to men who have fasted in view of promised doughnuts—received the procession which consisted of music, then the ladies, then the doughnuts. . . . Never was there such an aggregate since the world began. The circumambient air was redolent of doughnuts; every breeze sighed doughnuts; the soldiers ate doughnuts; the distributors cried doughnuts. There was the molasses doughnut and the sugar doughnut, the round doughnut and the square doughnut, the single twisted doughnut and the three ply doughnut, the light riz doughnut and the hard knit doughnut."

Despite the "Hurrah, boys" atmosphere, they were all dead in earnest. No one really thought war was fun. Most people were weighed down with a kind of horror of the tragedy that had befallen their country. And as the days passed, and the capital city could not be reached, there came into all this hullabaloo an ever-increasing grimness. Each regiment was sent off with a religious ceremony and escorted some distace on its way by practically the whole population of the district whence the regiment was drawn. A traveler who saw a regiment leaving Quincy, Illinois, escorted by six or seven thousand people, said that he had never seen anything more impressive. On Sunday evening, April 21, Mary Livermore, en route home to Chicago from Boston, saw the citizens of Auburn, New York, sending forth a regiment with a great religious service in a flag-decked church. On the evening air of that springtime Sunday, above the call of the peepers, singing outside in every bog, there rose from that great congregation the strains of the song, "It is sweet, it is sweet, for one's country to die," beautiful, solemn—and terrible.

For the moment every one was inspired with an energy that needed neither sleep nor food to sustain it. Mary's father had been so revived by the turn of events that on Thursday, when Mary received a telegram from her husband in Chicago, begging her to come home if she could, Mr. Rice said he was quite well enough to fend for himself. She'd better hurry home to Dan.

So Mary started, and made her way West through tumultuous throngs of men mobilizing for war. They were filling the railroad stations, eating and sleeping there, waiting to go on to some other place. They were whooping by on railroad tracks, in dirty cattle-cars, crammed as tight in them as the animals Mary had seen coming into the Chicago stockyards, and not half so well cared for, as regarded food and water. A week ago these men had been respectable citizens, sleeping between clean sheets, sitting down to well-cooked meals at well-set tables, hovered over and looked after by a wife or a mother. And now, here they were, sleeping on the floors of railroad stations or even on straw in stables, rumpled, dirty, and unshaven. They were eating God knows what. They were drinking—God knows how much. Mary's quick eye noted that some whom she thought at first to be drunk, were seriously ill. Altogether they were a sight to appal any good housewife. Suppose that she should see her Dan in such a condition!

But there didn't seem to be much a woman could do about it, war being the business of men. So Mary hurried home, and was relieved to find her Dan still safe in domestic respectability. That night she tried to discuss the state of the nation with Dan, while the children clambered on her knees, and pulled at her dress and insisted on talking about the new puppies, and Dan tramped up and down and wished she would get the children to bed so that they could really talk. This was home, dear, peaceful and secure, after that appalling mob in the railroad stations.

Everything was sweet and wholesome here at home, even though no woman can leave a house to a husband and children and a maid, and not find it all at sixes and sevens when she gets back. But to-morrow was another day, and she would pitch in and do some housecleaning. Thank Heaven home was a place where a woman didn't have to stand the revolting mess human beings seem to get into when they try to live together intimately, all day and all night, anywhere else. Home is a place a woman can really do something about.

So Mary settled down at home in Chicago. But she couldn't get all those men out of her mind nor stop worrying about the state they were getting themselves into. It kept her awake nights. It was keeping some 100,000 other women awake nights, too.

5

Though they had no central military command, and no central government to tell them what to do, in this fortnight of the great uprising, these amateur soldiers pitched in and did what they thought must be done, with crude common sense. And so they actually managed to take and make secure the two places that remained the strategic centers and principal mobilization headquarters throughout the war—the city of Washington, in the East, and the town of Cairo in the West. The way they did it was characteristic.

When the gilded gentlemen of the gold-plated Seventh New York regiment couldn't get to Washington by train, they took a steamer and so reached Annapolis. There they were joined by the Eighth Massachusetts, who had also taken a steamer when they couldn't get through by train. At Annapolis the two regiments found that the Confederates had destroyed the railroad to Washington. Annapolis was only thirty miles from Washington. Had these been European troops, they would, of course, have marched, and so would have reached the capital city in a day or two, on April 22 or 23. But being Americans, they had a constitutional objection to using their legs if they could fix up any sort of contrivance to carry them. So rather than walk, they decided first to

30

build a railroad train, and then to relay the tracks to Washington, and so to go forward in comfort!

Poking around in the railroad wreckage which the Confederates had left on all sides, they found materials with which they extemporized two platform cars, and mounted their little brass howitzers on them. Then they found a locomotive the Confederates had demolished, and tinkered with it till they got it going, and uncovered two old passenger cars in a railroad junk-yard and put them together again. After the many mechanical geniuses who can be found among any 2,000 Americans had put in a good day's work, they had fixed up an artillery, supply, ambulance, and construction train all in one, and were ready to start off. For the next few days the two regiments inched ahead, marching, scouting, laying tracks, and building bridges as necessary.

President Lincoln meanwhile was becoming daily more worried. Two or three messengers had got into the city, telling him of the great uprising in the North, and of the Seventh New York being on its way to help him. But where was the Seventh New York? It was reliably reported that it had arrived at Annapolis. But why hadn't these men come on to Washington? Someone replied that they couldn't come because the railroad was destroyed. "But haven't they got legs?" asked Lincoln impatiently. "It's only thirty miles. Can't they *march.*" April 23 passed. By this time the regiment could have marched to Washington. April 24 passed. There were reports that the Eighth Massachusetts had joined the Seventh New York. But where? On April 25, Lincoln was saying to the boys of the Sixth Massachusetts who were all he had to guard the capital, "There isn't any North. The Seventh New York is a myth. Only *you* are real." Suddenly there was wild commotion down near the Washington railroad station, and then a triumphant blare of first-class band music.

And there, sure enough, was the Seventh New York! Hearing that a Confederate force was approaching, they had left the Massachusetts regiment to guard the railroad, and had come on to the support of the President. Having built the railroad ahead of themselves all the way from Annapolis, they were now parading up Pennsylvania Avenue, with flying flags. Each company was gay in a remarkable regalia of its own, and ahead of them went the best regimental band in America, led by a classy and high-stepping drum-major whose evolutions had long been the pride and delight

31

of holiday crowds on Broadway. Having often served as the military stars in public processions in New York City, the Seventh New York knew how to march. And here it was, swinging along with a firm military tread, and a broad and triumphant collective grin on its sunburned face. And so President Lincoln was rescued, and the capital was saved!

Meanwhile, out in the West, the army of Chicago had decided to conquer Cairo. In Illinois no one had either the money or the leisure to develop the military showmanship of the Seventh New York. There were only a few companies of young men, here and there, who had done a little parading on Fourth of July or who had shot a few squirrels. There were about 500 stands of miscellaneous arms in the state, most of them thoroughly antiquated. And there was one man who actually held a commission as brigadier-general, though when he got it or why no one seemed able to remember. But this general—General Swift—thought that the boys had better take Cairo. And so they did.

Cairo was a miserable sink-hole of a town at the junction of the Mississippi and Ohio Rivers. Eastward from it stretched the Ohio River, the great water highway between the free states and the slave states. It flowed westward from its sources in the Appalachian System for 1,000 miles, drawing on 6,000 miles of tributary rivers, that came down to it from the parts of the country in which were concentrated the greatest available natural resources and the largest industrial cities west of the Allegheny Mountains. To Cairo this great river brought traffic from Pittsburgh in Pennsylvania, Wheeling in West Virginia, Cincinnati in Ohio, Louisville in Kentucky, and from the valley of the Wabash in Indiana. At Cairo the Mississippi stretched northward for 1,000 miles through the great grain and cattle country of the northwest, and southward for 1,000 miles to New Orleans, through the heart of the now seceded South. To Cairo the Illinois Central Railroad brought the traffic of the Great Lakes from as far east as Buffalo and the Erie Canal, and linked it with the river traffic.

There was as yet no High Command in Washington to determine that Cairo was the military key to the West and to most of the resources of the United States, and no one who could give the amateur soldiers from the farms and villages and from the streets of Chicago any authoritative orders except the Governor of Illinois. But he agreed with them that it would be too bad

32

if the Confederates got to Cairo first. So they all talked it over in Chicago, and then General Swift started off with 595 men and four six-pounder pieces of artillery and with all the rifles, shotguns, muskets, and carbines they could find in the shops of Chicago. On April 23 they arrived in Cairo. They had neither shot, shell, nor cannister for their batteries, but they hastily prepared some slugs, and these, they reported, "answered the purpose of all." At Cairo they were joined by Colonel Benjamin Prentiss, who had served in the Mexican War, and who had picked up seven newly organized companies of which he had assumed command. Occupying Cairo, they proceeded to stop all vessels on the river, and to take possession of supplies and munitions which were being carried to the Confederates from St. Louis.

When, shortly afterwards, the capital at Washington was delivered from its immediate danger and its isolation by the regiments that had fought their way through to it, and the telegraph communication with the rest of the country was re-established, the first thing Lincoln had to deal with was a lot of telegrams from Kentucky, Tennessee, and Missouri complaining of the highhanded procedure of the lads at Cairo. The senders of these telegrams wanted to know if the President had ordered this movement. The President had not ordered it, and when the first telegrams arrived he had known nothing about it. But he rose handsomely to his position as Commander-in-chief. To a state senator in Kentucky who wrote from Paducah, protesting against the behavior in Illinois, Lincoln replied through a secretary: "The President directs me to acknowledge the receipt of your letter of the 26th ultimo, protesting against the stationing of United States troops at Cairo. He directs me to say that he would never have ordered the movement of troops complained of had he known that Cairo was in your Senatorial district!" Thus was one of the greatest strategic advantages of the Union army in the war achieved.

Though as fast as he could find out what his volunteers were doing, Lincoln tried to take responsibility for it, he was somewhat embarrassed by the numbers and the enthusiasm of the People's Army. The Governor of Iowa who had been asked for one regiment, and had ten ready, telegraphed, "We have the men. For God's sake send us arms." The Governor of Ohio telegraphed that he didn't dare repress the people's patriotism by enlisting only the thirteen regiments that had been called for his quota. Thus far he had accepted twenty regiments and was trying to put them into camp, and more were still coming. The War Department at Washington replied to such telegrams that it could use no more three months' volunteers. All it could use were men who would volunteer for three years. Forthwith the three months' volunteers began to re-enlist for three years.

On May 3, the President issued a proclamation calling for 64,-748 three years' volunteers, and 18,000 recruits to the navy. But by that time some 250,000 were already gathering in camps, or were on boats or freight-trains going somewhere. And 100,000 more were assembling in little knots of six or seven or eight, parading on the village green, with sticks for muskets, and calling on their neighbors to join them and make a "company." Meanwhile the telegraph wires to Washington were jammed with conflicting calls for siege guns and field batteries, for gunboats and transports, for officers to muster in regiments, for supplies, for credit, and for cash.

To mobilize 200,000 raw recruits in two weeks, and get them into camp and under discipline, would be a task even for a large modern nation, with a standing army, and an efficient military machine. But these 18,000,000 Americans of the North, thinly spread over a geographical area measuring roughly 2,000 miles from east to west and 1,000 miles from north to south, had as yet no stable government and no standing army that could be depended on. They had only a man they were determined to keep in the White House in a city they were determined to guard against the objections of 12,000,000 Americans just as brave and ingenious as themselves. Somewhere on the frontiers, and mainly out of reach, the national government had had a standing army that numbered on paper 17,113 officers and men. But some of it was in Texas, some in Utah, some in California; and how much of it was going to fight with the North and how much with the South no one could surely tell. The most that could be known was that all its good officers, beginning with Robert E. Lee, appeared to be rapidly resigning to take command of the enemy!

Yet here they were from 200,000 to 300,000 men, crowding into the cities, jamming the railroad stations, all determined to fight, and all ready to go somewhere, provided that it seemed to be in a southerly direction. 200,000 to 300,000 men, herding in masses, without toilet facilities, without adequate water, without change of clothing, without medical care, without food. It was all very wonderful, and patriotic, and glorious. But, after all, they were but men. And within a few days after leaving home, most men were hungry, and some of them were running a temperature from the germs they had picked up.

The only people that seemed to be in a position to do anything about it were the women. When men arrived in town, and the women heard that they had not had anything to eat for twenty-four hours, there was action at once. Long board tables were set up in a church parlor, or even in a railroad station, and on them promptly appeared ham and eggs, preserved fruits, homemade bread and butter, doughnuts, and hot coffee. When men came through a town, looking hot and dirty, women met them with tin basins and soap and clean towels. If some fellow was dragging along with a flushed face, or turning away to vomit wretchedly, some good woman insisted on taking him home with her and putting him to bed.

The roads were full of men who looked like tramps, but who were going somewhere, with the hope of joining the army. Some of these were only runaway boys of fifteen or sixteen. Some were simple-minded fellows who had started off to fight the enemy without knowing what and where the enemy was, nor what military unit to join. Here and there something like this happened:— A young man knocked at a housewife's door, and said, "Would you kindly let me get a drink from your well, Ma'am?" He was tired. He didn't want anything to eat, but he'd like to sit down and rest awhile, thank you kindly. The housewife let him alone, even when she saw him lying full-length on her porch. She hoped that he was getting a little nap, poor lad, and expected that he would wake up after a while and be glad to have some coffee. But after he had slept on and on for what seemed a very long while, she tiptoed out and looked at him more closely. He was dead. He was dead—and not a mark of identification on him to tell who he was and where he had come from. A nice-looking lad. He could not be more than seventeen. He did not look rugged. There ought to be some way of weeding out the sick and weak boys. They shouldn't try to be soldiers. This was somebody's boy—a boy who, by the looks of him, had been loved and cared for and spared hard work. But whose? There was nothing in his pockets or anywhere about him to tell who he was and where he had come from. There was no way to get in touch with his folks or to tell his poor mother! Things like that were beginning to happen in this great uprising.

Everywhere the women were forming into groups to do what had to be done for all these men in a more systematic way. The women usually called their groups "The Ladies' Aid Society." Such a society was organized at the home of Mary Livermore. She agreed to be its president, provided that her lively friend, Mrs. Jane Hoge, would do most of the talking. Mary Livermore did not feel very much at ease in addressing a group of women. But Jane loved to talk, and was always clever and amusing. She could explain anything. Jane said she would do the talking, and Mary would do the doing. And so they would get along. This society at Mary Livermore's house was only one of several thousand that were being formed in the same way.

On April 25, 1861, there were as yet no high command, and no military machinery. There were as yet neither generals nor quartermasters in a position to be of service. Congress would not meet for another two months. But the Ladies' Aid Society was meeting in every American town and electing a president, a vice-president, a secretary, and a treasurer, and appointing a ways and means committee. Of all the people who were working against time to organize this war, the Ladies' Aid Societies got down to business first, with precision, and on a really grand scale.

3. One Hundred Thousand Nightingales

The brains of women are naturally unfitted to comprehend the mysteries of warfare. But these hoop-skirted dames and damsels of 1861, gathering in some neighborhood church, or schoolhouse, or private parlor, to draw up a constitution for the Ladies' Aid Society, did not seem to realize the fact. On the contrary, they felt themselves persons of weight, and even of authority and wisdom, in relation to what the first report of the first Ladies' Aid Society called "our young army now gathering." And they had good reason to feel so. For in those simple days, a man's chances for military advancement depended primarily on the number and competence of his women friends.

For a man who aspired to the rank of captain had to maintain his own recruits until they reached the number of 84, and could be mustered in as a company. This privilege the captain usually divided with his subordinates. A man who wanted to be a lieutenant, for example, had to enlist and maintain fifteen men. Since few of the aspirants for military leadership could afford to pay a local innkeeper or grocer to serve as the Commissary, they fell back on the services and culinary contributions of interested women. Where there was a close competition between two men to form and head the local company, the housewife's talents a man could commandeer might make all the difference in his military future. If Joe Brown and Fred Smith both aspired to form a company, and Mrs. Brown was a good cook and Mrs. Smith wasn't, other things being equal, the men tended to gravitate in the direction of Joe Brown's outfit. They wouldn't put the reason for their choice in so many words. But somehow the boys gathered at Joe's and talked afterwards about the good rhubarb pie they'd had there, incidental to getting their first lesson in tactics.

Even a Colonel's chance of filling and heading a regiment of 1,000 was somewhat influenced by the character of his wife. If she was popular and a good manager, and was going to be with him in camp, people had a feeling that the men would be well looked after in that regiment, and there was a rush to join it. Naturally there was some competition among women, too. A woman who wanted her husband to succeed was likely to bestir herself to organize her women friends, and to set up some kind of army auxiliary service, "so's the boys will be satisfied."

Though there was a good deal of competition in recruiting companies and regiments, there was also much whole-hearted collective action. There were mass meetings attended by everyone in town. Well-to-do citizens subscribed money to outfit the local boys. Storekeepers made contributions. Barracks, recruiting offices, depots for stores, and transportation were contributed free. And the women banded together to make one co-operative job of seeing that the men were fed, clothed, kept clean, and nursed if they needed it, until the state or the national government could take them over. Having determined to do the job all together, the women usually got some kind of center, to which supplies and contributions for the boys might be sent, and which served as a general information headquarters and workroom.

By the time they got to this point, they figured that they'd better organize as a regular corporate body, with a constitution and by-laws and officers. This was the more important since the ladies, having set up a center in some obvious place, rapidly acquired considerable property. It was no uncommon thing for some one to walk in, and to hand the woman who happened to be in charge fifty or one hundred dollars, to "be used for the boys," without asking for a receipt or giving a name or inquiring what became of the money. So the women bestirred themselves to get a treasurer and a finance committee, and to make suitable banking arrangements, and to appoint a responsible board of distinguished citizens who could advise them in their rapidly expanding business. Many of these societies had, from the first, associate male members. They thus became, in effect, a means of mobilizing the business and professional resources of the people for war. This arrangement whereby women became the directing and dynamic force in utilizing the civilian services of men, especially of the older men who had property and ripe experience, proved to be one of the most effective combinations of man-and-woman-power ever devised.

The first Ladies' Aid Society was organized by the women of Bridgeport, Connecticut, on the afternoon of April 15, the day Lincoln called for the first volunteers. The ladies drew up a statement of the objectives of their society. They were to meet every day to sew for the army, to explore means of providing food, clothing, books, and comforts to supplement whatever the government might do, to serve as a channel of communication between volunteers and their home-folks, and to keep a record of each volunteer who left their city.

The Soldiers' Aid Society of Lowell, Massachusetts, and the Soldiers' Aid Society of Northern Ohio, with its headquarters in Cleveland, are typical examples of the way these societies started and were put to work.

On April 18, just as the mayor of Lowell was drawing a long breath after getting off to Washington the Massachusetts Sixth regiment, which was full of Lowell men, the postman handed him a letter from Judge Crosby. Opening it, he found a check for $100 and a letter from the Judge. Judge Crosby confessed that he was worried about these men they had just sent off. He doubted whether the government at Washington was in a position to feed and care for them properly. Through haste and inexperience in providing for them, they might suffer considerably, and some of them might get sick. Wouldn't it be a good idea to put some extra money in the hands of the paymaster of the regiment, to be used for food, clothing, comforts, camp facilities, or medicines as needed? And wouldn't it be a good idea, too, to form a society at home to keep in touch with the men as to fill their needs as they arose? To set the ball rolling, he was enclosing his own check for $100.

A letter from an interested citizen may be ignored. But $100 is a responsibility. So the mayor called a meeting of the City Council that evening, and read the letter to them. The gentlemen of the City Council said that it was an excellent idea, and wrote out checks, themselves, to the total of $500. They now had money for the boys, but where was the Society? The Society should consist of the persons in closest touch with the men, persons to whom they would write the truth about that far-off and not very civilized part of the United States to which they had gone. These persons were naturally the wives, mothers, sisters, and sweethearts of the men. To them men would write what neither mayors nor governors could elicit from a man otherwise. So the ladies were called into council, and helped to set up an Aid Society, of which, more and more, they assumed the executive direction.

As soon as such a society was established, its activities expanded rapidly. For the state government, receiving the men in companies from the communities, was nearly at its wits' end to provide for them. On April 20, for example, Mrs. B. Rouse of Cleveland, "a lady who combined in her character more than ordinary intelligence and force with true feminine purity and tenderness," and who "had been a leading spirit in every benevolent enterprise in her city for twenty-five years," called a mass meeting of women in Chapin Hall. Mrs. Rouse was worrying about the situation of families in which the breadwinner had volunteered. What happened when a man left a woman with a brood of young children behind? Or suppose a man's wife got sick while he was away, or his mother was left in want? Somebody ought to be ready to look after the families of our soldiers.

So Mrs. Rouse got together "nearly all the most intelligent and estimable ladies of the city." Gathered in the hall, on such a "sacred impulse," they quite touched the heart of the chivalrous reporter. "There were flushed faces, aglow with exalted feeling; troubled brows, shaded by vague apprehension; grave countenances, pale with nameless forebodings; eyes that sparkled with excitement, and eyes with startled outlook or dim with gathering tears." But there they all were, and they got right down to business and organized the Soldiers' Aid Society of Northern Ohio, and elected Mrs. Rouse president of it by unanimous acclamation. They chose as a treasurer Miss Ellen Terry who had "enjoyed the benefits of a refined intellectual culture," plus a "mathematical education."

Though they had organized to minister to the families of soldiers in trouble, no sooner was the existence of such an aggregate of willing fingers known, than the state government produced a job for them. On the outskirts of Cleveland the state was setting up a camp of instruction for recruits. Many of these recruits were coming in from outlying farms and villages with insufficient clothing. The government as yet had no uniforms or blankets to give them. Could the ladies uniform them and find bedding? The ladies could.

40

So, having started as good Samaritans and family visitors, they soon found themselves running an army uniform industry instead.

Everywhere it was like that. Women, going through the good-hearted housewife's motions of taking an interest in the neighbors, were catapulted into large army jobs. Two years later a member of the War Department, commenting that Mrs. Rouse and Miss Terry, president and treasurer of the Soldiers' Aid of Northern Ohio, were women of great business ability, added thoughtfully, "But, after all, the various activities of that Society have assumed dimensions reached only in the transactions of our largest commercial establishments. A woman would have to be the equivalent of our greatest men of business to keep all the things they run going."

The fact that the first great modern war, the war that over-topped all the wars of history in geographical scope and in the men and materials involved, began as a people's movement was to have momentous consequences for civilization. The first organization of the largest national army ever assembled was accomplished by civilians who had to depend on women to meet the elementary needs of food, clothing, and comfort. Hitherto war had been mainly the affair of professional armies, and its real character and problems had been screened in pomp and circumstance. The business of bloodshed was shrouded in hocus pocus; the life of the soldier something quite apart from that of the ordinary citizen.

But here was war developing on a colossal scale right in the housewife's front yard. She saw the defenders of her country and of a cause she earnestly believed to be "sacred" not as an army with banners, but as a collection of the various Joes and Jonathans of her own household and neighborhood. She suddenly realized that knights and heroes and warriors bold are nothing but a large crowd of men who will get into dreadful trouble, and probably die quite needlessly, if they aren't looked after better than most men can be trusted to look after themselves.

For about three days after Lincoln called for troops, women were humble and trusting and were just trying to help out until the government could take over the men and organize them properly. Then they began to inquire what the government would do for the men when it got them. What did governments usually do for soldiers? What had Napoleon done? What had the British government in the Crimean War done? In less than a week after they had begun to feed, equip, and find quinine for their local boys, women were asking these questions, and they were beginning to get the answers. And with that, man, as a military mammal, fell down with a crash from the pedestal on which he had placed himself. For seen thus, at close range, it could not but strike an ordinary housewife that the procedures of war, as it had been carried on from time immemorial, were not only barbarous and brutal. They were simply asinine!

Up to 1861 there had been little advance in the soldier's standard of living since the days when Caesar camped with his legions in the woods of Gaul. Camps were pitched for military reasons without regard to drainage or a safe water supply. The great outdoors was the latrine. There was no general provision for cooking. Men were furnished with "salt junk" and "hardtack" and expected to hunt or forage for anything else.

Salt junk or "salt horse" was salted beef, penetrated with saltpeter, yellow-green with rust from having lain in the brine, and a stench in the nostrils. Salt pork, which sometimes alternated with salt beef in the army ration, was more palatable, if it was reasonably fresh. But often it was musty and rancid, or flabby and stringy. Hardtack was a biscuit made of flour and water. The standard army hardtack of 1861 measured three and one-eighth by two and seven-eighths inches and was nearly half an inch thick. Nine of these biscuits constituted a ration. Hardtack was so hard that only a strong set of teeth could risk it. It could not be soaked soft. Long soaking reduced it to a tough, rubbery consistency. Hardtack was bad enough if it was sound and fresh. But it was not the habit of those who provisioned the army to take much pains with the goods. So hardtack was often mouldy, from having been packed too soon after baking. Moreover there was a belief that hardtack would last forever, and that no particular pains need to be taken to preserve it. So when it was finally issued to the soldier, it was likely to be thoroughly riddled with weevils—slim, brown little bugs, whose capacity to eat through hardtack when a strong man couldn't, was a professed object of admiration to seasoned soldiers. Old soldiers said they didn't very much mind the weevils. If you didn't look at what you were eating, you couldn't tell a whole sound piece of hardtack from one inhabited by a couple of hundred weevils,

42

except that the latter crumbled more easily. The weevils didn't have any particular taste, even if you did eat them. So you might as well swallow the bugs with the victuals and not be too fussy.

Salt junk and hardtack was all that an army could be expected to serve its soldiers. If they got anything else, it was by the grace of God or by taking it from the countryside.

The soldiers of the regular army were outfitted with uniforms, blankets, and almost every type of small arms then known, but not with underwear, towels, or bed-linen.

Each regiment of the regular army had a surgeon, and generally one or more assistant surgeons. These surgeons enlisted young, and were sent to places on the frontier far from books or contact with advancing medical knowledge. The few surgical instruments they took with them generally lasted them all their lives. Sometimes they could get medicine through the quartermaster. More often they could not. Apart from surgery, there was no provision whatever for the sick. When a man was wounded, the commanding officer said to the next man, "Get him out of the way." Sick soldiers were expected to care for each other. No special diet was provided for them. If they couldn't eat salt junk and hardtack, they ate nothing. When an army moved on, it dropped off men who could not keep up with the march without care or provision.

One of the best descriptions of army life in 1861 is that given to Mary Livermore by a young man who joined one of the first regiments as a chaplain. A chaplain, he said, is a Christian who sleeps in the open air in a government wagon with hungry mules foraging around and snatching at hay, with crickets, spiders, centipedes, and snakes crawling all over him, and who lives for weeks at a time on salt pork which he detests and hardtack which no water can soften. When asked what preparation he advised for a man who wanted to go as a chaplain, he said:

"To prepare to be a chaplain sleep on the floor of the attic a few nights without pillow or comforter, or in the garden wrapped in a couple of horse-blankets. Get a pound or two of the rustiest pork you can buy and some mouldy crackers and feed on them, eating nothing else for a week. Or treat yourself to a couple of herrings and drink your muddy black coffee without milk or sugar. Make up your mind to be a man among men, cheerful, brave and blameless. Trust in God, and keep your powder dry."

Small frontier armies of tough men used to the region where they were operating, such as the Indian fighters of the West, who constituted most of the American standing army of 1860, might get along in the traditional military style. But when large numbers of civilians were taken out of the comforts of home, and set in motion through populous districts or encamped in and around cities, in accordance with the living standards of the army, the result was pestilential. Even in a relatively healthy frontier army, where food could be supplemented by hunting and foraging and the men could always move on, and leave camp dirt behind, the death-rate of the soldiers from filth and malnutrition and from neglected hurts and infections was, in 1860, very high. This was becoming generally known because of widely publicized studies the British were then making of the sanitary condition of their troops in every part of the Empire, under the direction of a group of men known as the British Sanitary Commission. The British were doing a spectacular job of washing dirty military linen in public. At the washtub stood a woman, a rich, high-bred, and lovely woman, "with dazzling complexion and bright gray eyes," not conventionally beautiful, but of an appearance indescribably "distinguished and elegant." She was Miss Florence Nightingale.

Only six years had passed since that November day in 1855 when Miss Florence Nightingale landed with thirty-seven English-women at Scutari, in the Crimea. Piteous and revolting stories of the condition of English soldiers, dying there not of wounds received in battle but of filth, malnutrition, and neglect, had been published in the *London Times*. It was estimated that of every 1,000 men encamped there 912 bade fair to rot to death in barracks and so-called "hospitals."

Miss Nightingale and the other Englishwomen had come to nurse the sick. Miss Nightingale ended by going after the whole army in the greatest orgy of feminine house-cleaning in history. And while she housecleaned, she wrote home to London. She was a spirited woman, who did not care what she said, and knew supremely how to say it. The Secretary of War was her personal friend. To him, and to the British public, through the columns of the *London Times,* she sent back such a description of food, beds, drains, transport service, medical service, and pompous officials completely tied up in red tape, as made decent, respectable citizens' hair stand on end.

She reported that hundreds of the wounded had contracted cholera and nothing was being done to prevent the infection from spreading. Refuse and rubbish had been thrown into the court-yard of the huge old building which was called a hospital. Sewers of the worst possible construction, loaded with filth, mere cesspools, were underneath the building. In the basement, directly over these sewers, several hundred women, wives and mistresses of the sol-diers, were huddled together. Here some of them were confined. Others were dying of various diseases. The blankets and beds were stiff with filth and dried blood. One small fountain was the only source of water, so that, even if enough orderlies had been on duty to wash the men and their wounds, there would not have been enough water to keep them clean. The lack of proper medical and surgical equipment was as appalling as the inadequate sanitary ar-rangements. Sick men lay on hard, lumpy, and dirty pads and suffered terribly from bedsores. And there were not enough band-ages—men were simply allowed to bleed to death.

Part of the difficulty was due to the fact that military men had never even dreamed of applying ordinary human standards of comfort and cleanliness to soldiers. Part of it was due to red tape and administrative inefficiency. The transport of army stores was so tangled up in clearance papers, bills of lading, and the like that goods were constantly shuttled back and forth on the sea, unable to land though desperately needed. When Miss Night-ingale finally succeeded in getting bedsteads she found that the iron legs had been put on another ship and sent back to Balaclava. Though Miss Nightingale began as a nurse, she ended by running a sort of importing business for a distracted army that seemed unable to feed or clothe itself. "The fact is," she wrote, "that I am now clothing the British army. . . . I am a kind of general dealer in socks, shirts, knives, forks, wooden spoons, tin baths. . . . cab-bages and carrots, operating tables, towels and soap, and small pillows."

Working twenty hours a day, tramping through four miles of hospital corridors, overseeing everything, Miss Nightingale made decency and order, imposing relentlessly on the slovenliness and pompous self-importance of current military administration a well-bred woman's notions of good housekeeping. She cared for sick and wounded men as a mother cares for her own children. She saw to it that they were fed as a lady feeds the guest at her

45

board. Two of the many popular descriptions of Miss Nightingale's methods caught the fancy of the public. They were almost always read aloud at the first meeting of the Ladies' Aid Society in every American town and village, in those spring days of 1861.

One of these was a letter from the Commissioner of the fund which the *London Times* had started to provide Miss Nightingale with means of carrying out her reforms. "Wherever there is disease in its most dangerous form and the hand of the despoiler distressingly nigh, there is that incomparable woman sure to be seen. ... As her slender form glides quietly along each corridor, every poor fellow's face softens with gratitude at the sight of her. When all the medical officers have retired for the night and silence and darkness have settled down upon these miles of prostrate sick, she may be observed alone, with a little lamp in her hands, making her solitary rounds."

This had been turned by Longfellow into a poem, which was usually recited at the first meeting of the Ladies' Aid, by the town's most gifted elocutionist.

> *Lo, in that house of misery*
> *A lady with a lamp I see*
>   *Pass through the glimmering gloom*
>   *And flit from room to room.*

> . . . .

> *On England's annals through the long*
> *Hereafter of her speech and song*
>   *That light its rays shall cast*
>   *From portals of the past.*

> *A lady with a lamp shall stand*
> *In the great history of the land*
>   *A noble type of good*
>   *Heroic womanhood.*

This was very touching and beautiful, and after the more susceptible members of the Ladies' Aid had paid it the tribute of wiping their eyes and sniffing a little over it, they perked up and listened to the description of Miss Nightingale's methods which was *really* their favorite. This was Harriet Martineau's description of the way Miss Nightingale could cook.

"The very idea of that kitchen was savory in the wards; for

out of it came, at the right moment, arrow-root, hot, and of the pleasantest consistence; rice puddings, neither hard on the one hand, nor clammy on the other; cool lemonade for the feverish; cans full of hot tea for the weary, and good coffee for the faint. ... The meat from that kitchen was tenderer than any other, the beef tea was more savory. One thing that came out of it was the lesson on the saving of good cookery. The mere circumstance of the boiling water being really boiling there, made a difference of two ounces of rice in every four puddings, and of more than half the arrow-root used. The same quantity of arrow-root that made a pint thin and poor in the general kitchen made two pints thick and good in Miss Nightingale's."

This description was a great favorite with the ladies. Wherever, in the years to come, they set up a kitchen that ministered to soldiers, you would be likely to see a copy of this hanging on the wall.

Miss Nightingale's heroic work in the Crimea was only the beginning of a continuing influence that reached its height at the time when the American ladies were forming their Aid societies. For the British people had subscribed 44,000 pounds ($220,000) for her to use as she thought best, in developing proper care of the sick and wounded in the army, and in raising the standards of health and well-being for soldiers. In 1857 the Queen had appointed a commission to inquire into army camps and hospital arrangements in co-operation with Miss Nightingale. In 1859 a similar commission had been appointed to work with Miss Nightingale in surveying the problems of the British army in India. This Englishwoman had become easily the most distinguished military figure of her time. Her observations were constantly quoted and she minced no words.

So the ladies of the Ladies' Aid, having paid due tribute to Miss Nightingale as the flower of heroic womanhood, could get right down to brass tacks, and learn that the British Sanitary Commission found that 354 out of every 1,000 soldiers had venereal disease, or more than one soldier in three. The principal cause of this, said Miss Nightingale, was boredom and want of interesting occupation. But she thought over-rigid discipline and an harassing amount of drill tended to drive the men into vicious courses as a means of distraction. As for wives and other female camp followers, Miss Nightingale was not for abusing or even banishing

47

them as contaminators of the British army. The best thing, she thought, was to establish laundries and sewing rooms where they might do some real good, keeping in decent order a lot of men who needed it, and meanwhile earn an honest penny. This might limit their attentions to one man of their choice, and prevent them from acquiring and spreading disease. As for the soldiers, some coffee-houses, schools, recreation halls, reading rooms, and money order and home-communication arrangements might fill their time with something besides "vice." Drunkenness, Miss Nightingale admitted, was the curse of the British army. She thought decent living conditions, good food, sports and outdoor exercises of an interesting kind might alleviate conditions that caused drunkenness. But apart from raising the general intelligence and wellbeing of the soldier, the best thing she could suggest was plenty of good beer. If they could get good beer, they were not so likely to drink rum.

Ideas like this—honest, forthright, tolerant, and kind—were poured forth by this great exemplar of mid-Victorian womanhood, and were circulated among the American Ladies' Aid societies. She kept the old generals of Europe purple with blushes. There was nothing she wouldn't talk about, and nothing she wouldn't say, in the plainest words and no mincing matters. Yet in every word she said, she remained a lady—not only a lady, but a great lady. She seemed to think that the humblest soldier, the man who had hitherto been only cannon-fodder, and the lowest female camp-follower was entitled to exactly what she, as a great and rich woman, would offer her guests in her own house. She would talk about the most intimate and secret habits and ailments of a drunken, diseased soldier, quietly stripping him down to his bowels, letting the light of day in on his unmentionable vices, and when she had finished making hash of the mystery and hocus-pocus with which men have tried to veil their masculine indulgences, one realized that, in every word, she had been giving that poor fellow back his dignity as a man.

In the later days of the Civil War, Miss Nightingale's observations were constantly published in the *Sanitary Commission Bulletin,* the magazine of the aid societies. But in those early days of April, 1861, when the societies were holding their first meetings, they circulated in the form of clippings from English publications. And of course ladies everywhere possessed copies of

48

Miss Nightingale's *Notes on Nursing,* which had been published in England in 1859 and in Boston in 1860. They often quoted from it such remarks as, "People talk about the effect of the mind on the body. I want to talk about the effect of the body on the mind"; or "Management is the art of multiplying one's self, so that what is well done when one is there is equally well done when one is *not* there."

For every man on his way to join the army, there was now a Florence Nightingale at home, sitting in the rooms of the Ladies' Aid Society, stitching on army shirts, tearing old linen into bandages, scraping lint, and listening to items about the way the British Sanitary Commission was putting a woman's reforms into the British army. And under her scoop bonnet each Florence was tucking away a great idea: if a woman just made enough fuss, the Government would have to appoint a Sanitary Commission to do what she said!

4

Not all the Ladies' Aid groups had to depend on newspapers and books for their guidance from Miss Nightingale. In Boston, Newport, R. I., and New York, they were in direct touch with her personally, through Americans to whom she had been writing for years. Chief among the American friends of Miss Nightingale was "dear Doctor Howe." The Ladies' Aids of Boston, Newport, and New York all consulted Doctor Howe. Miss Nightingale herself had consulted him for years.

Doctor Samuel Gridley Howe of Boston was described by Miss Nightingale as "one of the greatest and best men of our age," a man with a "noble horror of helpless pity," and "indomitable faith in progress." To charity and good works he had contrived to give the highest splendor of romance. Of him Whittier wrote:

> *Wherever outraged Nature*
> *Asks word or action brave,*
> *Wherever struggles labor,*
> *Wherever groans a slave—*
> *Wherever rise the peoples,*
> *Wherever sinks a throne,*
> *The throbbing heart of Freedom finds*
> *An answer in his own.*

When he was a young man of twenty, just graduated from medical school, and the handsomest youth in Boston, he had been fired, like Byron, with enthusiasm for the Greeks in the War of Independence and had set out to help them. He served with the Greek army both as surgeon and soldier, and made himself so beloved that all sorts of legend and balladry gathered around the chivalrous young American. People called him "the Chevalier." Ladies who saw him on horseback declared that he was the perfect image of the knight, *sans peur et sans reproche*. When he returned to America, he might have had anything and done anything. But he settled down to a humble and hard-working career, as a physician to the blind. As such he devised a system of education for blind persons which finally culminated in his great triumph of teaching Laura Bridgeman, born deaf, dumb, and blind, to speak.

He captured the imagination of the public again when he married Julia Ward, "the pretty blue-stocking," a belle of old New York admired by Longfellow and Sumner and other distinguished men for her charm and her gifts. The Wards were among the most respected members of the small but sacrosanct aristocracy of New York, and had a hospitable home, well supported by the ownership of large blocks of real estate in the center of the growing city of New York.

All social doors here and abroad were open to the famous doctor and his charming wife. When they went to England, Florence Nightingale's parents invited them to stay at Embley Park, the stately old country estate of the Nightingales in Hampshire, England. This was in 1844. Florence, then an eager young woman of twenty-four, was thrilled, like most young Englishwomen, to meet the romantic American doctor. He was so handsome, so unassuming and kind. He had always done daring and noble deeds in a matter-of-fact way. But when she asked the doctor to let her read his scientific reports on the care of the blind, the quality of the writing in those reports—so much like the quality she herself later achieved—struck a deeper note in the gifted girl's soul. She would read again and again such a sentence as this: "The sight of any being in human shape, left to brutish ignorance, is always demoralizing to the beholders. There floats not upon the stream of life any wreck of humanity so utterly shattered and crippled that its signals of distress should not challenge attention and command assistance."

50

Observing that the doctor used to rise early, and take a turn up and down the long and beautiful garden paths of Embley Park, Florence took her social courage in both hands, and asked him one evening if she might meet him in the garden next morning before breakfast.

He assented in that kind, unsurprised, matter-of-fact way that made him the chosen confidant of so many women for so many years.

"Doctor Howe," she said to him, next morning, walking with him among the roses, "you have had much experience in the world of philanthropy; you are a medical man and a gentleman; now may I ask you to tell me, upon your word, whether it would be anything unsuitable or unbecoming to a young Englishwoman, if she should devote herself to works of charity in hospitals and elsewhere, as the Catholic sisters do?"

Doctor Howe replied, "My dear Miss Florence, it would be unusual, and in England whatever is unusual is apt to be thought unsuitable, but I say to you, go forward, if you have a vocation for that way of life; act up to your aspiration; and you will find that there is never anything unbecoming or unladylike in doing your duty for the good of others. Choose your path. Go on with it, wherever it may lead you, and God be with you."

So he had talked to her, and so both he and his wife talked to her for years in letters across the Atlantic, encouraging her in her studies of hospitals and in her struggles to find or devise some kind of training for nursing, at a time when there was no such thing outside the charitable efforts of some religious sisterhoods. Those were the days when hospitals were only places where one dumped the paupers who were ill, when, as Florence Nightingale said, she could find no nurses who were not drunkards, and few who did not carry on sexual intercourse in the wards with any male patient who wanted them. Those were the days when the nurses at Bellevue hospital in New York City were described as "drunken prostitutes." But Miss Nightingale would be a nurse, and when her English family and friends disapproved, she could always write to the good American doctor and his wife, and receive their sensible, kind, brave answers.

Doctor Howe was a Boston institution. Mrs. Howe was a New York institution. They spent their summers at Newport, Rhode

Island, where the rich and great of both cities congregated. So nearly everybody knew the Howes, and as the various leaders in towns along the Atlantic seaboard from Boston to New York began to form soldiers' aid societies, almost everybody consulted the Howes, and so heard what Florence Nightingale had said about this, and what she would do about that. Some of them wrote Miss Nightingale letters asking for her advice in regard to the new American army, which the doctor said she would surely answer. And in due time she did.

Meanwhile there was another friend of Miss Nightingale's who was prepared to take immediate action. She was Doctor Elizabeth Blackwell who had made a place for herself in the circles in New York City to which the Howes belonged—those circles in which the most progressive reformers and social and intellectual radicals of all kinds met and joined hands with the old blue-bloods. Doctor Elizabeth Blackwell was a quiet, stubborn little woman of forty who had been the first woman in the world to achieve a degree as Doctor of Medicine. Her long and determined fight for full medical training had made her an international figure. She had completed her training in Paris with the respect and admiration of French intellectual circles, and had been acclaimed in London. Florence Nightingale sent her a message of congratulation on her long battle, which started a friendship that went on for years in a copious correspondence across the Atlantic. Since other women who were trying to follow in her footsteps were finding it impossible to get a chance to practice in hospitals, Doctor Blackwell, and her sister Emily, who had also graduated from medical school, established in New York City the New York Infirmary for Women and Children. This was supported by the Quakers (who believed in the equality of men and women in all types of work) and was completely staffed with women doctors.

Years of battle had taught Doctor Blackwell to be very quiet, very unobtrusive, and to let somebody else, preferably a man, take credit for what she did, if possible. But a large proportion of New York's "most respected gentlewomen," the daughters and wives of the rich and the great, had come to have great faith in her.

So it happened that, on April 25, in a room in the New York Infirmary for Women and Children, a large company of these ladies gathered to form a Ladies' Aid society, with immediate reference to the encampments of volunteers who were coming down with measles on Staten Island. And what they did at that meeting made history. For then and there they took up the work of Florence Nightingale, and began to turn it out, in a truly American style, on a mass-production basis.

4. *Ninety-two Respected Gentlewomen*

On the morning of April 25, the family coaches of the Roosevelts, the Astors, the Schuylers, and others whose stately passing could always make the city cab-driver sit up and take notice, were all drawn up before a neat, modest little building on the lower end of Manhattan Island. And each was unloading such a cargo of frilled and fluted hoop-skirts, fashionable mantles, and superlative spring bonnets as could not be seen elsewhere outside of *Godey's Lady's Book*. For the Astor, Schuyler, and Roosevelt coachmen had been instructed to circulate among the brownstone residences, under the rows of maple trees just feathering out in red and green, and to pick up the ladies for Doctor Blackwell's meeting.

It was pleasant to see the flowers of New York society entering the New York Infirmary for Women and Children that morning. Their hoops swayed gracefully as they walked, with a rhythmical, billowing motion. And in their wake there was a faint fragrance of the best cologne water. In those days, when Miss Nightingale had made *sanitary* a word to conjure with, few ladies cared to use a perfume stronger than cologne water. For had not Miss Nightingale remarked that a perfumed lady was too often *dirty?* The thing to do, said Miss Nightingale, is not to disguise the *smell* but to remove the *thing that smells*. So, immaculately fresh, and only delicately cologned, the ladies moved into the Infirmary and looked around with approval, because here there was no smell of disinfectants. Miss Nightingale had said that to disinfect a sickroom is too often an excuse for not *cleaning* it. Here in the Infirmary everything shone with pure elbow grease, and smelled pleasantly of April odors drifting in through the open windows.

For had not Miss Nightingale said that windows are made to open, and doors are made to shut!

There were three generations of ladies in the company that rippled through the corridor of the Infirmary that morning. There was gray-haired Mrs. Dix, Mrs. General Dix, they called her, wife of General John A. Dix who had till March 4 been Secretary of the Treasury at Washington, and who would soon be Major-general of the New York Volunteers. And there was Mrs. William Cullen Bryant, wife of the venerable poet and editor. But there was also a bouncing group of very young women, among whom there was one who stood out with clean-cut distinction. She was Louisa Lee Schuyler, aged twenty-four, great-granddaughter of Alexander Hamilton, and doubly descended from General Philip Schuyler, since her mother, the granddaughter of Alexander Hamilton and Betsy Schuyler, had married a Schuyler cousin. Brought up on the Hudson River estate, in the security of unpretentious wealth, she was a healthy, vigorous, natural young woman, so much like a modern college girl that an observer of to-day would want to strip off those unsuitable-looking hoop skirts and get her into tennis shorts. In contrast to the cascading spring frills of the costumes all around her, her simple, fawn-colored spring outfit, with its crisp linen collar, was smart and functional. And she walked with a direct stride that gave a dancing buoyancy to her hoops, and carried her forward as if on a strong gust of wind. Going ahead of the others, she was pointing out with enthusiasm the various features of the Infirmary.

Some of the ladies wanted to linger in the corridor, and look into the rooms where poor women and children were receiving a care that no invalid, on a millionaire's great curtained, four-poster bed, could yet command. Some were curious to see the white iron bedsteads. The idea of sleeping on iron, even if it didn't come in contact with your body, was pretty cold and forbidding. But they did say no vermin could get into these beds, and here in New York, even an Astor or a Schuyler could never feel quite safe from a bedbug. The rooms looked very fresh and pleasant, with their white iron beds, and starched white covers, and ruffled white curtains, and tables and window sills filled with flowers. Miss Nightingale approved of flowers in a sickroom, and the ladies of New York delighted to send the surplus of their conservatories and the flowers they had ordered for balls and large

55

parties down to the Infirmary. Here and there a lady stopped and asked pleasantly for one of the nurses, and chatted with her a moment. The nurses looked very nice, though a little odd, in their full brown skirts without hoops, their large ruffled white aprons with bibs, and their enormous white mob-caps of dotted Swiss. Here at the Infirmary, Doctor Blackwell was demonstrating that a nurse could be a good, kind, even a well-educated human being, and keep herself tidy no matter what she had to do.

So they passed on down the corridors and congregated in a large room decorated with a skeleton and some physiological charts. Settling down there, in little circles and groups, they pulled out their sewing and all began talking at once. Though most of them had the low-pitched, well-modulated voice which was the hallmark of a lady, and was systematically taught in the fashionable girls' schools, their vocabulary was crisp and downright. A certain kind of high-flown verbiage which passed for elegance in current publications was practically never heard when elegant females spoke their minds in private. Though literary fashions in America have come and gone, the vernacular has always remained much the same. So, despite the literary style in which these dear angels were sometimes described, in current pieces of literature written about them, when they spoke for themselves, they talked just like to-day's meeting of the League of Women Voters or the American Women's Voluntary Services. From many diaries, letters, and reminiscences of the day, it is not difficult to piece together just about what they were saying that morning.

They started with the news that measles had broken out over on Staten Island where several thousand soldiers were gathering. Had they quarantined the cases? Doctor Ellis had tried. But all he could get to use as a hospital was a dreadful old building simply foul with dirt, and when the storm came up the other day, the roof leaked so that he had to move the men back into their tents, where they are now infecting every one else.

"And unfortunately," amended Doctor Blackwell, grimly, "the disease over there is of a malignant variety."

Three ladies then volunteered the information that they had gone over to Staten Island to look at the troops and their camps through the connivance of Mrs. Dix. Here Mrs. Dix, seated under the skeleton, paused in her sewing and began to listen intently, as the report on the Staten Island camp prattled on.

"Some of the men have tents, but men come in so fast that there are not enough tents to go around."

"What kind of tents? The Sibley tents? The ones that look like Indian wigwams."

"Oh no, these are just the little wedge-shaped tents—you know—the kind they call dog-tents?"

"Why dog-tents?" asked an inquiring female.

"Because a dog wouldn't live in one," said some one else.

"Better call them pup-tents," said another. "They are only large enough for a pup. They can't be more than five feet each way."

"And my John is six feet tall," murmured a voice. "What can he do with the other foot?"

"Cut it off and add it to his waistline. That's the old army way. Never fit a tent to a man. Fit a man to a tent."

"I think the tents are all right—or anyway they serve—but I don't see why they should be so mouldy," observed a voice.

Mrs. Dix spoke suddenly, "My dear girl, when you have had to do with the army so long as I have you'll know that everything in the army is mouldy. Mould just naturally adheres to the military profession."

"Mouldy or not, if I was a man," said another, "I'd want something between me and the rain. It's rained every other day since they've been there, and half of them are lying right out in the mud all night."

At this there was a titter that grew and grew from group to group, as they kept passing a piece of paper on from one to another. It was a letter written to one of the younger women present by her fiancé who was captain of a company now over on Staten Island. It ended with *A Soldier's Prayer.*

> *Now I lay me down in mud,*
> *And wrap me in the roaring flood.*
> *If I'm not here, when you awake,*
> *Just look for me with an oyster rake.*

"But don't they get colds or pneumonia or something out there in the wet?" asked an anxious-looking little woman.

"They do," said Doctor Blakwell grimly. "Present indications are that a third of this army will be taken off by respiratory and pulmonary diseases before it ever sees action."

There was a horrified silence. Finally Mrs. Dix said soothingly.

"Really, every one is working just as hard as he can to see that our soldiers are provided for. Look at the general—and at his age, too—he didn't come in till three last night. We must be patient."

"While we are being patient," said Miss Louisa Schuyler, "our army will be dead."

"But really," said Mrs. Dix, "the state is doing absolutely everything it can. Look at the food allowance. They aren't asking those men to eat hardtack. They are allowing $.40 a day for each man, to be spent on a good and varied diet."

"$.40 a day!" exclaimed several women present, for, at the current price of food, this was indeed a munificent allowance.

"On $.40 a day," said Mrs. Astor, "I could feed myself, my butler, and my maid."

"Yes," said a young woman who was staying with the Roosevelt family. "And look what is happening to that $.40. The government has let the contracts for feeding the men to private restaurant keepers. They are pocketing the money, and giving the men only what the army ration amounts to—only worse, because, bad as salt junk is, I do think it possible to make it even worse by bad cooking. And did you hear what happened last night? The men got so angry at the kind of swill handed them for supper that they organized a big riot and smashed the cook house, and ran all those fellows and so-called cooks who are supposed to be feeding them right off the island. Al came over to New York on a mission to General Dix this morning. And he told me about it."

"The men must have been drunk," said Mrs. Dix.

"I don't think they were drunk," said Miss Schuyler. "I think they were intelligent."

At this point Doctor Blackwell seized the conversation with a firm hand. "All these observations of the army camps are very smart," she said, "but, frankly, they are scatter-brained. All over the country women are forming societies, and they're just meddling with the army without being in the position really to do anything about it. And that's why I got you all together here this morning. As you know, I have had a lot of experience in getting my own way when nobody wanted me to have it. And I've found that there's just one way to do it. You do it by bringing up all the available strength you have, in any quarter, and concentrating it all, firmly and persistently and continuously, on just one thing at a time.

"So I suggest that instead of just forming another Ladies' Aid, we proceed now to set up a central agency in New York with which all the aid societies everywhere can affiliate themselves in one concerted effort to bring all civilian resources to bear on winning our war. I suggest that we get a full list of all existing societies, enter into correspondence with them, get as many of them as possible to agree on one concerted line of action, and then try to see that future societies are organized, within the fold, so to speak, with our advice and co-operation.

"And having got this pooling of the people's power started —you notice I don't say *woman power*—I think what women are good for is to organize all the people's power for what women care about, which is really what men care most about, too, only they don't know it—as I was saying, having got started on organizing everybody everywhere, let us concentrate first on one single object."

She paused. Every one was now listening intently. Finally Mrs. Dix asked, "What object?"

"The object of getting a complete, generous, and scientific preparation now for the care of all the sickness that may develop in this army, and all the wounds that may be received in battle."

"If we do that," said Mrs. Dix, "we do something never yet achieved by man. There never has been any preparation on any adequate scale for the care of the wounded in any battle yet fought."

"That's no reason why it shouldn't begin right here on the American continent in this year of grace 1861," said Miss Schuyler.

And at this point they settled down, and began mapping out with pencil and paper the methods by which they would proceed with their campaign.

Meanwhile, outside of the Infirmary, a troubled young man was walking up and down. He was Doctor Elisha Harris, a bright young doctor from Vermont, still in his thirties, who, for the last five years had been superintendent of the quarantine hospitals for immigrants on Staten Island. He had been invited to come to the meeting of these great ladies. He did not dare to refuse, and he did not dare to go in. The ladies would ask him too many uncomfortable questions. Things were in a mess over there on Staten Island now that the volunteers were being put there, with

59

no preparation, but he didn't see what these women could do about it. And yet they were so cussedly powerful, with their social connections and all. They might make him say anything, and then it might be used against him—which certainly would not be good for a young doctor with his way to make.

Slowly and thoughtfully up the street came another gentleman, a substantial scholarly figure with graying hair. He was Doctor Henry Bellows, aged fifty-three, pastor of the First Unitarian Church of New York. Here indeed was a tower of strength! Doctor Bellows could champion more radical causes, and keep more snugly on the right side of the conservative powers that were in the great city, than any man then going. He paused a little uncertainly before the Infirmary. So he had been invited to the ladies' meeting, too, and even he didn't want to go in! Then Harris spoke to Bellows. They fell into conversation. Each thought that he should tell the ladies to be patient and to wait "for government to act." But which of them had the courage to do it? In union there is strength. They combined forces, and shoulder to shoulder they marched in. They were immediately overwhelmed by bonnets and hoop skirts. When they finally spoke it was to promise weakly to help the ladies to organize a mass meeting for Monday next, and to get some of their gentlemen friends to come!

2

The day after this meeting, while the ladies were still trying to work out with Doctor Blackwell a means of enlisting the New York medical profession in their cause, they received some providential assistance. This was in the shape of a letter in the first mail from Washington that had got through for a week. It was addressed to Doctor Blackwell, from Miss Dorothea Dix.

Dorothea Dix was the nearest American equivalent to Florence Nightingale. She lacked Miss Nightingale's charm, and high social position, and her great wealth of natural endowments. But her career had been, in many respects, more sombrely heroic. That career had begun twenty years ago, in Boston. Miss Dix was then a modest member of the intellectual circle that included Longfellow, Charles Sumner, Doctor Samuel Howe, and Doctor William Ellery Channing. She had been a governess to Dr. Channing's children, and had had a fashionable girls' school of her own. She had written, in 1824, a little book entitled *Conversations on Common Things,* that had become a household classic. It went through sixty editions between 1824 and 1860 and brought her a steady income. This income, added to her savings from her earnings as a teacher, and some inheritance from her grandparents had, at the age of thirty-nine, made her independent of the need of earning her daily bread, and had given her a chance to invest her abounding energy in good works. She was at that time a tall, slender, blue-eyed woman, of some natural beauty, with a soft voice, a gentle manner, and great dignity and "elegance." But the will-power and mental downrightness under this pleasing feminine exterior made her a holy terror. "I have no great love of my species," she said, "but I confess to an exhaustless fund of compassion."

One day Miss Dix undertook to teach a Sunday School class in the East Cambridge gaol. There she discovered, to her horror, that insane prisoners were confined in an unheated room and subjected to cruel physical suffering. She talked to Doctor Howe about it. He talked to Charles Sumner. They wondered if insane persons were treated in that way in other places. Miss Dix undertook to find out. For two years she toured her state, looking into every town and village, and when she had finished she had a social exhibit that made the Boston intelligentsia sick. So they combined with her to put through the Massachusetts legislature a bill insuring more humane care of the insane and the mentally ill.

Miss Dix then carried her fight for the care of mental disease into other states. In the next seven years, she traveled 10,000 miles, from Nova Scotia to the Gulf of Mexico, by uncomfortable railroad trains, by river steamers, by farm wagons, by any and all conveyances, visiting 300 county jails, 18 state penitentiaries, and 500 almshouses. What she found she described in 1848 in a memorial to the United States Congress asking for the passage of a Federal bill to assist the states in reforming these abuses. "I myself have seen more than 9,000 idiots, epileptics, and insane in these United States, destitute of appropriate care and protection, and of this vast and miserable company, sought out in jails, in poorhouses, and in private dwellings, there have been hundreds, nay thousands, bound with galling chains, bowed beneath fetters and heavy iron balls attached to drag chains, lacerated with ropes, scourged with rods, and terrified beneath storms of profane execration and cruel blows; now subject to gibes and scorn and torturing tricks, now abandoned to the most loathsome necessities, or subject to the vilest and most outrageous violations. These are strong terms, but language fails to convey the astonishing truths. I proceed to verify these assertions, beginning with the state of Maine."

In 1854 Miss Dix secured the passage by Congress of a bill granting to the states 12,250,000 acres of public lands to be used for the benefit of the insane, deaf and dumb, and blind, but President Pierce vetoed it. She had got insane asylums established in twenty states; and she had meanwhile got lifesaving service introduced on Sable Island off Nova Scotia to reduce the frightful death-toll of ships on the North Atlantic. Going to England in 1854, for a rest, she interested herself in the problems of the mentally ill there, and started a European campaign which, in the next few years, covered the continent as far as Turkey. She was in Europe when the furor about the conditions in the Crimea broke out in England. She herself made a complete independent investigation of the military camps, and of Miss Nightingale's reforms.

When Lincoln called for 75,000 volunteers, Miss Dix started for Washington with the first troops. She was then fifty-nine and intended to rest. But not until she saw to it that the ills of the Crimea were never repeated here! She got through to Washington on the train that followed the Massachusetts Sixth out of rioting Baltimore. Her first concern was for the 17 wounded men the Massachusetts regiment were carrying with them. But in this she was forestalled. For another Massachusetts woman had taken them in charge. This was Clara Barton, a slim little midget of a woman, only five feet tall, with brown eyes and a wide, expressive mouth, who had been a schoolteacher in Massachusetts, and then a clerk in the patent office in Washington, until she was fired for entertaining abolition sentiments. Miss Barton had met the tired men from Baltimore and their casualties with five negroes carrying baskets of food and drink. She hovered over them while they were being barracked in the Senate Chamber, and then stood on the steps of the Vice-president's chair and read them the account of their battle and their present fortunes that she was going to send back to the papers at home. As soon as she could get word through to New England, she was going to advertise in the home press for everything they needed. Meanwhile if there was anything that could be done for these boys, in besieged, distracted, and demoralized Washington, Miss Barton was doing it.

Leaving the Massachusetts Sixth to Miss Barton, Miss Dix saw the Surgeon General and pointed out that Washington was not equipped to handle 17 wounded men. They were surviving only by the grace of God and Clara Barton. A great and bloody battle might develop in and around the city at any moment. To-morrow they might all be fighting for their lives in the streets. What was the Surgeon General going to do about it? The poor Surgeon General didn't exactly know. Miss Dix said she'd do something about it if he'd let her, and if he didn't let her, she would do it anyway. She would begin by recruiting and properly training one hundred women in the Nightingale techniques, and meanwhile she'd find all the buildings in Washington that could be put into passable hygienic condition for hospitals and would see that they were equipped. If the government could equip them, very well. But anyway they would be equipped. Miss Dix, referred to President Lincoln, told him the same thing. John Hay, Lincoln's secretary recorded, "She makes munificent offers."

Miss Dix was an old hand at pushing the officials in Washington around. They didn't exactly encourage her. They merely knew that it was hopeless to stop her. So Miss Dix assumed that if she produced the one hundred nurses, the army would take them, providing pay, subsistence, and transportation. Such a thing had never been done in the history of warfare. Miss Nightingale's nurses in the Crimea had been interlopers without official status.

Miss Dix's proposal was distinctly embarrassing to the War Department. Women as angels were one thing, but women as regularly enlisted personnel were quite another. This raised all sorts of questions a gentleman could not discuss with a lady, though the lady, soft-voiced and elegant, would quite unblushingly have discussed them with him—toilet facilities, for example, and—er—immorality. The War Department could not discuss the matter, and it could not stop Miss Dix. So she went ahead and wrote to Doctor Elizabeth Blackwell, saying that she could place one hundred nurses in the army just as soon as they were recruited and trained. Would Doctor Blackwell recruit and train them?

While the ladies in New York were still getting out their invitations to Monday's rally, Doctor Blackwell held a conference in which she laid the letter from Miss Dix before a few select spirits.

63

Some of these ladies were jubilant. They considered this the opening wedge in getting official recognition of the place of trained women in war. They were glad the opportunity to train the first army nurses in Miss Nightingale's techniques had come to Doctor Blackwell. She could do much better at it than most medical men. Forward under the banners of Florence Nightingale!

But Doctor Blackwell pointed out that New York was full of ambitious physicians. Some were young men who had been trained in new methods of healing, such as the use of anesthetics. Some were distinguished older men who had kept up with all the marvelous advances science and medicine had been making in recent years. These men had followed with interest the reports of the British Sanitary Commission. They were quite ready to put in practice Miss Nightingale's reforms and even to better them, but they did hate to have things thrust down their throats by a woman! Most of the modern well-trained doctors were just like the women themselves, longing to get their hands on the army camps, baffled by military red tape and traditional practice. And how would they feel if the first chance to do something really modern and efficient in providing for the health of the soldiers should be monopolized by a woman doctor?

No, said Doctor Blackwell. Leave her out of it. Take this assignment, and put on their prettiest smiles and their most humble female need of "guidance," and run around to the men doctors and ask if they wouldn't help Miss Dix out by starting a class for the nurses at Bellevue Hospital. Doctor Blackwell would tell them just which medical men to approach, and just what to suggest. And meanwhile she was writing to Miss Nightingale for her suggestions.

The doctors, assured that this wasn't just a wild pipe-dream of the ladies but that a person of Miss Dix's power had actually got encouragement for it from President Lincoln's office, took the idea up with enthusiasm. Between April 25 and April 30, they held two meetings and organized two associations to co-operate with the association the women were going to form. These were the: Advisory Committee of the Boards of Physicians and Surgeons of the Hospitals of New York, and the New York Medical Association for Furnishing Hospital Supplies in Aid of the Army. The doctors were looking for an opening wedge, too, and suddenly saw the enthusiasm of women as a professional godsend. The introduction of female nurses into the army, under the powerful championship of Miss Dix might be made the beginning of a good many other sanitary reforms!

3

On April 29 every newspaper in New York published a call to the women of New York City to meet in Cooper Institute at eleven o'clock on Monday morning, April 30. This call was signed by the city's "Ninety-Two Most Respected Gentlewomen." Next day 4,000 women gathered in the auditorium of the handsome new adult education center recently built by Mr. Peter Cooper, who was New York City's most colorful self-made millionaire, the owner of more than half the telegraph lines in the United States, and the husband of one of the ninety-two gentlewomen. The meeting was opened by the Honorable Hannibal Hamlin, Vice-President of the United States, and briefly addressed by two members of the garrison of Fort Sumter. The ladies present then formed themselves into the Women's Central Association for Relief, with a Board of Managers of which Dr. Valentine Mott accepted the presidency.

Doctor Valentine Mott was the dean of American medical men and one of the world's greatest surgeons. His seventy-six years of life, thus far, had spanned practically the whole history of the American Republic, and had seen great changes in medicine. His intellectual arteries had never hardened. Vivid, active, young, with a mind as fresh as a girl's, he perceived the medical opportunity Miss Dix and Doctor Blackwell were opening, and brought his immense professional influence to their support.

While Doctor Mott was placing the highest authority of American medicine behind the ladies, Peter Cooper was setting them up with an office in his Institute. Every afternoon a committee of doctors, including Doctor Elizabeth Blackwell and Doctor Harris, interviewed candidates for the position of army nurses in the Philosophical Rooms of the Institute. Mrs. Hamilton Fish and a committee of ladies with financially powerful masculine advisers began to raise funds. Doctor Bellows and a group of ladies began to draft a constitution.

The office of the new association, which soon came to be known as "The Women's Central" was in charge of Miss Louisa Lee

Schuyler, the Corresponding Secretary. "We began life," reported Miss Schuyler later, "in a little room which contained two tables, one desk, half a dozen chairs, and a map on the wall. . . . We sent out circulars, wrote letters, looked out of the windows at the passing regiments, and talked about our work, sometimes hopefully, sometimes despairingly."

They might well despair. For it soon appeared that all these generous and flattering supporters among the men were accomplishing exactly nothing. "They think to humor a temporary excitement, and to conduct it to speedy nothingness," remarked Miss Schuyler. Gradually even the flattery ceased. The War Department informed them that no arrangements whatever had been made to receive women as nurses. General John Dix, in command of the New York volunteers, threw cold water all over them, even though his wife was one of the "Ninety-two most respected gentlewomen." And finally Doctor Bellows, dear Doctor Bellows, their brave and powerful backer, felt bound to say publicly that the women's efforts were ill-advised and could only do harm.

5. *"A Fifth Wheel to the Coach"*

"There is one institution of government we are still privileged to use," said Miss Schuyler. "And that's the United States post office."

The first use they made of it was to send a letter to Miss Dix. Miss Dix made a forced march against the War Department and opened up all her guns. The Medical Department of the War Department thereupon wrote the ladies a letter, saying that they would accept Miss Dix's nurses with thanks, but begging them not to embarrass an overworked government with any other offers of assistance.

Meanwhile Miss Schuyler had opened correspondence with other women's groups from the Atlantic to the Mississippi. From the first, the women had taken the measure of their power as the principal correspondents of the army. Never before had there been an army in which almost everybody could read and write. The first thing that the men did with their literacy was to write home to the women they loved best—mothers, wives, sweethearts, or sisters. The information in these letters the ladies pooled, passing it around from one to another as they sewed. The essence of it, and the women's opinions about it, was then distilled and sent on to Miss Schuyler.

Alexander Hamilton's great-granddaughter, at her desk in Cooper Institute, was enlarging her correspondence with every mail. As the letters came in from aid societies farther and farther away, she was greatly touched by their spirit. "Only those who have seen our letters," she said, "all breathing the same spirit of love and patriotism, from the little villages and homes hundreds of miles away, can appreciate the sacrifices and noble spirit of these true-hearted, loyal women."

These letters presented an appalling picture of incompetence and inexperience in the commissary, quartermaster's, and medical departments of the army. Women who had gladly sent their only breadwinners or their only sons to fight for a "sacred cause," had learned that these men had had nothing to eat for thirty-six hours, except some coffee the kind Cleveland women brought down to the cars. A boy in Pittsburgh who had had nothing to eat for twenty-four hours, was finally served some soup, "which was so burned as to be nauseous. I ate a good quantity of it, however, and consequently *unate* it, and ate no more till the next night."

The first government uniforms issued were so bad that they fell to pieces on the first wearing. Men were actually standing guard on the Potomac without trousers. Some said this was just a rumor. *Harper's Weekly* made a joke of it and published a picture of the Union Soldier sans anything below his ragged shirt-tails. But the report was verified. Ten days after receiving their uniforms a Wisconsin regiment had to be completely refitted with blue jeans, "for decency's sake." Women asked for samples of the disintegrating fabric and went on a furious tour of the clothing mills to which the government, in great haste and for good prices, had let the clothing contracts. "The uniforms are made of shoddy," they reported. "Shoddy consists of the refuse and sweepings of the shop, pounded, rolled, glued, and smoothed to the external form and gloss of cloth but no more like the genuine article than the shade is like the substance. . . . Our soldiers on the first day's march found their clothes, overcoats, and blankets scattering to the winds or dissolving under the pelting rains."

The profiteering in food was just as bad. Outraged citizens, observing government agents trying to buy everything in a hurry, reported: "For sugar it (the government) got sand; for coffee, rye; for leather something no better than brown paper; for sound horses and mules spavined beasts and dying donkeys; for serviceable muskets and pistols the experimental failures of sanguine inventors or refuse of shops and foreign armories." The regular army provender of salt beef or "salt horse" was described as a "half de-salt-peterized, half-washed, half-cooked article." In answer to loud protests against this time-honored military diet, the government tried to get fresh pork. What it got was described by a newspaper man thus: "Its unclean stench crowds one's nostrils

68

at every hour of the day as its smoke rises from a hundred frying pans. Its scrofulous, greasy, foul-looking slices cover every platter. It reposes in superlative nastiness in every barrel."

The profiteering in horses was even worse. Boys began to write home for "just a few drops of your cologne, Sis." Why did they want cologne? Because, in addition to the smells of open drains, human offal, and accumulated camp filth they suffered from "dead horse." The disintegrating carcasses of horses were everywhere in Cairo and Washington and other centers of mobilization because every man who had an old, diseased horse, unfit for other uses, brought it to army headquarters to sell to the government. An inquiry was instituted at Chicago. Of 2,500 horseflesh offerings there assembled, there were only 27 which were not diseased, maimed, or dying.

Meanwhile contagious diseases, brought into the army camps because of insufficient medical inspection and quarantine at the outset, were spreading among ill-fed, exhausted men in daily mounting fatalities. When the first feverish heat of spring struck overcrowded Washington, the sewerage from the army encampments was washed into Rock Creek and the Potomac by the thundershowers, and the men drank the water. When they got sick, as they did in appalling numbers, they were piled into churches, without running water or toilets, into office buildings, and into shacks along the river hastily cleared of Negro refugees. And there they died.

Hardly a day passed without bringing news of some boy's death to his home town. The pitiful announcement came not as a notification from the government, for the government had as yet no adequate registration of the 250,000 men who had so ardently answered its call—but in a letter from a comrade, telling of the last minutes with crude pathos, and begging some kind woman to break it easy to his mother or his girl.

When, frantically, women inquired what the army did for boys who got sick, they were told by Mrs. Mary Livermore who went down from Chicago to Cairo to see what was done for sick boys there. "The fetid odor of typhoid fever, erysipelas, dysentery, is rendered more nauseating by unclean beds and unwashed bodies, while from the kitchen which opened into the hospital wards, came the smell of boiling meat and coffee, befouling still more the air of the unventilated apartments. The nurses were convalescent soldiers, wan, thin, and weak, and requiring nursing themselves, and though they were kind to their comrades, they were wholly worthless as nurses."

2

Though Doctor Blackwell was opposed to offers of amateur help and wanted all women to concentrate on preparing really trained nurses, these nurses could not be ready under six weeks. And meanwhile boys were dying for lack of a little cleanliness and common sense. So, following the meeting at Cooper Institute, Henry J. Raymond, publisher of the *New York Times,* aided and abetted his wife and other ladies in rebellion against the high professional ideals of the doctors by equipping four women to start at once to nurse boys in Washington. On May 3, Raymond himself put them on a troop train in Jersey City, armed with a letter to Surgeon General Wood.

"There is only one military hospital in Washington," said the Surgeon General to the ladies, "and we've put the smallpox cases there. Do any of you ladies want to nurse smallpox?"

The four ladies held a consultation. The youngest and prettiest said she couldn't possibly because her husband would never forgive her if she got the disease and spoiled her complexion. The oldest lady said she didn't feel strong enough to do such severe nursing. She had come because she thought she would be useful in reading the Bible to the poor fellows. But smallpox patients would be too sick to listen to the Bible. The third hesitated and said nothing. The fourth, Miss Adelaide Thompson (later Mrs. Spurgeon) a childlike little girl, said, "I will nurse the smallpox."

"The hospital," reported Miss Thompson later, "was a small, two-story-and-a-basement brick building, located on First Street east, between B and C North. It contained six rooms and a medium-sized closet, which was fitted up as a sort of dispensary. The front basement was used as a dining room for the steward, a rattle-brained Southerner. The doctor remained but a few hours daily, and as soon as he left, the steward generally started for the city, and returned somewhere in the small hours grossly intoxicated. The only other inmates who were able to walk around were the Irishwoman who pretended to wash the clothing, and another to cook. The cooking and washing were both carried on in the same room, on an old stove."

Miss Thompson began with a war upon the food. "Never have I seen such meat. It would require the power of a Hercules to masticate it. The sugar was of the consistency of mud, and about the same color. Butter was not to be thought of and vegetables were out of the question. No dishes; nothing but tin cups and tin plates and so few of them that the food of two or three men had to be served on the same plate."

However, there was a barrel of flour. Miss Thompson baked some good bread, and then tried in vain to get the old Irishwoman to make some decent soup. The doctor, arriving, heard the argument and saw the boys pouring the soup Miss Thompson objected to into the cuspidors. He told the Irishwoman that if he saw such cooking again, he would throw it out of the door and her after it. She got angry and left Miss Thompson with no cook.

Miss Thompson spared no words in her reports to New York City's most respected gentlewomen. She wrote that she was alone night after night, except for the sick men. Often four or five dead men lay all around her in the darkness waiting for light to bring the undertaker. A man died of blood poisoning because of "the impure vaccine put into his arm before he left Michigan. The weather was warm, and before his comrades arrived to bury him, the body burst." The old laundrywoman died at her post from overwork. Finally Miss Thompson herself came down with blood poisoning, which invalided her for life.

These and other reports like them came into the office of Cooper Institute where Louisa Schuyler sat at her desk, day after day, trying not to remember how the spring flowers were blooming now on the ledges above the Hudson, up there on the old family estate. She was determined to resist all persuasions of her family to come up to the country. She intended to stick right here, receiving stories of ever-increasing and sordid misery, and passing them on in loaded mail-bags day after day.

Now and then Doctor Bellows looked in on Miss Schuyler and the other girls at work in the office. Though he publicly discouraged their efforts, he continued to oversee them, like a good father who does not approve of what his children are doing, but stands by, ready to help them out of any trouble they may get into. Gradually the sheer weight of the evidence in the women's letters, confirmed by increasing protest all over the country, forced Doctor Bellows and the medical advisers of the women to take a step which, they feared, might make them ridiculous. They determined to go to Washington, and to ask that the Board of Managers of the Women's Central be appointed by President Lincoln as a United States Sanitary Commission, with power to advise the army with reference to matters of health, well-being, and personal morale. They made bold to do this because the women had already assembled, as their advisers, the professional men who were most suited by reputation and experience for this position.

"It must be well known to the Department of War that several such Commissions followed the Crimean Wars," said the petition of the Women's Central, which was to be carried by Doctor Bellows to Washington. "The civilization and humanity of the age, and of the American people demand that such a Commission should *precede* our second War of Independence—more sacred than the first. We wish to prevent the evils that England and France could only investigate and deplore. This war ought to be waged in a spirit of the highest intelligence, humanity, and tenderness for the health, comfort, and safety of our brave troops. And every measure of the Government that shows its sense of this will be eminently popular, strengthen its hands, and redound to its glory at home and abroad."

On May 17 Doctor Bellows and Doctor Harris, and two other medical men set out for Washington. There they were received with an almost pitying politeness. They presented their petition to the War Department. They were respectfully bowed in and bowed out. "The Department regarded us," said Doctor Bellows, "as weak enthusiasts, representing well-meaning but silly women."

For twenty days the four gentlemen cooled their heels in Washington offices and studied the camps around Washington. At the end of that time Doctor Bellows and Doctor Harris appeared to have undergone a moral transformation. The puzzled, amiable, insecure gentlemen who could not say "No" to a woman, had hardened into steady, shrewd, ruthless reformers, whom no woman would ever again have to set in motion. With their own eyes they had seen the utter incapacity of the War Department, and the tragic demoralization of the volunteer army. They knew, with a desperate certainty, that the success of the Union forces,

72

and the future of the whole country now depended on an immediate and drastic change in the method of handling the volunteers.

3

The War Department was headed by a new Secretary of War, Mr. Simon Cameron, a politician from Pennsylvania. But the general control of arms, munitions, equipment, clothing, food, medicine, the construction of vessels, steam machinery, and engineering, was still in the hands of such members of the old bureaucracy as had not joined the Confederates. These were mainly men of sixty or over, who had once graduated from West Point, but who had had no practical experience of war, and little more practical experience of life. They handled everything by "regulation." A request for anything from a rifle to a dose of quinine was referred to an appropriate official who made a "report," and who, in turn, handed it on to another official who made another report. After a certain amount of reporting, it was decided that the request was contrary to "regulations." If it was not contrary, nothing in particular was done about it. It just died a natural death.

Naturally, a nation rushing at top-speed to fit itself for war, was not leaving these bureaucrats in perfect peace. Quite the contrary! At the moment Doctor Bellows and his committee tried to present their petition, the whole War Department was rocking with explosions. The few capable and experienced army officers whom the government was locating and bringing on to Washington as fast as possible were unable to get attention to their request for some new Enfield rifles instead of the old smooth-bore muskets of the Revolution which, modified by a few changes, had been the arm of the infantry so far. All sorts of discards from European armies had been passed off on the volunteer forces by the profiteers in arms. Army officers were expressing their opinion of this matter in such terms that the atmosphere of the War Department was, at the moment, sulphuric.

Meanwhile, suffocating heat fell on the feverish and overcrowded city, and through the humid, hot air there penetrated even to rose-bowers in old gardens in Georgetown the stench of the army camps. The inquiring committee from New York traced that stench to its source. The sink or latrine, reported the gentlemen, is in most cases "merely a straight trench, some thirty feet long, unprovided with a pole or rail. The edges are filthy and the stench exceedingly offensive; the easy expedient of daily turning fresh earth into the trench being often neglected. In one case, men with diarrhoea complained that they had been made sick to vomiting by the incomplete arrangement and the filthy condition of the sink. Often the sink is too near the camp. In many regiments the discipline is so lax that men avoid the use of the sinks, and the whole region is filthy and pestilential.

"In but few cases are the soldiers obliged to regard any rules of personal cleanliness. Their clothing is shamefully dirty, and they are often lousy. Although access is easily had to running water, but few instances are known where any part of the force is daily marched, as a part of camp routine, to bathe. A careful daily inspection of the state of the men's clothing is probably made in few, if any regiments. Whatever good qualities they possess in other respects, our volunteers are, in many cases, really much dirtier than it can be believed they have been accustomed to be in their civil life; and it is obvious that neither they nor their officers comprehend in the slightest their duty in this particular, nor the danger and inconvenience they are bringing upon themselves by its neglect."

The primary difficulty was the "half political," wholly amateurish way in which captains and lieutenants first acquired their commissions. Knowing nothing of the duty of officers, they were now being rushed and harried to get the elements of military knowledge into their men, and, in most cases, to learn these themselves. After a day spent violently drilling, they had neither energy nor knowledge to apply to the detail of keeping their men in any kind of decency. So far as both comfort and cleanliness were concerned, the men were hampered by the clothes they had brought with them. Clothes, of a sort, they had in comparative abundance. Most regiments had outfitted themselves in fearful and wonderful uniforms of their own designing, which combined, in one homemade outfit, everything gaudy and inconvenient and ill-fitted for active life that had caught their eye in the traditional military parade uniforms. "The dress of the majority," said the Committee, "is inappropriate, unbecoming, uncomfortable, and not easily kept in a condition consonant with health." Most of the clothes were far too heavy. The men had set out from the North when the weather was still cool. They were now daily performing violent

74

exercise in extremely hot and muggy weather, with no change of garments. After a day of military practice, their clothing "from top to toe, is saturated with sweat and packed with dust, and to all appearance no attempt is made to remove this, even superficially." The truthful gentlemen of the Committee carefully verified the rumor about men standing guard without their trousers. "A New York soldier has been seen going on duty in his drawers and overcoat, his body-coat and pantaloons being quite worn to shreds."

The soldiers' discomfort was increased by the unsuitable diet. The government had been generous in its food allowances. The standard diet was coffee, beans, and fat salt pork. In cold weather, men leading an active life could do pretty well with this. But it was quite unsuited to the hot weather now upon them. All army surgeons agreed that the man should have fresh vegetables and fruits. But in an overcrowded city, more or less surrounded by enemy territory, with many lines of communication and means of access to the gardens and orchards southward disrupted, it had proved impossible to supply such highly perishable items. The Committee thought that a supply of dried fruits and vegetables should somehow be arranged.

The Committee believed that the situation was one which no purely military effort could relieve. What was needed was a complete system of civilian co-operation and re-enforcement, able to bring the best business and professional resources of the nation to the aid of the small under-officered and overworked corps of experienced military men who had their hands full trying to train this patriot mob in even the elements of fighting.

Withal the Committee found a few exceptions that only proved its general contentions. The Seventh New York, for example, who had been assigned to guard Arlington Heights, had a neat camp and a soldierly routine under their able and experienced commander, Marshall Lefferts. But these volunteers were largely recruited among well-educated and well-to-do men who were able to supplement the army issues out of their own pocketbooks. A Rhode Island regiment similarly recruited from among the well-to-do had provided itself with adequate living conditions and training.

There were also some less privileged groups who were not doing badly, mainly because they had enlisted women. In an era when a man's well-being was almost completely in the hands of his womenfolk, some regiments from the Northwest and from New England had assumed, in their simplicity, that they would need some women for housekeeping and nursing and "keeping the boys in order." So they had enlisted them, just like soldiers. The women thus chosen were generally of an excellent type for the purpose. They had had to pass muster with the Ladies' Aids which outfitted the regiment, and with wives, sweethearts, and mothers. They had been certified by the local clergymen as persons of character, and by the local doctor as possessors of nursing experience. Regiments that had had the foresight to enlist women might be relatively ignorant or poorly equipped, but they and their chosen female aides were generally tackling their problems of living and training with homely common sense and self-reliance. Many of these enlisted women proved to be remarkable characters who went with their regiments right through the war.

Bad as conditions were, the War Department did not know what could be done about it. It had enough on its hands, in the way of purely military preparations, without listening to philanthropic ladies in New York. But circumstances were working relentlessly in favor of Doctor Bellows and his committee. Every day brought weeping women to Washington to recover the bodies of their dead. Every day the trains left Washington station with an ever-increasing load of corpses packed in ice. Implacably Doctor Bellows faced the officials of the War Department. "We understand," he said,, "that on July 4, President Lincoln will go before Congress and ask for 400,000 volunteers. Our own investigations show that, of the men already recruited, one half will be dead of camp diseases by November 1. Do you think you can go before the country, and ask the wives, mothers, sweethearts, sisters, fathers, and neighbors of these men to send any more of them into this shambles?"

The harassed army officials gave up. "Turn the mess over to the women," they said, "and let them clean it up."

4

So on June 9, the Secretary of War approved a document providing for the appointment by President Lincoln of a United States Sanitary Commission, with power to oversee the health and welfare of the volunteer army, and to serve as a channel of communication between the people and the government. At the same time, Dorothea Dix, who had nearly driven the War Department crazy with her "hustling, poking around, and prying," was finally appointed United States Superintendent of Army Nurses, with authority to recruit nurses for the armed services and to oversee the housekeeping of the military hospitals. She was the first woman ever appointed to an executive position with the United States government.

Between June 9 and June 13, the Committee met almost continuously, in constant communication by telegraph with the Women's Central in New York, and reorganized itself as the United States Sanitary Commission by adding to itself a number of physicians, army officers, and scientists whose reputation qualified them to be of the highest service at the moment. Altogether there was probably not an agency in Washington, not excepting the War Department and the President's cabinet, that brought together in one group men of such outstanding ability and superior technical and professional background as these men on whom the women and Doctor Bellows' Committee agreed.

Notable among the physicians were Doctor Valentine Mott and Doctor Samuel Gridley Howe, who had been acting as a one-man Sanitary Commission for the New England troops, and who had a military background. Two of the proposed members of the Commission had been serving as technical experts for the government. One was Alexander Dallas Bache, a grandson of Benjamin Franklin. "Professor Bache," as he was called, was a graduate of West Point, and had been an instructor there. He had been an incorporator of the Smithsonian Institution, and was still one of its regents. In 1861 he was Superintendent of the United States Coast Survey. With the open-mindedness and imperturbability of his grandfather, he had solidly allied himself with the gentlemen from New York. He believed in their project and was prepared to give it as much of his time and influence as possible.

Another government expert who not only accepted the nomination as a member of the Commission but was prepared to work enthusiastically with it was Doctor John Strong Newberry, the War Department's authority on the geology of the Western Rivers. Doctor Newberry had a medical degree, and had done postgraduate work in medicine in Paris for two years. In his work in the West, Doctor Newberry had noted with admiration the efficiency with which the women were organizing themselves. He was a friend of Mrs. Rouse and Miss Ellen Terry, and the other energetic ladies who had established the Soldiers' Aid Society of Northern Ohio. He had noted the condition of the soldiers in Cairo, and had noted, too, that the people who appeared to be doing the most for them were several remarkable women. He was also impressed by some women's groups in Chicago. Latent in these women of the aid societies was some remarkable executive ability—a good deal more than he saw around the War Department.

So while other officials in the Department had cold-shouldered Doctor Bellows and his committee, Doctor Newberry had not only talked to them but had gone out of his way to make friends with them. "When you get this Commission of yours set up," he had said, "why don't you take me into it, and let me organize the West for you? There are Ladies' Aid societies out there I should consider it a privilege to represent."

There was therefore nothing amateurish in the list of fourteen members of the United States Sanitary Commission that Doctor Bellows proposed to present to the President for his rubber stamp. While the document of the War Department establishing the Commission particularly specified that the President should appoint the Commission, the New York Committee were determined to suggest names so outstanding and so obviously fitted for the proposed work that the President could do nothing but accept them. They were taking no chances with Commissioners nominated by any one but themselves.

On June 13, the reorganized Commission was introduced by the Secretary of War to President Lincoln. He took the document establishing the Commission and looked it over dubiously. "I'm afraid it's just a fifth wheel to the coach," he demurred. Doctor Bellows replied. Several others among the proposed Commissioners replied. Lincoln listened shrewdly. Then he took the document, and wrote across the bottom, "I approve the above. A. Lincoln."

5

A Commission had been appointed. But it had no actual power, except to make suggestions the War Department could ignore, and to write reports that could be laid away in government files. "The Commission was born paralytic," wrote Doctor Bellows later.

"Had it depended on Government, it would have died in its infancy."

But it did not depend on Government. It depended on the ladies, and they intended to make it work. Enthusiasm flowed warm in the correspondence Miss Schuyler sent out from the New York office in all directions, "In England those women who with Florence Nightingale did their work in the Crimea had no such channel through which every woman in the land might work with Government itself. As the men went to their work with the national army, so the women go with them, in an organization running side by side with the army, knowing its needs and meeting them."

Rapidly the Commission organized itself as the board of professional managers and technicians for the women's societies. Representatives of these societies met with it in New York City on June 22, and elected Doctor Bellows President of the U. S. Sanitary Commission, Professor Bache, Vice-president, and Doctor John Newberry, Secretary for the West.

Naturally the first necessity was money for operating expenses. For this they appealed to the life insurance companies. These companies had a special stake in the health and welfare of the camps because, in the enthusiasm of recruiting, many communities had taken out life insurance policies for all their volunteers—the premiums being guaranteed, for the duration of the war, either by the aid societies or by individual citizens. Pointing out that it would be good business for the companies to do everything possible to lessen the danger of premature death to their policyholders, the Commission proposed to have the whole army re-examined by physicians and the poor health risks immediately discharged and returned to their families. Fifty thousand dollars, the Commission figured, would save fifty thousand lives.

They did not get $50,000, but they got enough to set up a headquarters in Washington and to engage a corps of medical inspectors who, working on limited expense accounts but without personal salary, would make a thorough survey of the military camps.

The Washington office was established in the Treasury Building, in rooms donated by the government, and put under the direction of Frederick Law Olmsted, Executive Secretary. Olmsted was the choice of the Ninety-two Respected Gentlewomen. He was a protégé of Mrs. Peter Cooper and Mrs. William Cullen Bryant, and was greatly respected by the able young women working with Doctor Blackwell to establish high professional standards for nurses.

To a military eye Olmsted looked his part as the representative of "the sentimental feelings of women." He had a slight figure and walked with a limp. From his sensitive face, with its delicate features, burning blue eyes, and high forehead, his black hair was brushed back and fell to his collar, after the long-haired fashion affected by literary men and artists in his day. He was both a literary man and an artist, and, as such, he had an experience of more immediate value than that of most army officers. For he was the author of three books that are still credited with giving the best picture in literature of the ante-bellum South, embodying observations made during horseback rambles through the slave states. Much of the terrain over which the Union armies must fight he knew as only a young adventurer could know it. He had bivouacked under the stars, waded through swamps, and made the acquaintance, first-hand, of the malaria mosquito and the diseases that lurk in water. He had urged his horse over more than one route that might have to serve as an army supply-line.

As an artist, too, Olmsted had acquired useful experience. While earning his living, in New York City, on the staff of *Putnam's Monthly,* he had experimented with landscape gardening on his Staten Island farm, leveling, grading, making plantings, and meditating on what he would do to open up crowded city blocks, if he only had the chance. Every time he crossed to New York, on the Staten Island ferry, and entered the dense, crowded little city, with its low, graceless buildings huddled along crooked, narrow streets on the lower tip of Manhattan, he mentally took it apart, and disposed different pieces of it in a seemly and dignified style on other parts of the island. This concern for the New York landscape led to the alliance with William Cullen Bryant and Peter Cooper through which his abilities became known to the Ninety-two Respected Gentlewomen.

The venerable poet of Nature was at that time editor and principal owner of the *New York Evening Post,* and the self-appointed guardian of the wild natural loveliness of upper Manhattan Island. As the rapidly developing city sprawled northward, sullying the brooks and ruining the meadows, he began an agitation in his paper to have a piece of the original landscape reserved for ever as a people's park. Backed by Peter Cooper, who had invested heavily in real estate on the frontiers above Fourteenth Street, this agitation reached the point where a competition was announced for a design for a city park. It was won by a plan anonymously submitted by Olmsted.

Appointed as architect-in-chief of the proposed park, Olmsted soon showed such great executive and practical ability that Mrs. Cooper and Mrs. Bryant and all their friends were convinced that the man who had made the good burghers of Manhattan accept Central Park could make the army accept some improvements in military encampments. The originality of these ladies consisted in their perception of the possible usefulness in war of a kind of talent, temperament, and personal experience that had thus far been despised by most military men.

Olmsted set up the Washington office and began at once to translate the paper powers of the Commission into action. These paper powers gave him permission to inquire into the principles and practices connected with the inspection of recruits and enlisted men; into the sanitary condition of the volunteers; into the means of restoring the health and securing the efficiency of troops; into the proper provision of nurses and hospitals; and into subjects of like nature. The War Department had intended a "general permission," and no doubt expected it to remain general. But Olmsted, the members of the Commission, and the office of the Women's Central, working together, proceeded to make it devastatingly specific. Taking all the items mentioned in the thousands of letters from soldiers in the women's hands, and fitting them to the Commission's own informal observations of camps around Washington, they produced 180 separate questions. These questions they printed in a document distributed among the women's societies. Meanwhile they sent out inspectors, each armed with the 180 questions, to talk to the officers of twenty army encampments around Washinton, and to look at every detail with their own eyes.

The questions covered everything—the qualifications of surgeons and military officers, the method of recruiting that had been followed, the way the uniforms had been supplied, the location of the camp, the nature of the subsoil, the source of the water, the sources of the food, the military police, the temper of the men. They went into specific details. How far from the camp are the horses picketed? How far from the camp are the cattle slaughtered, and what disposition is made of the offal? Is there any special place for refuse and slops and are the soldiers confined to the use of such place? Are there trenches around the tents for drainage? Do these communicate with the general drain? How is the water thus collected disposed of? Are means systematically used to promote cheerfulness by games, entertainments, etc.? Is there a regimental band? Is there a regimental library? What is the character of the books? What about the number of men sent daily to the guardhouse? Is this mainly for intoxication? Are peddlers of eatables or drinkables allowed access to the men in the camp?

While Mr. Olmsted's inspectors were describing the army around Washington as no army had ever been described before, Doctor Bellows and Doctor Newberry set out on a trip through the West, to survey the troops there and to meet the women of the various aid societies. They were looking, among other things, for a western representative of Miss Dorothea Dix, able to recruit army nurses and to assign them to proper training.

The gentlemen were particularly anxious to see Cairo which, because of its position at the junction of the Mississippi and Ohio Rivers, had become the great army center of the West. The descriptions of Cairo that had been coming to the Women's Central had been very lively, especially those written by Mary A. Livermore, president of one of the dozen aid societies of Chicago that had taken the boys at Cairo under their wings. Mrs. Livermore had made a tour of inspection there. She reported that it was by no means a lovely place. "A levee built up around the south and west protected it from the over-flow of the Mississippi and Ohio. From the levee the town looked like an immense basin, of which the levee formed the sides and rim. It was partially filled with water; and the incessant activity of the steam pumps alone saved it from inundation. Vile odors assailed the olfactories as one walked the streets. If it chanced to rain, one was in a position to obey the New Testament injunction, 'to be steadfast and immovable' for the glutinous, tenacious mud held one by both feet. Go where I would, this was 'the order of exercises.' I went down a flight of crazy stairs, across a bit of plank walk, around a slough of unknown depth, behind somebody's barn, across somebody's back yard, over an extempore bridge of scantling that bent with my weight, then into the mud, at the risk of losing rubbers, boots, and sometimes, I feared, my feet, and at last, ferried over a miniature lake in a skiff, reached my destination."

"Mrs. Livermore said that the regimental hospitals were "established in small dwelling houses, carriage-houses, sheds" and that, "compressed within their narrow limits were more filth and discomfort, neglect and suffering than would have sufficed to defile and demoralize ten times as much space."

But when Bellows and Newberry observed the town with their own eyes, they were somewhat relieved to find that conditions there were not quite as bad as painted. This was apparently due to the ladies who had been working ever since the western troops occupied Cairo to establish decency and hospital care.

Two women in particular were already being enshrined in the saga of the western soldiers as "Angel" and "Mother." The Angel was Mary J. Safford, lovely young sister of a banker in Cairo. She had been the first woman in the West to organize camp and hospital relief. "When the boys first gathered in Cairo," wrote Mary A. Livermore, "there had been no system, no organization, no knowledge of what to do, and no means with which to work. As far as possible, Miss Safford had brought order out of chaos, systematized the first rude hospitals, and with her own means, assisted by her wealthy brother, had furnished necessities which could be obtained in no other way.

"Surgeons and officers everywhere opposed her, but she disarmed them by the sweetness of her manner and speech, and did what she pleased. She was very frail, petite in figure as a girl of twelve summers, utterly unaccustomed to hard work. She threw herself into hospital work with . . . energy and forgetfulness of self. . . . When she entered one of her hospitals the effect of her presence was magical. It was like a breath of spring borne into the whitewashed rooms—like a burst of sunlight. Every face brightened, and every man who was able to half raised himself from his bed or chair. . . . It would be difficult to imagine a sweeter sound than her educated and tender voice, as she moved from bed to bed, speaking to each one. Now she addressed one in German—a blue-eyed boy from Holland—and then she chattered in French to another, made superlatively happy by being addressed each in his own tongue."

Glamorous as the "little angel of Cairo" was, she was intensely practical. And what she told Doctor Bellows and Doctor Newberry

83

about the prospects that faced the armies of the West if, with transportation and food supplies as at present they attempted to move south was to be substantiated in the next year of war. It was confirmed by a newly made colonel of a new regiment of three-year volunteers who were just being mustered into the Federal army after a month of drilling by their shabby little commander. Dusty, sweaty, ununiformed, with a sash tied around his sack-coat to distinguish him, the colonel was drilling the men, using a stick for a sword, doggedly, persistently making them go through their military evolutions again and again. The name of this colonel was Ulysses S. Grant, and he was a graduate of West Point. Unimpressive as he was, he seemed, in a quiet way, to know his business. For Miss Safford and her efforts he seemed to have considerable respect, and, so far as an unimportant colonel could, he was backing her up with military authority.

Working with Miss Safford was a woman twice her age, "Mother" Mary A. Bickerdyke, a plain, substantial person about forty-five, with smoothly parted graying hair and steady eyes, and a kind of homespun, healthy comeliness. She seemed the embodiment of common sense, and of a vast, serene, maternal staying power. She was a widow, and had brought up four stepsons, but was without domestic ties. Quietly she had dedicated herself to mothering Miss Safford and the whole western army, backing up the intelligence, charm, and frail physical strength of the younger woman with her inexhaustible reserves of female horsepower.

Like the Women's Central in New York, the western societies had achieved smooth and willing teamwork across all social and practical barriers. Whatever Miss Safford and Mother Bickerdyke called for—from a surgeon to a lemon—was dispatched to them by the women of Chicago by the next train on the Illinois Central.

Looking for the directing center of the widespread and efficient network of women's activities in behalf of the army at Cairo, the two gentlemen from Washington found their eyes slowly coming to rest on Mary A. Livermore. Could it be that here, in this unassuming somewhat literary housewife, was that western mate they were seeking for the stupendous Dorothea Dix? Yet army surgeons constantly spoke of her with respect. Her perception of what a hard-pressed medical man might need, and her skill, precision, and ingenuity in getting it to him were uncanny. However, nothing was settled in this western journey. It would be necessary to wait till, one by one, these various aid societies, and their women leaders, held meetings and made up their minds formally to accept the Sanitary Commission as their representative to the army and their board of professional managers. However, Newberry and Bellows were greatly impressed by the quality of the western troops. "A nobler, manlier, a more intelligent, earnest and valuable body of troops was never gathered on the earth's surface," reported Doctor Bellows. . . . "Sick or well, in camp or on parade, I have seen only one spirit—a profound love of country, a solemn sense of the necessity of this war, a willingness to die in defense of the sacred interests at stake; with a most assured sense that God was behind them and victory ahead. Since the earliest and best days of the war of the Reformation no such spirit has stirred soldiers in the field as that which now animates our troops."

But he went on to deplore the fact that this native heroism might be worn down by anything so sordid as bad cooking and improperly located camps. "The perils of the actual battlefield are nothing to such men; the injuries their open enemies can do them almost not worth thinking of; but will malaria, fever, pestilence—irrational and viewless enemies—be as little dangerous? No. It is before these inglorious and deadly foes that our brave boys will flinch. Before their unseen weapons they will fail. Their generous and self-devoted officers are likely to be the first to suffer. They share the hardships, they more than share the labor and exposure of their commands. They have the best purposes. But they know not yet how to control the diet, the personal habits, the ventilation and police of their quarters and camps. They are studying war *tactics,* intent on making soldiers; they rashly assume that intelligent men know how to take care of themselves; and they are finding camp dysentery seizing their regiments with a most threatening grasp."

The western trip was interesting, and Doctor Newberry and Doctor Bellows had seen a good deal, and had made friends with a good many women in the western aid societies. The two men made an interesting and impressive report both to the War Department and to the Women's Central. But back in Washington, they felt a little discouraged. The whole war was a chaos, and everybody's authority uncertain. The ladies who were their bosses did not want fine words or excellent academic reports. They wanted to know how to get all these opinions and conclusions "*approved* by the Medical Department, *ordered* by the War Department, and *carried out* by the officers and men." That was what the Sanitary Commission was for. The housewives of the aid societies had no intention of wearing themselves out collecting funds and sending out publicity merely for the purpose of maintaining distinguished gentlemen who should waste themselves on "the barren and thankless task of merely counselling lazy, ignorant, or worthless subordinate officers."

They wanted action, and circumstances soon enabled them to get it.

6.   *Banners in the Dust*

On the morning of July 15 there was great excitement in front
of the Treasury Building. Lines of covered wagons were drawn
up there—each wagon covered with a dome of white canvas,
like the market wagons of the Dutch farmers, or the prairie
schooners, and each drawn by from four to six frisky little mouse-
colored mules. Within the wagons were beds, made up with clean
white sheets. A large number of people were bustling around,
mostly women in calico dresses and white aprons, and medical
students in white coats. Behind the covered wagons, some big
baggage wagons were waiting to be loaded with a pile of bales
and boxes stamped "U. S. Sanitary Commission." Through this
general impediment to traffic, an Adams Express wagon and two
telegraph messengers were trying to snake their way.

At the same moment there was equal excitement in an empty
store fronting on Third Avenue, in New York City, at 10 Cooper
Union. The dusty windows were being washed down with rivers
of water. Other rivers of water were being pushed around with long-
handled scrub-brushes and mops, over a board floor stained with
tobacco juice. Shelves were being nailed up along the walls. Some
barrels and boxes were being carried in, and others carried out.
Three Adams Express wagons stood in front of the door. Four
telegraph messengers were running down the street. And pre-
siding over all this were New York's most respected gentlewomen,
their faces streaked with dust, their fair hands red from having
taken a turn at the scrubbing brush themselves. Safe in a far
corner which shone with a sanitary application of soap and water,
Doctor Blackwell was opening boxes of surgical instruments
and bandages, and carefully inspecting them. Some she threw

out and some she passed on to a committee headed by Miss Schuyler, who was directing the careful wrapping of the same.

All this meant that the first great battle of the Civil War was soon to be fought between the Union men and the Confederates. It was destined to be a defeat for both armies. It was not to be a defeat for the ladies.

For the first time the Sanitary Commission would test out all its theories by going along with the army, prepared to minister to the wounded. Their ambulances and wagons, under the personal direction of Mr. Olmsted, would leave from Washington, following the army. And meanwhile, night and day, the Women's Central in New York would be on duty, constantly in touch with the field-unit by telegraph, with an express service always functioning between their headquarters and the train to Washington, and another from the Washington station to the battlefield. Thus supplementary stores could be dispatched the moment they were called for. To this end the women had hired an empty store from Peter Cooper, and were moving in and setting up machinery for action. The days of merely sitting at a desk and sending out letters were over.

The Sanitary Commission had expected to have secret advance notice of military movements from the War Department. But everybody had had advance notice of this battle. The Union army had to fight and for a very good reason. The time of the three months' volunteers was about to expire. It would be a nice how-to-do if, after all the excitement of recruiting and getting the boys off, and all the work they'd done drilling and studying tactics, they should disband and go home without having had one chance to lick the enemy.

The newspapers were carrying on a big "On to Richmond" campaign. Nothing was more annoying to the good people of the North than the fact that the Confederates had moved their capital to Richmond, Virginia, only a hundred miles from Washington itself. The government at Washington would never be able to hold up its head until it had at least driven these rebels back to the cotton-fields and the cane-brakes. In Richmond on July 20 the rebel Congress was to meet. Such a proceeding could not be allowed. By July 20 Richmond must be held by the national army.

To this end a force of some 30,000 Union soldiers encamped at Alexandria and Arlington, under General Irvin Macdowell, had

been in training since May 27. That is to say the _____
ing had been established there, but the army ha_____
from day to day, one or two regiments at a ti_____
coming.

One of the first things Congress did when it c_____
was to urge Macdowell to pitch right in and fi_____
urged him. Macdowell, somewhat embarrassed b_____
men he was supposed to fight with were country pumpkins _____
route to him on railroad tracks all over the country, objected that
his troops were too green. "But," said Lincoln, with a shrewd little
smile, "the enemy is green, too!"

Meanwhile the Confederates under Beauregard were establishing themselves on the other side of Bull Run, a winding sluggish
stream with steep and wooded banks, some thirty-two miles south-
west of Washington. Three miles beyond the stream was Manassas
Junction, where the railroads from Richmond on the south and
the Shenandoah Valley on the west united. To take the junction
would be the first step toward taking Richmond. To do this it was
necessary to defeat the 22,000 Confederates who had been building fieldworks to protect the junction, behind the natural defense
of the stream.

By July 15, everyone knew that the noble army of the Republic was now setting forth to get those rebels out of there. Of
course everyone wanted to go along. Livery stables in Washington
were doing a thriving business renting carriages for $1,000 a
day to gentlemen and ladies who wished to see the great battle.
"$1,000 is cheap for a battle," they said. Congressmen, sena-
tors, and well-to-do ladies in crinoline invested heavily in conveyances, and set out, taking picnic lunches with them. One of these
carriages carried Benjamin F. Wade, Senator from Ohio, and
six Ohio congressmen and politicians.

Of the military adventures which followed, many records have
been written. But there is one story, the story of the battle as
seen from the distaff side, which yet remains to be told.

2

In the army in Alexandria, which received its marching orders
on July 15, there were several enlisted women. They were the
women enlisted at the outset by some regiments in the capacity of

nurses," *vivandières,* or "daughters of the regiment." One
ese was Kady Brownell, wife of a sergeant of the Third Michi-
n regiment, and color-bearer of the regiment. The boys were
very proud of Kady. She could ride and shoot with the best of
them. She was an English girl, born in a British army camp
in Africa, and full of astonishing army lore. She had notions
about courage and discipline and soldierly behavior. She felt
herself responsible for seeing that the boys were well looked after,
and took lessons from the army surgeon in wound-dressing and
care of the sick.

With Kady riding up in front, with the colors, the boys felt
twice the men they would have felt without her. She wore a costume of her own designing, consisting of loose trousers, with a
full tunic falling over them to the knees and belted with a wide
cartridge belt. Her sunburned face topped by a sort of cowboy
hat, she rode astride, handling the wildest horse with easy as-
surance. Altogether a gallant and picturesque figure, and as good
for the soldier's morale as a regimental band!

With the troops under Colonel S. P. Heintzelman, there were
a pair of women who had given another interpretation to the
idea of women in war. They were S. Emma Edmonds and a lady
who preferred to be known in the record afterwards only as Mrs.
Kate B., wife of Chaplain B. S. Emma Edmonds was an assumed
name. Girls of conventional family background who joined the
army frequently did so under a false name, keeping their army
careers separate and distinct from their social relations as women
before and afterwards. Emma Edmonds was an attractive, dark-
eyed Canadian girl, evidently well-educated and well-bred, with
a gay, lively manner and a great gift of mimicry. Her companion,
Kate B. was also very much of a lady—tall, slender, with fine
blue eyes in a clear pale face. With the chaplain, Mrs. B.'s husband, and two doctors, these girls had formed a morale and nursing
unit according to their own ideas, which corresponded very nearly
to the ideas the ladies of the Women's Central were trying to introduce into the army through the Sanitary Commission.

Mrs. B. and Emma had tried to see that proper drains were
dug, even taking a turn at the spade themselves. "Here's how the
Northern *shovelry* will beat the Southern *chivalry,*" Emma had
said. They had tried to get suitable diet for the sick, writing back
to the ladies in Chicago about it, and getting some money and sup-

90

plies which they used to help the boys. Emma had even gone fishing in a stream near Washington, in an effort to get fish with which to vary the diet of ailing men. She and Mrs. B. had a little wagon with which they had gone from door to door in Georgetown begging for delicacies, wines, and even medicines for sick men. So far as they could, they tried to apply the ideas of Florence Nightingale in nursing the sick. Who had outfitted these girls in the first place, and who sustained them it is difficult to tell. It was either the State of Illinois or various Ladies Aids. Apparently they could draw rations and share transportation with their men. They both had good horses. But, however they were sustained, they seemed to enjoy a position of dignity and respect in the division under the command of Heintzelman, and it was apparently taken for granted that they would go right along with the boys into battle.

These girls wore an outfit at once ladylike and professional. It consisted of a black riding habit, shortened to street length by use of a silver ornament, and a small black leghorn hat. They carried silver-mounted seven-shooters in their belts, had a flask of water swung over one shoulder and a flask of brandy over the other, and a haversack with provisions, lint, bandages, and adhesive plaster and other first-aid materials hanging by their sides.

On July 15 Emma recorded in her diary: "Marching orders received to-day. Two days more and the Army of the Potomac will be on its way to Bull Run." Interrupted here, she did not take up her pen again for many days. She was too busy. She and Mrs. B. had to see that all the sick in camp were sent back to Washington, their clothes changed, their knapsacks packed, their letters written home, and packages sent to the express office for them. After all was done, and each man had been laid tenderly in an ambulance, Mrs. B. said to Emma, "The ambulances are starting back now. Let's go to every ambulance and bid the boys good-bye." So they passed from one to the other. "God bless you! God bless you!" the men kept murmuring. Some drew from their bosoms some treasured remembrance and wanted one of the girls to keep it "to remember me by."

About one patient the girls were much worried. He was a boy of sixteen, with clear blue eyes, curly auburn hair, and a broad white brow, his mother's only son. When, two weeks before, he had come down with typhoid fever, and the girls had insisted on giving him special care, the surgeon had said, "You may do what you can for him, but it is a hopeless case." Mrs. B. had devoted much of her time to him, while Emma took over her friend's duties in addition to her own. Through days of violent delirium both girls had fought to keep him in bed. Finally, knowing that they themselves would have to go with the army, and knowing that, without them, one more sick boy would probably get very short shrift from the overworked surgeons, they telegraphed his mother, begging her to come and take her son away. She was expected to arrive about the time that they were loading the ambulances. "What shall we do?" asked Emma. "If we send him to Washington, the poor woman will never find him." Mrs. B. thought they could keep him without bothering to argue with the surgeons about it. So they had him carried to a nearby house, and got one of the volunteer nurses among the local women to stay with him.

With their freight of emaciated, suffering men, the ambulances started back to Washington, looking to the girls like a great funeral procession. And then the girls had to run to their tent to pack their saddlebags and get ready for the march.

Suddenly they heard a woman's wail. "Oh, why did you send my boy away? I wrote you I was coming. Oh, why did you do it?" Then they heard the embarrassed army surgeon trying to explain the necessity of obeying orders, sick or well, mother or no mother.

Emma and Mrs. B. hugged each other in relief and delight. "Quick, Emma," whispered Mrs. B. "You get the doctor into conversation, and I'll draw her aside and get her to the boy!"

And so she did, and got back just in time to mount her horse which Emma had ready and was holding for her. "I left her kneeling by his bedside," she whispered. It seemed strange that accomplishing a little feat like that should make two girls so happy. But no matter how often they managed to perform some kindness for the men or their families, in the face of all military restrictions, they were just as excited and pleased with their latest performance as with their first.

The first day's march was great fun. Over the country roads, through the scrubby country, past run-down Virginia farms, they clattered, sun shining on their arms, flags waving, bands playing intermittently. Soldiers broke ranks and picked blackberries. Every time they saw a little stream twinkling in the grass, they made a rush for it. Most of them were intent on providing themselves with a chicken or two against the evening meal. Emma and Mrs. B. saw soldiers arrested for shooting chickens, but they knew that there were more dead birds than the military police would ever know carefully concealed in that army. Some men were even out gunning for a cow. They must have got her, too, for when Emma and Mrs. B. made their rounds that night, they detected a generally savory atmosphere of broiling steak.

Next day the reveille sounded early, and with only a light breakfast on the crackers and pork in their haversacks, the men started off. The day was hot. Water was scarce. Many men limped painfully. New shoes had been issued the day they started. In many cases their feet were now literally raw. Emma and Mrs. B. rode back and forth, seeking out the men in greatest torture, and binding up their feet with ointment and bandages, and improvising soles on which they could flap along without so much agony. Here and there they noted a man had dropped out and was lying by the roadside. Most of these cases were sunstroke. Whatever they were, the girls, assisted by Mrs. B.'s husband, the Chaplain, tried to see that their comrades helped them into wagons or ambulances and sent them back to Washington.

The army camped that night near Centerville, the girls and the Chaplain being nicely quartered in a log cabin which had been evacuated by the enemy. The three of them worked till late that night, helping the surgeons turn the little stone church in Centerville into a hospital and medical center and trying to clean and equip as hospital annexes a number of other buildings near the church. Returning to their cabin toward midnight, they took a turn through the camp to see how the boys were, on the eve of their first battle. The great mass of them were stretched on the ground wrapped in their blankets, fast asleep. Some were writing by the glimmering light of their campfires. Some were reading their Bibles by the same light, or sitting in groups, talking in low, earnest tones. Just as the three turned toward their cabin, they heard several voices singing in a grove nearby.

O for a faith that will not shrink,
Though pressed by every foe,
That will not tremble on the brink
Of any earthly woe.

That will not murmur or complain
Beneath the chastening rod,
But in the hour of grief and pain
Will lean upon its God.

"Ah," exclaimed Chaplain B. "I recognize Willie's voice. It is his prayer meeting night for the boys. Apparently he has remembered it even here."

Silently they stood together among the trees, listening to the prayer meeting, bowing their heads with the prayers, and then they stole quietly to their own hut.

They started on the march again before dawn on the next day, which was Sunday. Column after column moved forward, over the green hills and through the hazy valleys, the late light of the moon gleaming softly on their arms. There was not the sound of a drum or a bugle—only the muffled tread of thousands of feet and the subdued hum of thousands of voices, and far off where the Confederates lay—the sound of artillery. Soon the morning rose bright and clear, and there was the enemy in plain sight of them posted on heights that rose in regular slopes on the further side of the stream. The woods which interfered with his cannon ranges had all been cut away, and his guns had a clean sweep of the Union army as it approached.

3

Emma, Mrs. B. and Chaplain B. took the station assigned to them in Heintzelman's division. The two girls were on foot, having given their horses to Jack, the Negro groom, who was keeping them under a nearby tree, ready for instant action. But Chaplain B. sat his horse, looking, wrote Emma afterwards, "as solemn as if standing face to face with the angel of death."

Their call to duty came instantly. A shell burst into the battery, killing one man, and wounding three men and two horses. Kate and Emma rushed to them. The first man Emma reached was Willie, the Christian soldier who had held the prayer meeting in the grove the night before. He was weltering in blood. Emma got him out of the way on a stretcher, carried by soldiers, who deposited him under the big tree where the army surgeon had established himself.

Henceforth Emma knew nothing except the fierce struggle with blood, dust, noise, and heat until hours later, she was aware of a messenger who said, "The medical supplies have given out. You are to go back for more." She took her horse and raced him back to the little stone church at Centerville.

Returning with emergency supplies in her saddlebags, and more following, she plunged through bursting shells across a field where, she said, "legs, arms, and bodies were crushed as with thunder bolts," looking for Kate. Terror possessed her. Was Kate killed already? How could she work without Kate? They had been partners ever since that April morning when they arrived with the first troops from the West in Washington. Together they had fought dysentery, malaria, and typhoid from camp to camp. Everything had become unreal to Emma except this partnership with Kate in the never-ending battle with the physical disintegration of war. If Kate were gone!

But suddenly Kate came riding at top speed. "Emma," she cried, "No time for the wounded. The men are famishing for water. They are beginning to fall back. Keep them fighting."

Chaplain B. rode up with the same message. Collecting the canteens strewn over the field, and taking some from the nearest dead soldiers, they raced for the spring, a mile away. The enemy knew of this spring, and had it covered with sharpshooters, so that the Union men might not get water. But under the rain of bullets the Chaplain and the two women dashed back and forth for three hours, bringing water to the troops. The Chaplain's horse was shot from under him and bled to death. Colonel Cameron, brother of the Secretary of War, rode up to speak to them, and, as he opened his mouth, was shot dead. There was no time to drag him out of the way. But Emma stopped a moment and closed his eyes and folded his arms over his breast.

The girls knew that the men were in torment, from causes which, to their limited female intelligence, seemed preventable. The men shouldn't have been issued new shoes for the march. They should have had some breakfast this morning. There should have been a better water supply. But just where the break came, and the wild panic on the field began, they could not tell, nor what exactly was its immediate cause. But suddenly their own army turned in a wild swirling mass that caught them up and pushed them on with it, no matter what they could do. They turned their horses. They looked to officers for orders. They got none. Madly, wildly, whipped on by hysterical, yelling demons on horseback, the Union army was running away!

In another part of the field, Senator Wade and his friends from Ohio, looking on from their carriage, were lifted bodily by the swirling mass of men. "Come on, boys," said Wade, "we'll stop this damned runaway right here!"

He and the other six gentlemen leaped from the carriage, grabbed pistols from the nearest runaways, and formed a line against the furious onslaught. And they held the line until the Second New York, one of the regiments which was still retaining its wits, came to their relief.

Kady Brownell, bewildered, saw her regiment suddenly melt away. She shouted. She waved a flag. She leaped from her horse to the ground, resolutely turning her face where she thought the enemy must be, lifting a shrill feminine voice which suddenly choked into silence. "I must have been yelling so hard I lost my voice," she thought desperately. What should she do? She saw a flag dragged along on the wheels of an artillery wagon rushing by. That wasn't right. She tore at the flag, caught a piece of it, and standing furiously in the field, turned round and round, trying to find where the enemy was, damn him! She waved the torn scrap of red and white and found her voice again in one faint, long-drawn squeak.

A soldier from a Pennsylvania regiment caught a glimpse of her, in his own headlong flight. He stopped, and grabbed her hand. "Come on, Sis," he said. "No use standing there to be killed." He pulled her with him down a gully, amidst small pine trees, she struggling all the while. A ball went through his head. He collapsed, dead on her shoulder, his blood staining her dress. She extricated herself and climbed back to the open space where she thought they should be fighting, grabbed another piece of torn and trampled flag from the dirt, and held it up, trying to yell. An officer on horseback whom she recognized came by, and spoke to her in a tone of authority, "Your regiment has gone on," he said. "Go and find it." Grateful for something that sounded like an authentic military order, Kady seized a riderless horse, leaped on his back, and rushed off.

Meanwhile Emma and Mrs. B. and the Chaplain, swirling round and round amidst rattling artillery wagons, mules, horses, baggage

96

wagons, and masses of men crammed together in one panting, pushing mass on foot, kept trying to find what to do, looking for some officer to give orders, looking for some sign that somewhere there was orderly advance—or retreat—or something to guide them. Finally they extricated themselves and headed back to the stone church in Centerville. They found dead bodies stacked waist-high around it, but the surgeons who had been in charge here were all gone. Everywhere on the floor lay wounded men.

A feeble voice spoke to Emma. It was Willie, the Christian soldier. As she tried to care for him, he snuggled up to her gratefully, and died. She kissed his forehead, and cut off a lock of his hair. She intended to send it to his mother if ever she got out of here. It was quiet in the church and almost dark. The two girls and the Chaplain, taking possession of the abandoned medical stores, went to work to care for the patients themselves, as well as they could. After aeons of intense work, Emma, as if far off, in a feverish dream, heard the Chaplain saying, "The Union army is gone. The enemy have surrounded us. We are prisoners."

She came to life with a snap. "I don't believe it," she said. "They were confused. But they wouldn't retreat!"

Surely by this time, she thought, they had re-formed the ranks. Probably they had shifted their position for some good military reason. "We'll soon find out," she said.

She started out in the dusk to reconnoiter. Assured that the men approaching were indeed the enemy, and that the Union forces were nowhere to be seen, she rushed back to Centerville, dodging under the very hoofs of the Confederate cavalry, and made for the place where they had left their horses. She found that Chaplain and Mrs. B. had gone, taking her horse.

A slight female figure in a black dress naturally aroused little suspicion among the Confederates, who took her for one of the local ladies. So she dodged among their horses into the church. As she put her head in at the door, there came the cry she had heard all day, "Water." She put water where every one who still had the use of his arms could reach it, and took the names and addresses of the abandoned men. Finally, hearing the clatter of hoofs, she knew that the church was being surrounded. "Go," whispered the men. "Hurry! Go!"

She opened the door cautiously. It was pitch-dark now and raining torrents. She made a dash for it, climbed a fence, fled across a field, and was out on the highway. She walked all night, and till noon of the next day, and reached Alexandria, where she collapsed, so lame and so spent that it was two days before she could go on to Washington and find Kate and ask her what she meant by running off with the horse!

4

Back into Washington streamed the runaway Union army, soaked to the skin, streaked with mud and blood, utterly worn out, sick, and ashamed. They were followed by some regiments who marched back in good order, and raised a big laugh against the runaways, pointing out that, even with this utter demoralization of their ranks, the Confederates had not been strong enough to pursue and overpower them. "The Rebs were just as soft and green as we were, you fools," said these courageous brothers.

Washington was full of groups of men wearing only parts of military uniforms. Some were clothed with garments taken from dead soldiers who had been left on the battlefield. Some were armed with muskets. But as a whole they were a woebegone rabble. "All are excessively dirty, unshaven, unkempt, and dank with dew," reported Frederick Olmsted, who circulated through town continually, noting all that he saw and reporting it to the Women's Central, which sent it out all over the country. Some men stood around street fires made of boards wrenched from citizen's fences. Some were asleep in gutters and on doorsteps or sitting on the curbstones resting against the lamp posts. Some were begging from door to door. Some, Olmsted reported, appeared to be "ferocious, others sick and dejected, all weak, hungry, and selfish." Olmsted saw no commissioned officers amidst these mobs, seldom a non-commissioned officer. But at Willard's Hotel, the officers swarmed. They, too, were dirty and ill-conditioned, but appeared "indifferent, reckless, and shameless, rather than dejected and morose."

Emma and Mrs. B. also moved about ceaselessly, trying to find the boys whom they knew, and many of whom they surmised to be ill, and to get them to bed somewhere. "Measles, dysentery, and typhoid fever were the principal diseases after the retreat," wrote Emma." The hospitals in Washington, Alexandria, and Georgetown were crowded with wounded, sick, and discouraged soldiers. That extraordinary march from Bull Run through rain, mud, and chagrin, did more toward filling the hospitals than did the battle itself." In her diary she wrote: "Oh, what an amount of suffering I am called upon to witness every hour and every moment. There is no cessation, and yet it is strange that the sight of all this suffering does not affect me more. I am simply eyes, ears, hands, and feet. It does seem as if there is a sort of stoicism granted for such occasions. There are great strong men dying all around me, and while I write three are being carried into the dead room."

"All is lost—including honor," ran the telegraph messages to crowds surging around the telegraph boards as they had not surged since the fall of Sumter. "The gloom in this city is funereal," wrote Horace Greeley, from New York. "For our dead in Bull Run were many, and they lie unburied yet. On every brow sits sullen, scorching, black despair." Lincoln called this "pusillanimous." But when some one tried to find some mitigating circumstances in this disgraceful rout, pointing out that the Confederates got nothing out of it, and seemed pretty well taken by surprise themselves, Lincoln drawled sarcastically, "So it's your idea that we whipped the rebels, and then we ran away from them!"

Meanwhile the people, rallying, began furiously to demand a congressional investigation. Senator Wade, the doughty senator from Ohio who, with his friends, had tried to stop the runaway, was made chairman of a Committee of Congress for the Conduct of the War. This Committee was empowered to take hold of the whole military situation and see that it was set in order, no matter whose head came off. Grimly the people abandoned their idea of quick and easy victory, set their faces to the prospect of a long war, and prepared to bring the strength of the army up to a million.

5

The only people who were ready either to do anything or to contribute anything to the explanation of the whole debacle were the Sanitary Commission. Sixteen wagons started from Washington by the Sanitary Commission reached Bull Run just as the army deserted it. Under a flag of truce the inspectors and relief agents went on to the battlefield, and for days they worked there, trying to locate and care for 8,000 wounded men. Around the open field, in woods, and in depressions in the ground, they found little groups of men who had crawled out of the way or had been car-

99

ried there by their companions. In one such group all had died. In another the only living man was one poor fellow who lay with his head pillowed against a rock, looking at the bodies of five companions that he had seen die. A little on one side of the field were a number of living, in a fairly comfortable state. The Confederates had filled their canteens with water, had killed an ox and a sheep for them, and had shared with them their own scanty bread. On the third day after the battle, the wounded were released on parole, and were slowly gathered into the hospitals at Centerville, guided and aided by the Sanitary Commission.

Meanwhile the Washington office, under the cool and forthright direction of Olmsted, was busy pointing out to the War Department that had the report the Commission had made on twenty military camps around Washington been heeded, and its recommendation for the improvement of those camps put into execution, this might have been avoided. For the regiments that had broken were the particular ones which the Commission had reported as being in a poor condition, and those that had stood their ground or had re-formed and behaved in a soldierly fashion were exactly the regiments they had reported as being in a good condition. Within a week the Commission also made a systematic and detailed inquiry into the exact causes of the runaway. The inquiry was in the form of seventy-five questions put to officers and men representing a fair cross-section of the whole army. The answers to these questions contained 2,000 separate items of information.

The Commission ascertained that only eight regiments were in good physical condition. In eight others men were described as exhausted, partially exhausted, or evidently suffering. In twelve regiments practically all the men were described as much exhausted. In six regiments a number of men had completely given out, from sunstroke and other causes. Part of this was due to a long course of unwholesome food, overwork under unhealthy conditions for weeks before the battle, and generally poor morale and lax discipline. Much of it was due to bad management directly before the battle. The men had started with no breakfast. Their last meal was on the evening before. The distance marched on the morning of the battle was from four to twelve miles, one and one-half to three miles in double-quick time. There was no adequate supply of water. The men were in battle from five to six hours. Their retreat was due to lack of faith in their leaders. The leaders in many cases left their commands first. Altogether the whole military organization was imperfect, and this so-called "army" little better than a mob. "The depressing effect of long abstinence from food," wrote Olmsted, "exhaustion before the battle, over-tasking of their physical powers in it, and the horrors of retreat were wholly unchecked by the force of discipline. Men who never had been taught their duty as soldiers now became a hungry and ferocious mob."

The army, said Olmsted, is suffering almost equally from lack of instruction in cooking and lack of instruction in the elementary duties of officers, especially of captains. A resolution passed by the Sanitary Commission and ordered sent to the President, the heads of departments, and to members of both houses of Congress, called for the immediate establishment of adequate military discipline, in accordance with the best professional standards, throughout the volunteer army. Soldiers, said the Commission, would welcome such discipline over themselves and their officers. Self-elected captains and lieutenants should immediately be put through a course of training in the duties of officers. Those who could not qualify, by the best military standards, should either be demoted or discharged, no matter how active they had once been in getting their neighbors to enlist in the army, nor how popular they still were with the folks back home.

"The first thing we have to prove in this war," Lincoln had said, "is that popular government is not an absurdity." The people were ready to prove it. The big-hearted, self-confident populace of this raw land had for the first time really looked at themselves in the mirror. Bitterly, steadfastly, persistently they were ready to put themselves to school. And their own creation, the Sanitary Commission, offspring of the untutored benevolence and common sense of the women, stood ready to be the schoolmarm in one of the best courses of systematic self-training that a free people ever had.

7.   *Scrubbing the Lords of Creation*

Bull Run had proved the truth of what Dorothea Dix and the
Sanitary Commission had been saying about the miserable inade-
quacy of the hospital provisions of Washington. Every church,
every government building, every building of the District of
Columbia that could possibly be spared was crowded with sick and
wounded. Every family that had a spare room or could double up
and sleep—no one asked how many to a bed!—was urged to take
a suffering soldier in. Miss Dix came down from the high professional standards she was trying to establish and let almost
any woman take her turn at nursing, trusting to heat, foul odors,
the constant sight of blood, and back-breaking toil to weed out the
unfit and make them depart of their own accord.

Tents for the sick were pitched in all the parks. Yet many
lay for days in the streets, exposed to heat and rain and insects,
until they could finally be cared for. One of the largest of the
emergency hospitals was near the Smithsonian Institution along
the borders of the old canal. Half the drainage of the sweltering,
overcrowded city, already noisome with typhoid and dysentery,
seeped into that canal, so that it became one great cesspool. The
hospital that stood over it was a slaughter-house. It was said that
death from blood poisoning was certain if a man with the merest
scratch was lodged there.

Here again was a chance for the Sanitary Commission to go to
bat, and it lost no time in doing so. It began by establishing
friendly relations with the new commander of the army of the
Potomac, General George B. McClellan, a good-looking, fresh-
faced stocky little man with the highest standards of military
housekeeping and smart public appearance. General McClellan
had been a military observer for the United States government

in the Crimean War. He was familiar with the history of the Crimean camps. He had a fastidious distaste for anything sloppy or untidy. He loved not only to enforce but to multiply military routines. With such a man the Sanitary Commission thought it could work. McClellan, in his turn, was scrupulously and considerably polite to the officers of the Sanitary Commission—as he was to almost everyone—and occasionally interested in what they proposed.

On July 29 the Sanitary Commission sent McClellan the following resolution which had been voted by its constituent societies: "The Sanitary Commission assure Major General McClellan, in advance, of all the moral support and sympathy of their numerous constituents, and beg him to believe that the humane, the intelligent, the religious, and the patriotic, will uphold his hands in every endeavor to communicate a spirit of subordination, fidelity, and obedience to the troops, even by resort, if found necessary, to the utmost rigor of military law, believing that the health, comfort, and efficiency of the army are all united in their dependence on a strict, uniform, and all-pervading military discipline."

It was one of the merits of the Sanitary Commission that it never made a general suggestion without following it immediately with a concrete plan of action. Hence they backed up their plea for rigorous military discipline by appointing a Committee headed by Professor Bache, Benjamin Franklin's grandson who had been an instructor at West Point, to draw up a list of graduates of West Point who had retired to civil life, but were available for and physically capable of military command. Professor Bache and a committee of army officers also proceeded to lay out a plan for training the self-created captains and lieutenants with whom the army was cluttered. The merit of a plan of rigorous military discipline originating in this way was that it had the full cooperation of the folks back home, and through the correspondence of the folks with the soldiers, of the men themselves. Mamma, and sister and the girl he left behind him all informed themselves with regard to what Johnny would have to learn if he was going to be a good soldier. And if he couldn't show officer's stripes honestly earned by character, hard work, and knowledge, Mary and Jennie and the other girls at home weren't going to be interested in him.

Having established themselves as the right hand of the military in disciplining this raw army, the Sanitary Commission got back to their original business of seeing that the troops were made *sanitary*. The Commission drew up a detailed report of the exact character of the various buildings in Washington which Dorothea Dix had had to accept as hospitals. A typical report was that on the Union Hotel in Georgetown: "The Union Hotel Hospital, Georgetown, was occupied as its name implies, until recently hired for its present use. . . . Its halls and passages are narrow, tortuous, and abrupt, and in many cases with carpets still unremoved from their floors, and walls covered with paper. There are no provisions for bathing. The water closets and sinks are insufficient and defective, and there is no deadhouse. The wards are many of them overcrowded and destitute of arrangements for artificial ventilation. The cellars and area are damp and undrained, and much of the woodwork is actively decaying."

The Commission ended its report by pointing out that large old government buildings and hotels, in various stages of disintegration, do not make good hospitals. It recommended that, instead, the "pavilion plan" originally designed by Miss Nightingale be immediately adopted. "Hereafter, instead of hiring old buildings for General Hospitals, the Government should order the erection of wooden shanties or pavilions of appropriate construction and fully provided with water for bathing, washing, and water-closets, and ample arrangements for ventilation and for securing warmth in winter, to accommodate from thirty to sixty each, and to be sufficiently distant not to poison each other."

This plan, which was submitted to the War Department on July 31, 1861, was adopted, and orders placed for hospital accommodations of this type for 15,000 patients, the hospitals to be situated not in the crowded city, but in open country around it and readily accessible to it.

2

At the same time the Sanitary Commission began an offensive movement against the ignorance and stupidity with which the army had received the first nurses called for by Dorothea Dix, and carefully trained in New York hospitals under the best medical men in the country. Thirty-two of these women were now in Washington where from two to six of them had been assigned to each one of the emergency hospitals. But the ladies in New

York were up in arms, declaring flatly that not another woman should come until the status of army nurses was better defined, and decent personal treatment was accorded to them.

It had never been contemplated that any large part of the army nursing should be done by women. It was assumed that most of the nurses would continue to be soldiers, usually convalescent soldiers detailed for the purpose, and that a good many personal offices for wounded men could much better be performed by their own sex. What the women were agitating for was the appointment of women *head nurses,* carefully selected and trained by competent physicians in routines of cleanliness and comfort, after the standards set by Miss Nightingale. These head nurses were to direct and train the soldier nurses in those details of sickroom care which, it was assumed, no mere man would ever think of for himself.

Their idea that women were much better fitted than men to be the *superintendents* of nursing care was natural at that time. In those days food, drink, and medicine were all matters men left to the women. Hence the average man was much more dependent on women for daily sustenance and decency than he is at present. There were few prepared or processed foods, except salt meat, beef concentrates, and condensed milk. And both beef concentrates and condensed milk were still so new on the market that a man was inclined to regard them dubiously unless some woman served them to him and told him they were good for him. Hitherto there had been few hospital-trained nurses. But doctors had been assisted by good, practical, cleanly women that they had trained as helpers. In a typical family there was likely to be one chronic invalid and one dear angel who had learned to administer the sickroom under the doctor's direction. Though there were hospitals for the poor in the big cities, a hospital was looked upon with suspicion by the average healthy man. If he was to be sick, he wanted to be sick in his own bed, with his own woman looking after him.

To get any decency into army life, and especially into the army hospitals, it was necessary to have women as "lady superintendents," able and willing to keep their minds on a kind of detail hitherto beneath the intelligence of men. But the respected gentlewomen in New York, who were financing the training of women and publicizing to families the improved care that these women could give their boys, were not going to take any nonsense from the

105

army. In New York Miss Schuyler was mailing to the Ladies' Aid societies and to members of Congress and high government officials the following statement in which one detects the cool, incisive accents of Doctor Blackwell: "It is regretted that a more favorable account of the way in which the nurses have been received and treated in the hospitals cannot be given. They have not been placed as they expected and were fitted to be, in the position of head-nurses. On the contrary, with a very inefficient force of male nurses, they have been called upon to do every form of service, have been over-tasked and worn down with menial and purely mechanical duties, additional to the more responsible offices and duties of nursing. They have encountered a certain amount of suspicion, jealousy, and ill treatment, which has rendered their situation very trying.

"It must be confessed that the intrinsic difficulties of their situation are very great; that women nurses in military hospitals, though most grateful to the sick soldier himself, are objects of continual evil speaking among coarse subordinates, are looked at with a doubtful eye by all but the most enlightened surgeons, and have a very uncertain, semi-legal position, with poor wages and little sympathy, except from the sick and wounded men whom they comfort and bless. Nothing but the most patriotic and humane motives could sustain women in this position.

"These nurses have commonly, almost always, proved worthy of the confidence so carefully reposed in them by the society. They have been only *too refined* for their places. The association does not feel authorized to send on more from the same class of life from which these have come—certainly not until their position and relations are essentially improved. The society is deeply convinced of the wisdom of absolutely with-holding all nurses not over thirty years of age, and of sending none but those of settled character, with marked sobriety of manners and appearance. We are convinced of the value and importance of supplying the hospitals with women nurses. Those which have been sent have done a work of unspeakable importance; indeed, have been indispensable. It is impossible to tell what increase of suffering and mortality would have occurred but for their incessant exertions. Some of these women have brought the blessings of those ready to perish abundantly on their heads, and their names will be held in undying reverence and affection by wounded soldiers saved to their country and their families by their watchful and tender devotion."

It was not long before confirmation of the last words began to come pouring in from the families thus indirectly appealed to. Here and there the Sanitary Commission in Washington began to find the hitherto solid wall of opposition to its reforms crumbling. With Dorothea Dix ready to step promptly into any breach that was made, and Doctor Blackwell and the gentlewomen in New York ready to bring up re-enforcements, the campaign for better nursing was beginning to make progress.

3

The transition from the disorder of the improvised hospitals and the old system of hospital housekeeping to the new pavilion hospitals under the nurses trained in New York was amusingly described by Louisa May Alcott. As one of the emergency women nurses recruited by Miss Dix to meet immediate needs until more really trained women could be secured, she served for a while in the Union Hotel Hospital, which she called Hurly Burly House.

Five panes had been smashed out of the hospital windows, reported Miss Alcott. The mattresses were like plaster, the pillows in the last stages of consumption, the air foul with the steam rising from the washing of soiled, bloody, and muddy clothing in the washroom. For dinner nurses were served "beef evidently put down by the men of '76; pork, just in from the street; stewed blackberries like stewed cock-roaches." Miss Alcott toiled for six weeks, and then, like so many of the first nurses, broke down and had to give up. But she dreamed of "some better establishment where the washing of 300 people is done out of the house, the food is eatable, and mortal women are not expected to possess an angelic exemption from all wants, and the endurance of truck horses."

When a new pavilion hospital was set up, according to the specifications of Miss Dix and the Sanitary Commission, with one of the new New York nurses in charge, Miss Alcott described it thus: "The long, clean, warm, and airy wards, built barrack fashion, with the nurses' room at the end, were fully appreciated by Nurse Periwinkle, whose ward and private bower were cold, dirty, inconvenient, upstairs and downstairs, and in everybody's chamber. In Ward K I found a cheery, bright-eyed, white aproned little lady, reading at her post near the stove; matting under her feet, a draft of fresh air flowing in over her head; a table full of trays, glasses, and such matters on one side, a large, well stocked medicine chest on the other; and all her duty seemed to be going about now and then to give doses, issue orders which well trained attendants executed, and pet, advise, or comfort Tom, Dick and Harry, as she found best."

Though it had at first been intended to use women mainly as supervisors of the soldier nurses, both the new head nurses and the army surgeons soon found that it was much easier to get efficient service out of a woman untrained in nursing—provided that she was a cleanly, responsible person with some knowledge of house-keeping—than to drive half-sick soldiers to unaccustomed activities with towels and saucepans. So more and more volunteer women nurses took over the immediate handling of the wounded. These women who firmly took the convalescent soldier-nurses and put them back to bed were hailed by the boys with astonishment and delight, not unmixed with embarrassment. This business of women caring for soldiers was all quite new, and bound to cause blushes on both sides.

When some wounded men were brought in, Miss Alcott's superintendent, who was one of the new New York head-nurses, said, "Come, my dear! Tell them to take off socks, coats, and shirts, scrub them well, and the attendants will finish them off and lay them in bed."

Miss Alcott gasped. "To scrub some dozen lords of creation at a moment's notice was really—really—" However, she drowned her scruples in the washbowl, clutched a towel and a large hunk of yellow soap, and tackled the first specimen, a withered old Irishman with a wound in his head. "He was so overpowered by the honor of having a lady wash him that he did nothing but roll up his eyes and bless me in an irresistible style. . . . We laughed together, and when I knelt down to take off his shoes, he wouldn't hear of my touching 'them dirty craters.' 'Bedad,' he said, 'It's hard to tell which is the dirtiest—the fut or the shoe.' " This, said Miss Alcott, was certainly the truth, "for boots, shoes, trousers, and legs were a mass of mud."

Relieved by her jokes with the Irishman, Miss Alcott took heart and soon was scrubbing away, "like any tidy parent on Saturday night."

"Some of them took the performance like sleepy children, leaning their tired heads against me as I worked, others looked grimly scandalized, and several of the roughest colored like bashful girls." One of the "scrubees" had a bad face wound. He insisted on seeing himself in a glass, "Gosh!" he said, "I warn't a bad looking chap before, but now I'm done for. What will Josephine Skinner say?" Miss Alcott assured him that if Josephine was a sensible girl, she would appreciate the honorable scar. Thereupon he blinked at her with his one good eye so gratefully that she decided that this scrubbing of twenty bearded masses of gore and mud was a very fine job after all.

The families of boys who began to be adequately cared for were profoundly grateful. The soldiers' letters home were lyrical with delight and gay with the fun of spirits restored, and through the towns and villages the fame of the Sanitary Commission began to spread. Local aid societies that had hitherto confined themselves to sending supplementary stores only to their local regiments were more and more ready to join the Sanitary Commission. It was a great comfort to think that through one's own village aid society one could support and be in constant touch with a great organization of the most capable specialists who knew just what to do for John if he was hurt, who had their agents and stores on all the battle fronts, and whose representatives could even talk to the President and tell him what ought to be done. Not only mothers but fathers liked the idea that there were women working with the Sanitary Commission. Almost everyone felt that if John were wounded or sick or in trouble, he would be much better off if there were "some good kind woman around."

4

While they were improving the hospitals, the Sanitary Commission was sending inspectors among the camps. These inspectors were highly trained physicians who were willing to work for $2 a day and their expenses. They were asked to give an exact report on the location of the camp, the training and qualifications not only of the surgeons but of the captains and lieutenants, the condition of food, water, equipment, etc. They were asked to report evidences of profiteering, in food or clothing, supporting their statements with affidavits, and to see that each camp had received the quota of tents, equipment, clothing, food supplies, and medicine to which it was entitled. They were to start thrift clubs among soldiers, persuading them to save and bank part of their pay, to encourage music, distribute reading matter, and make suggestions to the soldiers and junior officers for the improvement of the men's living. Each inspector kept what was called an "official diary," on sheets of paper with very wide margins where comments could be written alongside the text. In this diary he wrote down his own observations, the reports of the men, and his own and the officers' and surgeons' suggestions and judgments. The diary had to be turned in weekly to the local Sanitary Commission office.

Selections from the inspectors' diaries were sent out to the aid societies, and read and discussed at meetings where the women gathered to sew or knit for the soldiers. A typical selection read as follows: "The 22nd regiment, Illinois, Col. Dougherty, encamped near St. Louis, is in a wretched condition. It is encamped in a valley, beneath very shady trees, under the lea of some hills, which combine to make the miasmatic atmosphere stagnate at this spot. They have been there only 13 days, but have 250 out of 900 more or less sick with camp dysentery. This is due in part to the situation but in part also to the water, which is black and disgusting. It is taken from some pits, sunk in a kind of half stagnant gutter, in the other end of which pigs are rooting. All the water they have is from this wretched source, and they have not even enough of this. Of course they mix worse rum with this bad water, and the men are poisoned. The hospital is a room hired for the occasion which is a perfect pigsty for nastiness. The accommodations are only for, say, five and twenty, and the sick are 250. . . . The 22nd should be moved immediately."

Wherever the troops went, the inspectors went, armed with authority from the Secretary of War, sending back their pitiless reports to the home-folks. As winter drew on, the inspectors reported typhus fever among the troops. "Its appearance is traceable to the natural disposition of soldiers to shut themselves up in their tents or huts in cold weather. In many camps they have already been allowed to commence a system of suicide by excavating the

110

ground within lodgings and throwing up banks of earth against their walls or curtains. This practice which caused great loss of life among the British in the Crimea should at once be forbidden. ... It would be better that double or triple the usual allowance of blankets and of flannel shirts should be distributed to men in camps, even if these should be left behind or thrown away at the first movement, than that they should be indulged in their disposition to burrow or seal themselves into their lodgings."

The result of this type of exposé was that the Sanitary inspectors came to be feared by everyone from the General down. Rare was the officer who dared to brave the steady, circumstantial publicizing of the faults of his camp. Since most errors were due to ignorance, and not to wilful carelessness, the officers asked inspectors for instruction in digging trenches, pitching tents, making latrines, and disposing of garbage. Harris, Olmsted, Bache, Newberry, Howe, and the best specialists of the New York medical associations combined their knowledge to establish a set of standards in these matters and to drill the inspectors in them. The inspectors, in turn, taught the camps.

In addition, the Sanitary Commission had eighteen little booklets prepared by well-known medical specialists, dealing with the different camp diseases, and methods of prevention and of treatment. There were booklets on malaria, typhoid, venereal diseases, pulmonary and respiratory diseases, etc. Doctor Valentine Mott prepared a book for army surgeons on pain and anesthetics. There were instructions for pitching camp, and for maintaining health on the march. This was the beginning of those pamphlet texts now so widely employed in the instruction and guidance of soldiers.

Never, in the history of war, had wife and mother had such an opportunity to know just what was happening to John when he "went to the wars," and themselves to do something about it. They were commandeering the best talent of the country to look after the boys. But no matter how great an expert might be, the ladies held the strings of the purse which supported the Commission, and were indefatigable in employing their pens and the United States post office in finding out all about everything and passing it on to the next society. Great reserves of ability and professional knowledge had been discovered and turned on the army. But no man could forget by whose grace he was making this use

111

of his talents in the service of his country. And once a serious
abuse became known to the women's societies, woe betide the
colonel and the War Department and the President if it were not
corrected. For this was a war carried on right under the eye of
Mama!

8. *Unconditional Surrender*

In 1861 Chicago was a city of new homes and fancy new stores with large plate-glass windows, inhabited by 110,000 people, of whom practically no one had as yet a gray hair in his head, and by a very much larger number of cattle, pigs, and horses. It was the perpetually excited, hopeful, and rapidly improving crossroads of a thousand miles of prairie. Forty thousand hogs arrived in the city weekly, and were turned into so much sausage that the newspapers figured that every week they could lay a double line of new sausage between Chicago and Milwaukee.

Chicago was full of pride and boastfulness. "Lake Michigan is situated on Chicago," wrote the *Cleveland Plain-Dealer*. "The principal productions of Chicago are corner lots, statistics, and wind. The population of Chicago is about sixteen million and is constantly increasing."

Of nothing was Chicago prouder than of the new brick schoolhouses that dotted every city area and most of the suburbs. When the flag over Fort Sumter came down, the citizens of Chicago furnished each of these schools with a new flagstaff and a new flag.

On February 16, 1862, the boys in each school were raising the flag, the school band was playing, cannon were booming, and the church bell down the street was ringing. There had been a great victory—the first clean-cut military victory of the war on either side. Fort Donelson on the Cumberland River, the key to the Confederate defense system for the lower Mississippi Valley, had been forced by General Grant to "unconditional surrender."

Mary A. Livermore first noticed the excitement when she attempted, for the twentieth time that day, to open the window of the stuffy rooms in which her little aid society had set up shop—

113

under McVicker's theater, on Madison Street. She never would get used to living with the concentrated olfactory essence of all the stuff the folks at home insisted on sending to the soldiers—codfish and sauerkraut, pickles and ale, onions and potatoes, smoked salmon and halibut, ginger and whiskey, salt mackerel and tobacco, kerosene for lamps, benzine for cleaning. She shook out her wide sleeves and smoothed her skirts. She could stand anything about the war, except *smelling* of it!

Then three telegraph messengers rushed in. The next thing Mary Livermore knew she was slowly awakening from a feverish dream of wild activity, months later, to find herself important and famous, with people for a thousand miles south and east and west hanging on her every move.

2

While the Sanitary Commission had been employing the money and high professional talent commandeered by the gentlewomen of New York to make itself a power in Washington during the summer of 1861, it had been steadily wooing the able and self-reliant women leaders of the West. By September Doctor Newberry had persuaded his friends, the "admirable business women," Mrs. Rouse and Miss Ellen Terry of the Soldiers' Aid of Northern Ohio, to help him to set up a branch of the Sanitary Commission in Cleveland with their society as its backbone. He then resigned his job with the War Department to employ his full time as Secretary for the West. Working from Cleveland Doctor Newberry started branch Sanitary Commissions of business and professional men in every principal city to serve as associates of the local Ladies' Aid societies.

His next step was to persuade Mrs. Livermore and her friend, Mrs. Hoge to affiliate their aid society in Chicago with the Sanitary Commission. Catching a glimpse of great possibilities Mrs. Livermore engaged a governess for her children, took a headquarters for her group, and went to work there from early morning to night, with only brief moments to spend, for the next four years, in the home of which she thought constantly, with never-ceasing nostalgia. "My home," she wrote, "its pleasant order and quiet, its welcome rest, its cheerful companionship, its gaiety which comes from the prattle and merriment of children who have a thousand adventures to narrate—all seem strange and unnatural after the experiences of the day. When I return to it, it is as if I had left the world for a time, to refresh myself in a suburb of heaven."

Meanwhile Doctor Newberry came to Chicago and called together in his room in the Sherman House an army officer, two physicians, and several other distinguished citizens, and asked if they did not want to organize as a Branch Sanitary Commission to back up the ladies. Which ladies? That charming Mrs. Livermore and her group. Oh, Mrs. Livermore! And so it was arranged, and one little society, under a housewife whose greatest asset seemed to be only a sunny, unassuming, ladylike charm started on a career that was ultimately to make her office the headquarters of the Northwest Sanitary Commission, and a major factor in the military life of the West.

Mrs. Livermore had been accustomed to write a column for her husband's weekly. Now that she was running an aid society, she began to tell her readers, living way off in remote places, about the many things that were being done for soldiers. If the people of your village have an aid society, wouldn't the president of it like to write to us? We can send interesting bits of news about our boys from time to time, or make suggestions about places on the front where some help from the good people at home would make life ever so much better for our brave boys. If you don't have an aid society, wouldn't you like to form one? We will gladly help you. In this simple way Mrs. Livermore ultimately tied to her Chicago office no less than 4,000 aid societies, and organized the whole Northwest, farm by farm, and village by village.

Mrs. Livermore had a simple kind of executive ability whose effortless functioning was often the despair and admiration of harried masculine executives who never ceased to wonder how Mrs. Livermore got so much done. It was the kind of ability often developed by American housewives who, like her, manage to write a little, help the husband with his business, and act as president of a woman's club, while maintaining a charming home and bringing up three children with nothing but incidental maid-service.

What Mrs. Livermore was doing always seemed much more significant to people around her than it seemed to her. Dropping in at her office, her husband was shocked to see the casual way she was handling letters from important personages in Washington

115

and from high military officers. She would open a letter, read it rapidly, answer it immediately, and then crumple it up and throw it into the waste-basket—as if it were just a note from Alice Evans down the street about the church supper tomorrow night. Unable to stop his wife in her tracks long enough to make her heed his objections to her office habits, Doctor Livermore asked the other women in the office never to empty the waste-baskets hereafter until he had had a chance to go through them and see what historic documents Mary was throwing away. Then he set himself to the most exact and scrupulous filing of all her letters, all newspaper items about her, and records of those many matters that Mary attended to, finished, and never gave a second thought. The best of her writings, which she often dashed off in the form of a private letter, he retrieved and published in his paper.

3

The outbreak in the West of the first large-scale fighting of the war tested the mettle of all the women leaders and their aid societies. On the 15th of February, 1862, Grant attacked Fort Donelson on the Cumberland River. The first day a cold rain fell, turning the ground to deep mud. That night the rain changed to sleet, and the temperature dropped to zero. The men had thrown away their blankets and overcoats in the heat of their fight, and had carelessly used up the insufficient field rations they carried in their haversacks. Unable to kindle fires that bitter night, lest their position should be seen, the men, without supper, all of them without tents, many without blankets, bivouacked on their arms. By morning many were frozen to death.

The next two days were equally cold, and each night the men bivouacked in the snow. They consoled themselves with the knowledge that the enemy was worse off than they, because many of the Confederates had come from warm climates, and had even less food and clothing. The Yankees figured that in this ordeal by freezing the North could naturally outlast the South. And so it did. "What are your terms?" said the Confederate general to Grant. "No terms," said Grant, "but *unconditional surrender*."

On February 16 church bells in the North were ringing wildly, proclaiming the first decisive victory of the war, the fall of Donelson. But on the field lay 7,000 wounded of both armies covered by the drifting snow. Almost no provision had been made to bring off the wounded. Squads of soldiers brought some down and dumped them into two dirty old transports on the river. Some men had been lying for four days in the cold, their wounds undressed, smeared with filth and blood. Two or three army surgeons did all they could, but they had no extra clothing to give out, no blankets, bandages or dressings, few medicines, and no stimulants. The only food was corn meal, hard bread, and bacon.

But Grant had known Mary Safford and Mother Bickerdyke in Cairo. And quietly and immediately he opened the way for these women to follow him. Within a few hours after the victory at Donelson, Mother Bickerdyke and Mary Safford, with nurses, surgeons, and rescue agents on hastily outfitted steamships, came up the Cumberland River from Cairo, to bring back the wounded. Another steamer set out from Cincinnati with Doctor Newberry.

Meanwhile trainloads of supplies were started from Chicago on the Illinois Central by Mary A. Livermore. Every sewing machine company in Chicago turned over its machines, rooms, and operators to her, and she put women on them in shifts, in a round-the-clock sewing schedule, to reclothe Grant's army and provide hospital outfits. Mary Safford made five trips to Donelson with the boats, standing in the snow, her slight form whipped by the wind, directing men who with pick and axe pried and hacked the wounded out of the mud into which they had frozen fast.

When Mary Livermore came down to St. Louis from Chicago to oversee hospitals, supplies, and transports, and saw the wounded from Donelson, at the Fifth Street Hospital, she grew deathly faint, and rushed out into the air. "Oh, I can't go on with this. I can't stand it," she thought. Then she rallied. "What men can stand to suffer, you can stand to succor," she told herself firmly.

She went back and forced herself to talk to one poor fellow who had fallen the first day and had been pried out of the ice two days later. His frozen feet had been amputated; his lower limbs were paralyzed, and the flesh had sloughed off his frozen back and thighs. But he was quite conscious and even weakly cheerful.

"If you had been a rebel, you couldn't have been used worse," said Mrs. Livermore indignantly. "Whoever left you men to suffer like that?"

"Oh, they couldn't be bothering with us," he replied, speaking feebly in jerks, but with spirit. "We'd much rather they'd go on and take the fort. *Unconditional surrender*—that's what we were holding out for. We fellows on the ground all cheered when we heard they'd given in. I couldn't cheer much myself because I was most gone, but Jerry did," indicating a man on the bed next to him. "His left arm was gone, and his right hand shot away, but he threw up the stump and cheered for both of us, enough to split his throat."

After that Mary Livermore decided that there was nothing she wasn't going to stand. Mary Safford was of the same mind. She was coughing, feverish and threatened with imminent collapse, and her wealthy, devoted brother was desperately worried about her. But she went on doggedly, supported by the mountainous force of Mother Bickerdyke. "That little gal ain't got much heft," said a soldier, admiringly, "but she's got sand, and she's got grit."

Mother Bickerdyke, having brought down five loads of the wounded and placed them in hastily improvised hospitals, decided that something must be done about the desperate shortage of clothing and bedding. Clothes, sheets, and bandages used by wounded men on the transports were saturated with blood, and with discharge from healing wounds and often swarming with vermin. It seemed hopeless to clean them, they were to be burned or buried. But when materials ran short, Mother Bickerdyke sent to Mrs. Livermore's office in Chicago for washing machines, portable kettles and mangles, recruited laundresses from among the Negro slave women who had fled to the Union lines, and superintended the laundering of all that offensive clothing. What she did not need at once she packed in boxes and bales to be "ready for the next battle."

Mrs. Bickerdyke was assisted by Mrs. Eliza Porter, a mild, soft-spoken little woman of forty-five, the wife of a Presbyterian clergyman. When Lincoln first called for troops, she was at breakfast with her husband and three nephews, "Oh, that I had a hundred sons to go," she said. The family rose from the table. The boys enlisted, Mr. Porter got an appointment as army chaplain, and Mrs. Porter went down to Cairo to work in the hospitals with Miss Safford. Now, as Miss Safford's health failed, and Mrs. Bickerdyke's enterprises increased, she was prepared to step into the breach.

These women became a kind of independent auxiliary army corps, operating directly under Grant's personal command, and with almost unlimited authority to use government transports and cut military red tape. Mary Livermore went amidst the army encampments carrying an order from the Secretary of War which she could use, if necessary, to supersede any authority opposed to her. Mrs. Bickerdyke set up and organized one hospital after another, following Grant down the Mississippi. In these hospitals the cleanliness and ventilation were perfect. The men were tenderly nursed, and for the first time well fed. "Mrs. Bickerdyke is a large heavy woman of forty-five, strong as a man," reported one army surgeon. "Muscles of iron, nerves of steel, sensitive but self-reliant, kind, and tender, seeking all for others, nothing for herself."

Like most of the first great army nurses, she made herself the special guardian of the private soldier, protecting him against careless army surgeons, rascally quartermasters, and selfish officers. As Grant's offensive in the West progressed, she acquired such authority that she was often called "General Bickerdyke."

One day she came into a hospital at eleven o'clock in the morning to find that the men had had no breakfast. The assistant surgeon had been drunk the night before, and had failed to make up the diet list. She sent for him. He came in, jaunty and coaxing. "Dear! Dear!" he said, "What is the matter now, Mother?"

"Matter enough," she said. "Look at these men without a bite of breakfast, and every one of them worth to his country a hundred of such as you. Do you think they are going to go hungry any longer while you get drunk? Pull off your shoulder-straps," she said, walking up to him, and ripping the straps off, with an expert yank of her strong hand. "You are discharged."

The surgeon appealed to General Sherman.

"Who caused your discharge?" asked Sherman.

"That Mrs. Bickerdyke."

"Oh," said General Sherman, "if it was Bickerdyke, I can't do anything for you. She ranks me."

Mrs. Bickerdyke's enterprises in behalf of Grant's armies were many and resourceful. Finding it difficult to get fresh food for the hospitals at Memphis, she got Illinois farmers to donate a cow apiece or a dozen hens, and set up a farm with 200 cows and 1000 hens on an island in the river, to supply her with fresh milk, butter, and eggs. She commanded a veritable army of contrabands or escaped Southern slaves. Every likely Negro man or girl

119

who fled from a Southern master could come to Mrs. Bickerdyke, and be put into training, and sent out promptly on wages to be useful to the army. Negro girls were trained as cooks, laundresses, and nurse's aides in the hospitals. Negro men were trained as farm hands, transport workers, and salvage crews for the battlefields. After every battle she not only had her men rescue all wounded, Confederate and Union alike, but she sent her salvage crews to strip off all usable clothing from the dead of both sides, and to collect all arms and weapons and turn them over to the quartermaster.

Though Mrs. Bickerdyke had been a comparatively uneducated girl brought up on a western farm, she believed not only in system but in training for every individual job. She got her own training in nursing and hospital management by seeking lessons from physicians. She had anything she wanted done reduced to a system and drilled into those who were to do it. It was in this way that she was able to make the Negroes that others were likely to dismiss as ignorant or shiftless into capable workers of all types. Though she thoroughly trained her subordinates, Mrs. Bickerdyke, in the last analysis, trusted nobody but herself. Sentries and patrols became accustomed to the fact that long after night had settled on a battlefield, and all activity was still, and all wounded presumably removed, there would be the figure of a woman, with a shawl over her head, and a lantern in her hand, carefully traversing the field, turning over one body after another and peering at it, to be sure that not one living man had been left among the dead.

4

As Grant moved swiftly southward, Mrs. Bickerdyke and Mary Livermore set their wits to work not only to pick up after him, but to get ahead of the army in preparing for the next battle. They were able to do this, to some extent, in the case of the battle of Shiloh, which was fought in April, 1861. Mrs. Livermore had supplies for 20,000 wounded men collected, or manufactured, and sent to Cairo. Mrs. Bickerdyke cleared hospitals of convalescent men and prepared fresh beds. Then she went on a warpath, getting twelve surgeons discharged and new men put in their places.

Meanwhile Grant chartered four large and luxurious river steamers and turned them over to the Northwest Sanitary Commission, Doctor Newberry and Mary Livermore co-operating, to be outfitted and staffed with surgeons and nurses. Several cities like Cincinnati also furnished one or more steamers, outfitted and staffed by local members of the Commission. On Sunday morning, as the battle opened, a large fleet of these boats, each flying the yellow flag of the Commission, lay on the Tennessee River off Pittsburg Landing, ready to take off the wounded. With them had come Mary Safford.

To the women of the Commission the river bank "seemed a scene of wild and hopeless confusion. Soldiers hurrying to and fro, the countless throng of army wagons floundering through the mud, now inter-locking, now upsetting their loads; the wounded borne on litters to the boats; the dead lying stiff and stark on the wet ground, the busy crowds of grave diggers rapidly consigning the corpses to the shallow trenches." The battle lasted two days. Toward night of the second day the Confederates retreated, leaving the battleground so covered with the dead and wounded that, as Grant said, he could not walk on the field without stepping on a body.

Mary Safford came back with boatload after boatload of the wounded, whom she consigned to hospitals at Cairo, Paducah, and St. Louis. She was everywhere, dressing wounds, cooking, singing, and praying. A soldier said that, for the sight of that little gal, he'd be glad to stay sick for ever. But when the last man was safe in a comfortable bed, including all the enemy wounded, she collapsed with an injured spine, from which doctors said that she would never recover. Her anxious brother sent her to Paris to get the best treatment money could buy.

And meanwhile Doctor Daniel Livermore's paper was carrying to sympathetic homes all over the Northwest a description of the way the war was turning his Mary into a hard-working Martha. It was entitled *A Day at the Rooms of the Sanitary Commission* and was written by Mrs. Livermore. "It is early morning—not nine o'clock, for the children are flocking in merry droves to school. . . . With a good bye kiss I launch my own little ones, bonneted, sacqued, and ballasted with books, like the rest, into the stream of childhood that is setting in a strong, full current toward the school room. I then catch the first street car and hasten to the rooms of the Northwest Sanitary Commission. . . . A dray is ahead of me unloading its big boxes and little boxes, its barrels and firkins, its baskets and bundles.... Ladies are in waiting, desirous of information.... An express messenger enters.... The morning's mail must be answered—a work which is interrupted every five minutes by some new comer. A venerable man enters, walking slowly, and my heart warms towards him. I remember my aged father, a thousand miles away, who, like him, is white-haired and feeble. "Have you heard anything yet from my son in Van Buren Hospital, at Milliken's Bend?" "Not yet, Sir; you know it is only nine days since I wrote to inquire for him. I will telegraph if you think best...." A childish figure drags itself into the room, shuffles heavily along, drops into a chair, and offers a letter.... A messenger boy from Admiral Porter's gun-boats who is sent north with the request that the child be properly cared for. Not thirteen years old, he has been in many battles... Fever, too much medicine, neglect... have done their worst... his right side is paralyzed.... A bevy of nurses enter with carpet bags, shawls and bundles.... They receive their instructions, commission, and transportation, and hurry onward.... Soldiers from the city hospitals visit us to beg a shirt, a pair of slippers, a comb, or a well filled pin-cushion, something interesting to read, or paper, envelope, and stamps to answer letters from wives, mothers, and sweethearts.... And so the day wears away. More loaded drays drive to the door with barrels of crackers, ale, pickles, sauer-kraut, condensed milk and beef, with bales of cotton and flannel for the sewing room, all of which, speedily disposed of, make room for the arrivals of to-morrow. Men and women come and go —to visit, to make inquiries, to ask favors, to offer services, to criticize and find fault, to bring news from the hospitals... to make inquiries for missing men... to make donations of money, to retail their sorrows, and sometimes to idle away an hour in the midst of the hurrying, writing, copying, mailing, packing, and shipping of this busy place.

"The sun declines westward, its fervent heat is abating, and the hands of the clock point to the hour of six, and sometimes to seven. Wearied in body, exhausted mentally, and saturated with the passing streams of others' sorrows, I select the letters which must be answered by tomorrow morning's mail, replies to which have been delayed by the interruptions of the day, and again hail the street car, which takes me to my home.... Only by a mental effort do I shut out the scenes I have left and drop back

for a time into my normal life—the life of wife, mother, and
housekeeper. I try to forget the narratives of gunshot wounds,
sabre strokes, battle, and death that have rained on me all day.
This hour with my husband and children shall not be saddened
by sketches of the suffering men and women who have defiled
before me all day.... There comes to me the grand tonic of the
poet:—

What matters, brothers, if we keep our post
At truth's and duty's side?

9. *Heroines of the Peninsula*

One day in April, 1862, the gentlewomen of New York City were meeting with the gentlemen of the Sanitary Commission and the medical profession in the vestry of Doctor Bellows' church in New York. They were celebrating a great victory and planning a new and epoch-making campaign.

The victory they were celebrating was the final rout of the old Medical Department of the War Department. The previous October the Sanitary Commission had decided that it could get nothing adequate in the way of hospitalization and medical care for the volunteer army until there was a new surgeon general at the head of an enlarged and modernized department. This decision they had conveyed to the Ladies Aid societies. The ladies had discussed it with those army officers, physicians, and men of sound political and business experience whom everywhere they seemed able to bring into their councils. Then they had gone to work on a lobbying job. They spent the winter writing letters, paying calls on congressmen, senators, and other influential men, and keeping a steady stream of items going out through the press. In the spring the bill to reorganize the Medical Department passed both houses of Congress and was signed by the President. A new surgeon general, nominated by the Commission, was to be appointed by the President. His name was William J. Hammond.

This was all to the good. But some time would elapse before the new medical organization could co-operate effectively with the armies in the field. Meanwhile General McClellan was landing some 112,000 men—which was a large army in those days—at Fortress Monroe, proposing to advance up the Peninsula between the York and the James Rivers, and capture Richmond. Much of the region through which they had to advance was low, swampy, and pestilential. Some of it had never been adequately surveyed or mapped. The army had made almost no preparation for the care of the sick and wounded. It was still the opinion of military men that in active fighting, under difficult conditions, to allow any of the precious means of transportation to be used for medical stores or to burden the personnel with the care of the sick and wounded was to weaken the fighting power. By imperiling the outcome of a fight, it risked the lives of several well men for every one who was wounded or sick. Hence, regrettable as it might seem, any man who could not keep up with the march or the battle must be discounted immediately as dead, and dropped off. The army must keep itself unencumbered with anything save the means of fighting. Its function was not to save life but to destroy and kill.

"As many times as this has all been explained to me," said Mrs. Griffin, in response to Doctor Bellows' exposition of the army's point of view. "I still don't believe it. Most of the men that are left by the army to die in swamps, in wet and in cold, have nothing wrong with them that a little decent care would not cure. I can't see why one seasoned soldier, made good as ever and returned to the fight, isn't worth three raw recruits."

Mrs. William Preston Griffin was a beautiful creature, whose dazzling skin, blue eyes, and golden hair were enhanced by the freshness and expensive modishness of her spring costume and grooming. Everyone, including Doctor Bellows, listened to her with respect. She had worked in the hospitals all winter, turning the coarsest personal service into a delicate perfection of routine. She was the nearest thing that New York could yet produce in the way of a true Florence Nightingale, the woman who could do a charwoman's service with the dignity and grace of a great lady.

"They'd better preserve the men they have," commented a sprightly young woman whom the others called "Georgy." She was Miss Georgiana Woolsey, sister of Mrs. Joseph Holland, whose husband was one of McClellan's officers on the Peninsula. She and her sister were nieces of President Woolsey of Yale University. "If they throw these men away, they are not going to get new recruits so easily. How many men will enlist when they know that ten men die on the Peninsula of typhoid fever for one that is killed by the enemy?"

"Georgy, you know very well the officers don't *like* to drop off the men and just let them die of neglect," said Mrs. Howland. "Colonel Howland says that they will be only too happy to co-operate with us in every way if we organize relief and rescue work like the wonderful work the women have been doing in the West."

"I'm against it," said Doctor Blackwell, suddenly, "I think it is high time the army organized an adequate ambulance and hospital transport service of its own. This business of women trying to stand by and be dear angels while men keep on being stupid will have to end some day. It might as well end now."

"It seems to be the general feeling of our societies and of our professional advisers," responded Doctor Bellows, smoothly, "that, instead of trying to be an outside relief agency always ready to come to the rescue, we should now use all our professional resources to work out for the army an adequate ambulance and hospital transport service which they can take over and administer henceforth themselves."

"No army ever did it. The Colonel insists that, from a military point of view, it is impossible, especially where the terrain is bad, fighting is tough, and movements must be rapid, as he says they must be in this campaign," objected Mrs. Howland.

"It is true that no army ever did it, and true that the obstacles to adequate removal and care of the wounded by the army itself are very great," said Doctor Bellows. "What you ladies signify your willingness to do—to go right through a violent and difficult military campaign with the army, and prove the practicability of an ambulance service absolutely co-ordinated with military movements, not interfering with them but actually helping them— is a very great innovation in warfare. All rescue of the wounded hitherto, even the remarkable transport service this winter in the West, has been emergency service by civilians. Our proposal that, as civilians, we train the army, set up the machinery for transport and care of the wounded, and then hand it all over to the military authorities, is naturally somewhat staggering. On the other hand, if we succeed, every other army in the world may adopt our method."

"I am ready to try," said Mrs. Griffin, rising and shaking out her voluminous silk skirt. A pleasant whiff of cologne water emanated from her various fluttering bows and ruffles like the fragrance of a flower suddenly shaken by a breeze.

"And I," said Mrs. Howland.

"And I," said Miss Woolsey, her sister.

"Doctor Blackwell will certify our training," said Mrs. Griffin. "There isn't any sort of disease and filth we haven't toiled over in order to equip ourselves."

"I will certify you as well trained, and so, I think, will every other responsible physician in New York," said Doctor Blackwell.

2

This or something like it, in the way of feminine conversation, was the beginning of the Hospital Transport service which in the summer of 1862 made medical and military history on the Peninsula of Virgina. In behalf of the Sanitary Commission Mr. Frederick Olmsted made a contract with the War Department to remove from the Peninsula all wounded men that the army surgeons certified as incapable of being restored to action in thirty days. At the same time he agreed that the Commission would cooperate with and, where necessary, direct and equip ambulance service and hospitals in the rear of the army which could restore slightly wounded men or those temporarily ill to active service within thirty days. If the military authorities were convinced of the practicability of the routines and equipment devised by the Commission, the army would henceforth carry on this service itself.

In working out the service, full use was to be made of women as "lady superintendents" who could establish the standards of housekeeping and train soldier-nurses. A central executive staff of four women was to set up the work, under the direction of Mr. Frederick Olmsted and Mr. William Knapp, the assistant secretary of the Commission. The four women were Mrs. Griffin, Mrs. Howland, Miss Georgiana Woolsey, already mentioned, and Miss Katherine Wormeley. Miss Wormeley was a vivacious, fashionable young woman of thirty, from Newport, Rhode Island. Her father, though American born, was a Rear-Admiral in the British navy. Miss Wormeley ran the Sanitary Commission offices and workrooms in Newport, and was, at the same time, the proprietor and manager of a shirt factory which she had set up to help women who had been left by soldier husbands without adequate support. She had got working capital from Newport summer residents, obtained a contract for 50,000 army shirts from the War Department, and had put the women to work.

Miss Wormeley could not join the other three ladies immediately because she had to make arrangements for 10,000 army shirts to be made up. But the other ladies prepared to go to Washington, in company with a band of medical students who had been trained as wound dressers and surgeons' assistants. Mr. Olmsted in Washington had been told by the Quartermaster General that the Commission might take over any transports it found lying at Alexandria. Armed with an order to this effect, he went to Alexandria, expecting to find a fleet. He found only one filthy old boat, the *Daniel Webster,* and on this the Commission was expected to take ninety convalescent soldiers and eight officers down the river immediately to Fortress Monroe. Nothing daunted, Olmsted telegraphed to Mrs. Griffin to come on with the other ladies and the medical students. They took the next train out of New York. From the railroad station in Washington they went directly to the boat, where they were joined by Mr. Olmsted and Mr. Knapp. The men had re-enforced themselves with three carpenters and twelve Negro contrabands to serve as workmen.

On April 25, a "lovely day, peaceful and shining," they steamed down the river, and, having taken stock of their ship, held a meeting on deck at sunset. There they divided themselves into two twelve-hour work shifts. Working alternately in two groups on a round-the-clock schedule, the two men, the three ladies, the medical students, the carpenters, and the Negroes all got busy together, and scraped, cleaned, and deodorized that old tub, while the contrabands entertained them with Negro songs. Then they rebuilt the interior, moving their passengers and cargo from place to place as they worked. Mrs. Griffin, as chief lady-superintendent, bossed all arrangements for sleeping, eating, and keeping clean. She had discarded her hoops and her fine spring clothes, and wore a gray calico dress which flapped about her slender figure, making her look, said the others, "like a gaunt Madonna." For a while Georgy and Mrs. Howland resisted Mrs. Griffin's orders to take off the hoops, but they had to yield, having agreed to outshine the army in the military discipline they imposed on themselves. Even so, they couldn't help remarking, strictly off the record, that without hoops they looked "truly mediaeval."

In this intimacy of manual work, side by side, hour after hour, the ladies were taking the measure of their commander, Mr. Olmsted. They had long known him in a social way, when they were all rigged out in the manners and habiliments of the best New York society. But this life side by side, dirty, toiling, sweating, was something different. They ate together with an old stove as table top, slices of bread for plates, fingers for forks, and carpet bags for chairs. They had agreed that Mr. Olmsted was commander-in-chief, and they would yield him implicit obedience. But they continued to look him over with appraising feminine eyes. A strange little man, "an autocrat and an aristocrat," they decided. He was reserved and reticent. His words were few, his orders absolute. His delicate, fine face usually looked severe, even sarcastic, except when he was caught off guard, and then there was something about it that touched a woman deeply. An odd man! Socially he was provoking, and made women want to tease him. But working side by side with him, they came to have a different feeling. They would obey him because they must. They would obey him because their shrewd feminine minds, which, in two days of such intimacy, would have stripped a stuffed shirt to nothing, respected him more every minute. And they would obey him also, with a careful tenderness, observing not only the letter but the spirit of the law, in all the difficulties into which they were going, because they couldn't bear to hurt him or put him into a difficult or humiliating position before the world.

They were five days en route to Fortress Monroe, where they received the equipment which had been sent on to them from New York. Then, gleaming white and clean, with fresh, well-made bunks, dispensary and operating room, nurses and doctors, and smelling faintly of cologne water, the *Daniel Webster* appeared among the forage boats and troop transports on the York River, the mother of all the Red Cross hospital ships that now sail the seas.

On its first trip back to New York the *Daniel Webster* brought back Katherine Wormeley, the fourth member of the central staff, and some other ladies who would man the various services. As fast as shipping could be released to them, they rebuilt other ships till they had a fleet of six hospital ships going up the York River and making trips to Boston, New York, Philadelphia, and Baltimore, taking away sick and wounded and bringing back stores and additional personnel as needed. In addition they had a steam launch, the *Wilson Small,* in which they would go up streams into the swamps, a variety of barges and water craft, and some kind of contraption, operated by themselves, that they could run up and down the railroad tracks.

Each ship had a staff of women whose duties were primarily those of housekeepers. They were responsible for the beds, linen and clothing of the patients, and had complete charge of pantry and store-room. They did all the cooking for the sick themselves and saw that it was distributed according to the surgeon's orders. They had a general superintendence of the wards, and of the nurses, who were all men. Most of these women had received careful training at the hands of physicians in Boston, New York, and Philadelphia, in accordance with the plans of the Ladies' Aids for a mass production of Florence Nightingales. Though any woman who could qualify was accepted, the transport service tended to be distinctly an upper-class service, manned by the daughters and wives of the well-to-do and the well known. "Mrs. M——'s mother writes dismal letters," reported Katherine Wormeley to her mother, "saying that a lady must put away all delicacy and refinement for this work. Nothing could be more false. It is not too much to say that delicacy and refinement and being a gentlewoman could never *tell* more than here. . . . As for the ladies among whom my luck has thrown me, they are just what they should be—efficient, wise, active as cats, merry, light-hearted, thorough-bred, and without the fearful tone of self-devotion which sad experience makes one expect in benevolent women. We all know in our hearts that it is thorough enjoyment to be here. It *is life,* in short, and we wouldn't be anywhere else for anything in the world."

It was not long before the officers of McClellan's army discovered that beautiful and clever women, women who were socially somebody at home, were manning the hospital ships. There was a rush to call, and to bring distinguished visitors to see the ladies and their ships, and to ask for a little entertainment here, and a little kindly feminine service there. Finally Mr. Olmsted issued word to the army that the hospital ships were neither floating hotels nor officers' clubs. He said that they would be glad to entertain important persons who came on genuine military missions, if the army had no other adequate accommodations available. But otherwise their business was the wounded. Mr. Olmsted also dealt severely with the epidemic of malingering that broke out in the army. Pressure was brought to bear to persuade the ladies to take on board all sorts of persons who had slight wounds or were only a little ill—because these persons were officers, or were known to the families of the ladies at home, or for a thousand other good reasons. Mr. Olmsted made it clear that only the most seriously wounded would be taken on the ships, and of the seriousness of the wounds the ships' own surgeons were the ultimate judges.

The duties of the men and women of the executive staff under Mr. Olmsted were to superintend the shipping of the sick or wounded on board the boats which returned from the North for fresh loads; to fit up those boats or others coming into the Commission's hands, and to see that they were kept in first-class condition; to receive at the landing, to sort and distribute, the patients who were sent down from the front; to feed, cleanse, and give medical aid and nursing to all these men, and otherwise take care of them until the ships should sail again for the North, and finally to be ready for all emergencies. And all the while they kept up a steady battle with careless military habits. It annoyed the ladies unspeakably that military men who never thought ahead for themselves should always be wanting to borrow from the thriftily collected stores and equipment of the ships. "It is our task," wrote one of them bitterly, "to build with infinite toil on shifting sands, to be called upon to fill leaky cisterns and keep them full, and to give our best strength to labors the results of which often fade while we work."

One night, for example, the quartermaster came on board, just as the ladies were going to turn in after a hard day's work. "This and all other available vessels," he said, "are to be ready at dawn for special transport service." All night the women worked, transferring their sick to another vessel. Two of the sick died under their hands. They trans-shipped their stores and coaled their ship. With dawn came another order. Their boat wouldn't be needed, after all! Miss Wormeley particularly hated to be called out at night for nothing. "No one can tell how it tries my nerves," she said, "to go toppling around at night on little boats, and climbing up ships' sides on little ladders!"

131

As the campaign progressed, more and more women came down with the ships, until practically every famous woman character of the Civil War east of the Alleghenies, except Clara Barton, was working somewhere on the Peninsula.

With the ships came Miss Helen Gilson, one of the favorite glamour girls of the soldier's saga. Miss Helen Gilson was in her twenties, the niece of Frank B. Fay, Mayor of Chelsea, Massachusetts, who, at the outset of the war, had organized a relief and medical unit for the battle front. Though Miss Gilson had been refused as a nurse by Dorothea Dix because she was too young and handsome, her uncle said that she might come with him, as one of his nurses. As such she had been through every battle fought by the Union army except the Battle of Bull Run. Mr. Fay had merged his unit with the Sanitary Commission, and Miss Gilson had been accepted as one of the front-line workers of the Sanitary Commission. She was sweet, merry, and kind. She nursed and entertained the soldiers with equal skill, and was one of those who had mastered Miss Nightingale's art of domestic perfection under the most unlikely conditions. Hot soup served by Miss Gilson was *hot;* iced lemonade served by her was *cold.* What she made clean was not only clean—it was dainty. She was, among other things, a heroine among the contrabands. Women who could attach to themselves the devotion of these runaway slaves who cluttered every Union army, and turn them into devoted and efficient workers, were always a power in the army.

Two other women well known to the soldiers arrived with the first hospital ships that returned from Philadelphia. The large and efficient Ladies' Aid organizations of Pennsylvania had remained somewhat aloof from the Sanitary Commission and continued to remain so throughout the war. But they would arrange to co-operate on specific projects. And now they sent their best in the shape of Mrs. Eliza Harris and Mrs. Mary Lee.

Mrs. Harris was a washed-out, melancholy, elegant invalid of uncertain years, the wife of a prominent physician. During the first year of war she had done the work of ten strong men, had survived shot and shell enough to knock out a regiment and controlled most of the army relief funds from the rich state of

Pennsylvania. She had been known to show up in howling blizzards on the most remote picket lines, and appeared in the front of battle as languid and elegant as in her own boudoir, and wherever she appeared, she made things happen. Her control of large sums of money was mainly due to the fact that she was an indefatigable writer for the newspapers. As such, she cultivated a peculiarly lugubrious style in which she unobtrusively dramatized herself as a refined and suffering woman who had arisen from a bed of pain to help the poor boys, as you would do, too, if you could see them!

Mrs. Harris was in charge of the service for the wounded at Fortress Monroe, efficient and suffering as ever, and was keeping the most remote Pennsylvania hamlet informed of what she was doing. For example, when the government transport brought off wounded men after the Battle of Fair Oaks, and Mrs. Harris hastened to meet the transport and have the men transferred to one of the Commission hospital ships, she wrote of the transport: "There were 800 on board. Passage-ways, state-rooms, floors, from the dark and foetid hold to the hurricane deck, were more than filled—some of the wounded on mattresses, others on straw; some in the death-struggle, others nearing it, some in their blood as they had been brought from the battle-field of the Sabbath previous, and all hungry and thirsty, not having had anything to eat or drink except some hard crackers for twenty-four hours."

After a circumstantial account of washing, wound dressing, feeding, and putting to bed on the hospital ship, with lists of all the supplies still lacking, she ended, "Disrobed and bathing myself with bay rum, was glad to lie down, every bone aching, and head and heart throbbing, unwilling to cease work where so much was to be done, and yet wholly unable to do more. There I lay, with the sick, wounded, dying all around, and slept from sheer exhaustion, the last sounds falling upon my ear being groans from the operating room." Readers of such a story would hurry off money, supplies, and workers on the next boat for "poor dear Mrs. Harris."

The other famous Pennsylvania character on the Peninsula that summer was Mrs. Mary Lee. She was a bouncing little Scotch-Irish woman, born in the north of Ireland, who had come to Philadelphia with her parents in childhood. Homely and sweet as one of her own famous apple-dumplings, she made comfort for the soldiers wherever she went. All over Pennsylvania, families had her picture hanging over the mantelpiece surrounded by the faces of the boys in the family who were in the service.

Mary Lee first became known to the soldiers as the leading spirit of the Union Refreshment Saloon, which was the army's favorite institution. It had started in this way: Back in 1861 on April 23, Sherman's battery of eight howitzers, manned by eighty very hungry and thirsty men, passed through Philadelphia on its way to Washington. As the troops appeared on the water front, in a shabby working-class district, women came running out bringing the plates off their own tables, and the saucepans and frying pans off their own stoves full of their own family dinners. Others came rushing with bottles from the pantry shelves, and bread out of the bread box. Loiterers on the street, seeing this, hastily bought up all the stocks of the pushcart men, who sold apples and oranges and peanuts, and added them to the food the women were assembling for the soldiers. A man passed around his hat and took up a collection which he spent buying out the nearest tobacco shop. The soldiers departing, replete with food, drink, and smoke, gave nine cheers for the Union, the Constitution, and the ladies of Philadelphia.

Mrs. Mary Lee, seeing the success of this spontaneous offering of the poor, immediately started to organize it. She set up a stove and apparatus for making coffee in an old boathouse, and hung over it the sign *Union Refreshment Saloon*. She organized the housewives of that whole area, so that at any time, day or night, when the signal gun announced that soldiers were arriving by train or by boat, bands of women appeared to serve them. Most of the women were poor. Some were so old that they could scarcely hobble. But Mary Lee used them all. It soon became known to weary and hungry men that, no matter how long they had to starve, en route to a military center, there was always food and comfort for them in Philadelphia.

Funds flowed in to the Refreshment Saloon from all over the city. The Saloon outgrew its quarters in the boathouse and took over one after another of the adjoining buildings as annexes. A rival institution known as the Cooper Refreshment Shop set up in a nearby cooper's shop. When soldiers complained that they hadn't had a chance to wash for days, bathing arrangements were improvised, and soon every soldier could get a wash or a bath. Then it was found that sick or tired soldiers, crammed for days in cattle cars, would appreciate a chance to lie down. Soon there were dormitories and bedrooms for the transients who needed them. Finally a hospital and medical center was established. By the end of the Civil War 4,000,000 men had been served in this simple way, in this working-class district.

Many people worked on this project, but Mary Lee was associated with it in the soldier's mind, and wherever she went afterwards in the army—and she seems to have been almost everywhere —she was hailed with peculiar affection. In the summer of 1862 she was looking after the soldiers at White House. White House was a little old cottage which had once belonged to the wife of George Washington, on the York River. Around it the Sanitary Commission had pitched 1,000 hospital tents, and Mrs. Lee was there, as some one reported, "talking all the time, cooking all the time, just as usual," and managing to be "always good company." She was accompanied by her daughter, who acted as her right-hand man. Her son was with McClellan's forces fighting somewhere on the Peninsula.

With the troops also were some of the most famous of the women soldier-nurses who had survived from the first days when some regiments had enlisted women. Neither the Sanitary Commission nor Miss Dorothea Dix nor the War Department approved of these women in theory, but no matter what rules were made about the use of women in the front lines, everyone, from the generals down, made exceptions for a few of them. One of these women was Kady Brownell of Michigan who had been at the Battle of Bull Run. Another was Mrs. Annie Etheridge, who was also a Michigan institution. "Gentle Annie," as she was called, was a quiet, reserved, virtuous young woman in her early twenties, said to be "of good family," whose military garb was a black riding habit. She was a dead shot, an expert swordswoman and horsewoman, and had the courage of a demon. She went with the boys into battle, rallied them in difficulty, sometimes snatched up the arms of a man who fell and took his place, nursed the boys, foraged for them, and fought for their rights at all times. She grasped at once what the ladies of the hospital transports were attempting and saw that her boys co-operated with it efficiently. She herself did heroic work that summer both in rescuing and nursing the wounded.

Another soldier nurse was Bridget Devan, an illiterate, tough, brown little Irishwoman whose husband was a non-commissioned officer. She could ride and shoot with the best of them, and saw that her boys got fed and looked after, no matter what. "Irish Biddy," the boys called her, and nothing could separate her "and me lads." She seems to have been intelligent and sensible, and threw all her weight on the side of the Commission and the new-fangled notions.

And there were Emma C. Edmonds and Mrs. B. and Chaplain B. still with Heintzelman's troops, encamped at first at Yorktown. Emma's career that summer was extraordinary. At first she was quietly nursing the sick at Yorktown, and riding out every day to buy up all the butter and eggs and milk she could find among the Virginia farms, for the use of the hospitals. And meanwhile she was falling very happily in love with a tall, dark-eyed young lieutenant and Christian gentleman, a Canadian, who came from her own province of New Brunswick, in Canada. But one day she rode back from one of her foraging trips to meet the soldiers soberly carrying a body to the place under the blossoming pear-trees, where they buried their dead. She did not have to ask whom they were burying. She knew. She rode on and went about her duties, but she was in the mood in which most of the suicide risks of war are undertaken.

Learning through Chaplain B. that McClellan was looking for someone to take the place of a Yankee spy who had been caught and executed in Richmond, she volunteered, suggesting that her gifts of mimicry and disguise, which she had often used to entertain the camp in dull moments, might be put to some military use. She was interviewed by seven different generals, given strict examinations in gunnery and military knowledge of all sorts, and asked to demonstrate how well she could ride and shoot. She was then required to test her capacity for disguise by getting a job as a colored boy with her own doctor and remaining unrecognized. Finally she was given a careful going over by McClellan's phrenologists, a phrenological examination being the Civil War equivalent of an army intelligence test.

At last her offer to go as a spy was accepted, and McClellan sent her several times into Richmond. Between these assignments she usually put on woman's dress and nursed demurely in one of the hospitals, at Williamsburg or White House. But sometimes she donned a soldier's uniform, took a boy's name, and, unknown

136

except to a few, served as an orderly to one or another of the officers, presumably to guide them with regard to matters which she had picked up as a spy. High spirited, plucky, and apparently attractive both as a girl and as a soldier, she was nevertheless a well educated and sensible woman who admired and rejoiced in the innovations of the Sanitary Commission and co-operated with them at all points.

4

Among the many accounts of feminine adventures on the Peninsula that were finding their way to absorbed readers in the North, none were more charming than those of Katherine Wormeley. The British admiral's daughter lived the nautical life of the ships as naturally and joyously as a sea gull on the wing, and took perpetual pleasure in the summer beauty of the Peninsula—"this garden land, . . . the lovely shores . . . belted with trees and shrubs of every brilliant and tender shade of green, broken now and then by creeks, running up little valleys till they are lost in the blue distance." On May 18, 1862, she wrote, "Yesterday, after getting off the *Knickerbocker* from Yorktown, with three hundred sick on board, we transferred our quarters to this vessel and started to run up the Pamunkey. It was audacious of us to run this big ocean steamer up this little river, without a chart and without a pilot. In some places we brushed the trees as we passed but we came safely up, and this morning as we came on deck, what a sight was there to greet us! The glow of the morning mist, the black gun-boats, the shining river, the gleam of the white sails and the tents along the shore. . . . We rewarded the three generals who had come over to meet us with a few miscellaneous luxuries— handkerchiefs and cologne to General M; hair-pins to General P— one button of whose cap was already screwed on by that feminine implement; linen thread and buttons to General F. The harbormaster wanting the room in the evening, we dropped down the stream and anchored by a feathery elm-tree."

Determinedly, day after day, the women patrolled the swamps in the rear of the army, with their staffs of medical students and Negro helpers, trying to see that all wounded and abandoned men were found and brought to them. The whole area over which the army was advancing was swampy and wooded, crossed by swollen rivers, full of malaria and typhoid. To make matters worse, it rained for days on end. Men were always being left behind in the marshes. Supplies would get soaked or lost in crossing swollen streams, and stranded men would be left without food or medicine.

The *Wilson Small* would nose its way up the creeks, crashing through the thick boughs of trees that hung almost to the black water. On its bow would be perched at least two of the young women, their full skirts, without hoops, clinging to them. Anxiously they would scan the oozy shores. Far off, beyond the woods, there would be the constant detonation of guns from the Union armies advancing toward Richmond against stubborn Confederate resistance. Suddenly they would find what they were looking for—a rude shelter of logs "on low and filthy ground, and within it a score of our men, piled in there, covered with vermin, dying with their uniforms on and their collars up, dying of fever." Or again they would find a dozen typhoid patients who had been lying outdoors in the pelting rain for twenty-four hours. "They were crazy and noisy," reported Miss Wormeley, "soaked with swamp poison, and in a sort of delirious remembrance of the days before the fever came, days of mortal chill and hunger. They kept screaming for warmth and food."

Whenever men were reported to be in trouble, by day or night, the women went to them. One day they heard that sixty men were lying along the railroad tracks without food. The women and their helpers got into their railroad contraption, which they could operate themselves. "With provisions, basins, towels, and blankets, we went up to the railroad bridge, cooking tea and spreading butter as we went." A tremendous thunderstorm came up, in the midst of which the men were found, put on freight cars and pushed to the landing; then washed, fed, and taken on the tug to the *Elm City*. Doctor Ware, the physician attached to the staff under Olmsted, found fifteen other sick men, located a shanty, and put the men into it for the night. In the morning, said Miss Wormeley, "we ran up on the tug, cooking breakfast for them as we ran, scrambling eggs in a wash-basin over a spirit lamp. And such eggs—nine out of ten *addled!*"

The more the army surgeons and officers learned to co-operate by picking up and bringing in sick and wounded men wherever and whenever they were found, the more trouble there was for the ladies. After ten or twelve hours of work, the women would turn in, hoping for sleep. "We are awakened in the dead of night by a sharp steam whistle, and soon after feel ourselves being clawed by little tugs on either side of our big ship, bringing off the sick and wounded from the shore. And at once the process of taking on hundreds of men—many of them crazed with fever—begins. There is the bringing of the stretchers up the side-ladder, between the two boats; the stopping at the head of it where the names and addresses of all who can speak are written down and their knapsacks and little treasures numbered and stacked; then the placing of the stretchers on the platform; the row of anxious faces above and below deck; the lantern held over the hold; the word given to 'lower'; the slow moving ropes and pulleys; the arrival at the bottom; the turning down of the anxious faces; the lifting out of the sick man and laying him into the bed; and then the sudden change from cold, hunger, and friendlessness into positive comfort and satisfaction, winding up with the invariable verdict, if he can speak, 'This is just like home.'"

5

It was in the techniques of evacuation that the Commission won its spurs that summer. One June 11, at four o'clock in the morning, the ladies on the *Elm City* heard the sound of cannonading, and knew that a great battle had commenced. Their boat was full of fever patients. Instantly they took it down to Yorktown, discharged their sick, had their boat cleaned and made up with fresh beds, sent all the rest of the fleet up to stand ready, and got back by sunset of the same day, just as the first wounded were coming down to the shore. As the Commission ships appeared, there was a wild rush for them, armed men with their officers coming out by boat or barge and scrambling up the side. No one on shore had charge of these men. It seemed to be a mob in retreat. The women and unarmed men Commission agents calmly stood on deck and gangplank, facing these men down, telling them that the ships could be used only for the most seriously wounded. Meanwhile wounded men in every condition of horror, the dead among the living, were being rushed down on the railroad, and thrown into government transports.

As the calmness of the Commission began to make order, word came from military headquarters asking them to take charge of the evacuation. Quietly, without hurry or confusion, the corps of medical students and Negro helpers who worked on the ships, filled up the Commission fleet and moved away. Then the women went to work for three days and nights, to get the rest of the men off, working not in their own well-organized service but trying to make the best of a bad case. On the government transports "not the smallest preparation was found for the common food of the men; and, as for the sick food, stimulants, and drinks, there was nothing of the kind on any government boat, and not a pail nor a cup to distribute food had there been any."

When the women said that men worn out by a hard battle should be fed, the quartermaster put up a large tent, the Commission opened its stores, and, working day and night for seventy-two hours, the women fed 3,000 exhausted and slightly wounded men. "Their intelligent, self-imposed duties were discharged with a courtesy and endeavor I have never seen equalled," said Doctor Ellis, an army surgeon.

Following this, Olmsted had quite a set-to with the War Department. The army officers reported that the Commission had "a judicious system, firmly carried out." A proposal was made either by the army or the War Department that the powers of the Commission should be greatly extended, and that it should be empowered to handle all future emergencies of this sort from the outset. Olmsted said the Commission didn't want any more power. It was looking forward to the day when it could hand back what it had to an army that had learned its business. He pointed out that all that the Commission did was actually to apply and constantly to practice the kind of system and discipline that were supposed to be the essence of good military procedure. If the ladies could act with precision, subordination, forethought, and patient endurance, he saw no reason why soldiers and military men could not do likewise.

"Conceive of the Medical Director of the army sending down over 4,500 wounded men without—yes almost literally without— anything for them," wrote Miss Wormeley, "without surgeons; no one authorized to take charge of them; nothing but empty boats to receive them; no arrangements made of any kind. . . . The boats which have been lying here idle for weeks, waiting for surgical cases, wholly unprepared and their surgeons off to the battlefield. No stores, no beds, no hospital stewards, no food, no stimulants. Then it is that the medical authorities fling themselves on the Sanitary Commission, and the Sanitary Commission gives everything with a generous hand. It has done all that it has done on three fourths of the Government boats, and that at the last moment, without notice and when its own supplies were heavily taxed in fitting out its own boats."

The protests of the Sanitary Commission to the office of the new surgeon-general brought specialists down from the War Department to go over the whole medical situation of the Army of the Potomac with Mr. Olmsted. The ladies on the transports thought it was high time. Under the extra strain that was thrown on them with every battle, Mrs. Griffin had already given out. Though she tried to keep on working, she was seized again and again with spells of fainting and mild delirium. Mrs. Howland was permanently disabled. Mr. Olmsted was working on sheer nerve. Two of the Commission's own surgeons were ill from overwork.

It was a happy day when they welcomed on board a "Great Medical Mogul" from Washington who "out-ranks all medical men on the Peninsula." "This," reported Miss Wormeley, "enables us to contemplate a great battle with less of a nightmare feeling than we have had while there was nothing to expect except repetition of past scenes." And indeed this medical mission from Washington was to be epoch-making.

6

McClellan failed to take Richmond. Instead, in seven days of battle, his men fought their way to a new base at Harrison's Landing on the James River, abandoning White House on the York River, where the Commission had a large hospital center and base of supplies. Mrs. Fogg, of Calais, Maine, who managed an advanced field-station for the Commission at Savage's Point, two miles behind McClellan's lines, kept it open till the last minute and then retreated with the army. Meanwhile the Commission fleet at White House, on advance warning of the army's plan, made a neat and skilful get-away. Under the direction of the ladies of the Central staff the sick and wounded were carefully gathered from tents and hospitals at White House and sent slowly down the winding river.

Miss Wormeley and the other ladies remained behind on the *Wilson Small,* to be sure that everything was done, "lingering as long as possible, till the telegraph wires had been out, and the enemy was announced by mounted messengers to be at Tunstall's; in fact till the roar of the battle came nearer and we knew that Stoneman with cavalry was falling back to Williamsburg, and that the enemy was about to march into our deserted places."

All night they sat on the deck of the *Small,* as they slipped down the river, "watching the constantly increasing cloud and the fire-flashes over the trees toward the White House; watching the fading out of what had been to us,' through these strange weeks, a sort of home, sacred to some of us now for its intense living remembrances."

Miss Wormeley took dispatches which had been entrusted to her to Fortress Monroe. Then, after coaling off Norfolk, they steamed up the James, enjoying the fact that they were in the High Command's secret and knew—what most people did not yet know—that the army was shifting its base. "This gave us the special fun of being the first to come leisurely into the panic then raging at Yorktown. The *Small* was constantly surrounded by terror-stricken boats; the people of the big *St. Mark* leaned over their bulwarks to question us, pale with fear. Nothing could be more delightful than to be calm and monosyllabic as we were. . . . We leave to-day for Harrison's Landing where our gun-boats are said to be. We hope to get further up, but General Dix warns us that it is not safe."

Thus girlishly the British Admiral's daughter reported an important assignment, coolly and skilfully carried out.

Meanwhile the visit of the Great Medical Mogul from Washington had borne fruit in the appointment, on July 1, 1862, of Dr. Jonathan Letterman as Medical Director of McClellan's army, ready to take over the Sanitary Commission routines, equipment, and as much of the personnel as wished to stay on, and to administer them as the first medical field service ever worked out, in detail, for any army. The plan was formally adopted by the Army of the Potomac on August 2, 1862, and by the armies under Grant in the West on March 30, 1863, and established for all the armed forces by an Act of Congress on March 11, 1864. It became the basis not only of our own medical field service, but of

142

that of every other army in the world, and is still followed, in essentials, wherever there is fighting in the present war.

The Commission that summer had set the general pattern, which has been followed ever since, of various types of mobile hospitals. When the ladies raised an outcry against bringing down the wounded in freight cars, Doctor Harris equipped cars with litters, swung on rubber bands, that could be lifted off without disturbing a suffering man. This plan was turned over to the railroad companies who proceeded to manufacture the famous hospital cars of the Civil War, with their swinging bunks, and operating room, and quarters for nurses and surgeons. Four hospital trains were put on the western lines, and several on the eastern lines. On them 150,000 wounded men from the western battlefields and 100,000 from the eastern battlefields were ultimately carried back with care and tenderness to the hospitals of the North.

So far had the American army come, in one short summer, from the first days of the campaign when the wounded were hurled carelessly, one on top of the other, into dirty freight cars, and then left there on the tracks, to fester in the broiling sun, because no one had given orders to move the train!

While Mr. Olmsted and the Medical Mogul were working out the field service, there was an exchange of letters between General McClellan and General Lee, in which they agreed henceforth to treat unarmed surgeons, Sanitary Commission agents, and other medical relief personnel as neutrals. At the same time the Sanitary Commission formally adopted the principle on which it had been working all along—to draw no distinction, in medical service and relief of suffering, between Union men and the Confederates. The various principles, first clearly formulated in discussions between the Sanitary Commission and the new medical corps of the Army of the Potomac, became the foundation of the Geneva Convention of the International Red Cross, under which relief work and care of the wounded and of prisoners of war are carried on to-day.

With the adoption by the War Department of its plans and routines, the Sanitary Commission felt that its work, in this respect, was over. It made over its fleet to the army, with its staffs of medical students and trained Negro workers. Three physicians who had been the Commission's inspectors of camps on the Peninsula joined the army, to carry on the reform of the camps from the inside.

Meanwhile the whole country was ringing with the praises of the heroines of the transports. 10,000 men rescued from the swamps, who, under the old army conditions, would have died, had been borne back to their northern homes by women on the transports. Every one of these men advertised the Sanitary Commission to their families and communities. Stories reached as far as California, and miners there, rough men who knew what it was to feed themselves and nurse each other without women, took up a collection and sent the Commission a gift of $100,000—the largest gift that it had yet received.

Word spread to foreign countries. Contributions came in from London, Belgium, Italy, Turkey, Chile, and the Argentine. All sorts of fine liquors, medicines, tools, and materials, at that time not obtainable in the United States, were offered to the Commission, through the interest of friends abroad. Inquiries came in about methods of setting up similar auxiliaries to European armies. Among those who were especially concerned was a committee in Geneva, Switzerland, which under the inspiration of the young Swiss, Henri Dunant, was trying to evolve an international version of the Sanitary Commission. In order to meet all these European offers and inquiries a European representative of the Sanitary Commission was appointed—Charles S. P. Bowles. Acting as the recipient of European contributions, and a purchasing agent in Europe for certain kinds of materials for the medical services of the United States army, he also kept in touch with the European committee in Geneva which became the nucleus of the International Red Cross.

"The Hospital Transport Service is ended," wrote Katherine Wormeley on July 25, 1862. "We left *Elizabeth* well supplied and moored to the long wharf at Harrison's Landing where the surgeons and chaplains and quartermasters can get at her with ease . . . I wonder who'll succeed to my cabin on the *Small* and hang his clothes on my gimlets (used for pegs) and inherit my other little inventions of that nature?

"Georgy and Mr. Olmsted and I sat up the greater part of our last night on the *Webster,* talking as people will who know that on the morrow they are to separate widely. Did I say somewhere that Mr. Olmsted was severe, or something of that kind? Well, I

144

am glad I said it, that I may now unsay it. Nothing could be more untrue; every day I have understood and valued and trusted him more and more. . . . We worked together under the deepest feelings, and to the extent of our powers, shoulder to shoulder, helping each other to the best of our ability. From first to last there has been perfect accord among us; and I can never look back to these months without feeling that God has been very good to let me share in them and see human nature under such aspects . . . The last I saw of Mr. Olmsted he was disappearing down the side of the *Webster,* clad in the garb of a fashionable gentleman. I rubbed my eyes and felt that then it was indeed *all over.* I myself had risen to the occasion by putting on a black lace teaspoon (such were the bonnets of the period) in which I became at once conventional and duly civilized.

"We are not yet forgotten on the James; at least I am assured of it in two letters—one from the Great Mogul, the Medical Inspector General; the other from the United States officer who did more than any other to make our work successful. They are characteristic. One writes: 'How I miss the dear ladies of the *Wilson Small* and their freshening drinks—animal that I am! But how can I forget that which comforted me?' The other says: 'The departure of the *Wilson Small* has left a sad blank in these waters. It always had a humanizing effect upon me to go aboard, if only for a moment.' I trust that when this weary war is over I may meet the friends I have made here under happier skies."

10. *Potatoes and Onions Conquer Vicksburg*

The great ladies of New York had won a brilliant victory in that campaign for which the United States Sanitary Commission was first mobilized. But the Commission, itself, and the Women's Central, and all the aid societies all over the land were only at the beginning of a career of usefulness which was to become greater and greater with the passing of every bitter month. For the women had discovered how long this war was going to be. As one solemn letter that circulated among the women's societies said, "Seeing our army sweeping up the Ohio and the Potomac, sending its wounded before it, and leaving its dead behind, we know that, for the sake of mankind on this continent, we must not have the experience of Europe repeated here. *We must go on and on and ever on, with this one war,* until such an end is reached as will prevent constant recurrence of war."

While the women were discovering the real character of the war, the army had been discovering the real character of the women. It knew now that it could no more dispense with the hard-working little housewife at home in the aid society than it could dispense with the private soldier. In the intricate network of war agencies of a nation now given over wholly to the necessity of fighting, no group had proved more orderly, exact, and responsible in its functioning than the little village aid society, largely manned by housewives. And at the heads of these societies, said Doctor Bellows, there were at least 10,000 *master spirits,* women of the highest executive capacity. Of these women, Bellows said, in words quoted with approval by Linus P. Brockett, a merchant of New York City: "No words are adequate to describe the systematic, persistent faithfulness of the women who organized and led the branches of the United States Sanitary Commission.

Their volunteer labor had all the regularity of paid service, and a heartiness and earnestness which no paid service can ever have. Hundreds of women evinced talents there which, in other spheres and in the other sex, would have made them merchant princes or great administrators of public affairs . . . Their work was distinguished by magnitude, system in operation, thorough co-operation with the other sex, distinctness of purpose, businesslike thoroughness in details, and sturdy persistency to the close."

Hence in the autumn of 1862, the gentlemen of the United States Sanitary Commission, in conference with officials of the War Department, determined to ask the women's societies for a very much larger volume of supplies than had at first been acceptable as "supplemental aid" to what the government itself wished to do for its army. The army now numbered well over a million, and a million more were to be raised as fast as they could be provided for. An army of a million had hitherto never existed in any land. There was no precedent for it in history. To provide even elemental subsistence and adequate arms for so many men, was taxing every regular channel of business and manufacturing. Adequate food simply could not be obtained. A government agent trying to buy 50,000 bushels of potatoes in the West could not get them. Every small and informal means of supply and manufacturing in the country must be opened up. And this job the government was ready to put on the women's societies because, as the official gentlemen said, handsomely, the remarkable success of every enterprise that the women had undertaken assured them that women could organize the voluntary work of citizens much better than men. Women "understand the principles and methods which insure success in such undertakings." In particular the women were to be urged to give free rein to their talents for publicity, because "their great ingenuity in discovering new methods of enlisting sympathy when the old have lost their freshness is very remarkable."

Hence Doctor Bellows called upon the men associates of the aid societies everywhere to assist in developing twelve key railroad centers to which the ladies could ship supplies collected by the local societies. From each center women executives would direct from 150 to 1,200 aid societies. Quotas of clothing, food, hospital supplies, and medical supplies that could be collected or manufactured locally were to be assigned to each town and village.

147

At the regional centers goods were to be unpacked, inspected, graded, and repacked. At every important station there was to be a Commission agent to see the goods safely on their way to the army. In other words the informal activities of the societies, which by this time were producing an enormous bulk of goods, were to be carefully co-ordinated into an immense shipping business run mainly by women.

In all this women's activity, the Sanitary Commission and the War Department were hoping to uncover the woman genius who could once and for all solve the problem of vegetables for the army. Though in those days nothing was known about vitamins, it was well understood that without vegetables men got scurvy. They would become muscularly weak, short of breath, greatly depressed. Their faces would get haggard; their gums would begin to swell and bleed; their breath would be foul. Then bruises would appear on their limbs; there would be bleeding from mouth and nose; terrible and offensive ulcers would break out on their bodies and begin to spread. Similar ulcers and bleeding would break out within the body, in the stomach, in the intestinal tract; and the men would collapse and die.

From the first the army had struggled desperately to supplement hardtack, coffee, and meat with vegetables locally obtained. The Sanitary Commission had strained every nerve to ship fresh and dried fruits to the army. Sanitary Commission agents and army surgeons alike had scanned the troops continually for symptoms of the dreaded disease. And now they knew that it was upon them. Man after man in the army of the Cumberland was failing. In General Grant's army on the Mississippi before Vicksburg, cooped up for weeks on steamboats among the bayous, there was a general and ominous decay.

Vegetables must be got and got quickly. Lemons and oranges were out of the question. They could not be provided in sufficient numbers. Sauerkraut would do, but where was there sauerkraut to feed a million men? The best possibility was potatoes and onions, both to be eaten raw. The Sanitary Commission had already demonstrated that raw potatoes sliced thin in molasses were an adequate antiscorbutic, and the soldiers liked the ungodly concoction. But the army couldn't get enough potatoes.

So early in November, 1862, a Women's Council of Relief was called in Washington, made up of the women leaders of the aid societies, to consider both the increase of general and miscellaneous supplies to the army and the solving of the problem of vegetables. To this meeting came Mrs. Mary A. Livermore, disliking the idea of this long journey away from her family in the dreary winter weather, but somewhat consoled by the fact that she could make a detour and see her old father in Boston. So she made her way east through throngs of soldiers all the way, soldiers cooking over open fires, lounging in railroad stations, soldiers singing, soldiers marching, and, too often, soldiers lying sick with no one to care for them. She noted with indignation that, to clear the hospitals, soldiers who should still be in bed, were discharged or furloughed and allowed to make their way home. Usually their pay was so much in arrears that they had no money for transportation or food. They would try to walk or beg their way, and somewhere would fall exhausted. Mary Livermore got so worried looking out for these sick lads as she came along that she almost forgot what she was going to Washington for. She was engaged in mentally renting and equipping soldiers' lodges or rest-houses all across the country.

So she arrived in Washington, and, with her thoughts still full of the sick boys, attended the Women's Council, talked to President Lincoln, and talked to Secretary Stanton. On the way back to Chicago she began to realize that the whole question of onions and potatoes and the prevention of scurvy in the army had been nicely laid in her lap.

2

Mary Livermore and her friend Jane Hoge knew where the potatoes and onions were, and so did every other good housewife. Potatoes, with onions as flavoring, were the staple of the average family's diet. They were served fried for breakfast, mashed or baked with meat for dinner, scalloped or creamed or made into potato soup for supper. A large proportion of the Americans raised these potatoes themselves. Most people then lived on farms. Business or professional people in the city or workers in factories frequently had large gardens on the land which lay cheap and plentiful around every urban settlement. People who did not grow their own winter vegetables usually laid them in in the fall, buying them cheap from the local farmers. Roads were poor in those days. The storms of winter blocked all traffic, and even isolated the dwellers in city suburbs for days. It was a thriftless family that didn't have plenty of potatoes to fall back on. By November 15, 1862, at the time when Mary Livermore and Jane Hoge put their minds on the potatoes, the season's crop was nicely stowed away in the nation's cellars.

Mrs. Livermore and Mrs. Hoge decided that the soldiers were going to have the potatoes and onions, even if the average family didn't. If Mrs. Housewife didn't know what else to feed her family, Mrs. Livermore and Mrs. Hoge would tell them. So household by household, farm by farm, village by village, from the Alleghenies to the Rocky Mountains, the women got the potatoes out of hiding. Local village talent gave shows—admission a potato or five onions. School children were organized into competing clubs, with a prize for the club bringing in the most potatoes. If you couldn't spare a bushel of potatoes from your winter's stock, you could give a peck. If you couldn't spare a peck, you could give a quart. If you couldn't spare a quart, you could give *one.* You could pass up the potatoes and gravy at dinner and eat bread and gravy instead.

Careful, detailed, and horrible descriptions of all the stages of suffering of the soldier who had no potatoes to eat were sent out to small-town papers, and passed around by word of mouth. There were signs and slogans. "A barrel of potatoes for every soldier." "Don't send your sweetheart a love-letter. Send him an onion." Mrs. Livermore and Mrs. Hoge toured the towns and villages—Mrs. Hoge dynamic and dramatic, Mrs. Livermore gentle and pleading, till the potatoes and onions piled up in mountains around them.

The climax of the great potato campaign, and the test of its efficacy, came in March, 1863. The six states of the Northwest were at that time a sea of mud. It rained every few days. The ground was thawing. A hard-surfaced road, in those days, was practically non-existent. But through the mud the potatoes were converging on the schoolhouses which had been made the receiving centers for them. They started in wagons. The wagons got stuck in the mud. Men heaved the potatoes on to their backs, and walked through the mud. But they brought the potatoes. Others, despairing of wagons, filled saddlebags with potatoes and came on horseback, twenty, thirty, forty miles through storms and floods. Others walked ten, twenty, thirty miles bringing all they had—a half peck of potatoes, a dozen onions. Even so, Mrs. Livermore did not trust the power of her publicity alone. In every town and village, the aid society had a wagon going around from door to door, through rain and mud, knocking at every kitchen, talking to every storekeeper, interviewing every farmer, making sure that if there was a potato or onion still extant, it started immediately for the army.

Somebody had to preserve and pack and safely transport all this produce. But that, too, was arranged through the aid societies. General Grant, who had taken all the shipping on the rivers, said he would gladly provide the boats to carry the potatoes if the ladies would see that they were manned. Mrs. Hoge became the commander of the potato fleet. And the potatoes and onions set out on their majestic way to the relief of Vicksburg. "With potatoes and onions, we conquered Vicksburg," said one lady proudly.

3

It seemed to Mary Livermore that it would be a good idea if the folks at home knew more about the day-by-day life of their army, and the soldiers knew that the folks at home were interested in them. So in March, 1863, Mary Livermore and Mrs. Colt, executive head of the aid societies of Wisconsin, were going down the Mississippi River, with a company of quartermasters, state surgeon generals, members of the state legislatures, and representatives of the Chicago Chamber of Commerce, together with nurses bound for the hospitals, and army officers returning from furloughs. What Mrs. Livermore and the eminent citizens with her were going to do was to visit every single hospital from Cairo to Young's Point, opposite Vicksburg, and to relieve right then and there such needs as were most pressing, making themselves useful in any way they could among the sick and the wounded. A full report of what each one saw and did, day by day, was to be published in the home town papers, in the Chicago press, and in the bulletins of the Sanitary Commission. Through the newspapers, the party had volunteered to take letters, messages, or small packages to persons on their route connected with the army, and to deliver them wherever possible.

Mrs. Livermore's own notebook read as follows: "Mercantile

Battery, Milliken's Bend, George W——. Saw his mother in Chicago. She is well, is not worrying, has gained thirteen pounds since the cold weather. Am to make particular inquiries about her son's habits, Does he drink, swear, or smoke? Tell him his mother would rather he be sent home dead than that he should return alive and dissipated."

"Young's Point, 113th Illinois, Peter R—— Wife and six children are well; gets plenty of work, good pay, and the county allowance of three dollars weekly. He is not to worry about them —*at all. Must never think of deserting.* Stand it like a man. All the family pray daily to the Virgin for him."

"Try to learn something concerning Herbert B—— of 15th Wisconsin. Has not been heard of since the Battle of Stone River."

"Try to get discharge for Richard R—— dying in Overton Hospital, Memphis, of consumption, and bring him home to his parents."

Her thick notebook contained scores of pages covered with such notes. The other members of the party had similar notes though not so numerous, because most inquirers naturally gravitated to Mrs. Livermore. As she said, she specialized in "the poor and the humble."

The party carried a considerable assortment of stores for hospital relief—especially potatoes, onions, sauerkraut, and vegetables for the scurvy patients, who constituted most of the sick in the military hospitals all up and down the Mississippi. Mrs. Livermore was graciously seeing to it that well-fed and important citizens from the home town were themselves kindly calling on boys in bed who were livid, faint, and covered with ulcers and open, bleeding sores because they had not had the right food. She was giving these persons a chance themselves to present to the boys, with their own hands, vegetables from their own cellars, and to learn from the surgeons and nurses the miraculous change which a few potatoes a day could make in a man's life. In addition, the party carried corn-starch, lemons, oranges, pearl barley, tea, sugar, condensed milk, ale, canned fruits, and a small quantity of the best brandy, together with hospital shirts, drawers, sheets, socks, and slippers.

The party traveled on a river boat put at their disposal by General Grant—a little rickety, wheezy, crowded, perilously unstable craft that had to poke along the river, towing in its wake three or four barges full of hay. The hay was always catching fire from the sparks of the steamship engine, or breaking loose and having to be recaptured and tied up again. One barge finally floated away down the river and was never seen again.

Behind this craft came a truly noble procession. For, inspired by Mary Livermore's stories about her party, the citizens of the Northwest were rushing to the Illinois Central, through the aid societies, everything they could lay hands on that could possibly help those poor boys. The army had ordered up all empty troop ships and transports to Cairo, and soldiers and rivermen were unloading from the trains boatful after boatful of antiscorbutic and hospital stores to follow the party down the river.

It was a truly wonderful journey. Not all the party stuck it out but Mary Livermore did, visiting every patient in every hospital. Day after day she went on through the melee of the Mississippi at war. She slept at the Gayoso House in Memphis, which had a reputation for style, secession proclivities, and discomfort, amidst nightly drunken fights, "the crash of glass, the ribald song, and fearful profanity." She was reviled by southern "ladies" as one of those "cold-blooded, white-faced, lank, lean Yankee women who are their own servants at home." Going among the army camps with a secret paper from the Secretary of War that she could use if she needed to, but well known to Grant and Sherman and all the higher officers, she was reported as a suspicious character. A complaint was lodged with the provost marshal saying that she was carrying contraband goods down the river to smuggle through the rebel lines. The goods named were morphine, quinine, chloroform, medicines in the package, and cotton cloth in the piece. The Yankees had a good laugh over that!

Day after day she floated on swollen rivers, whose turbid waters were all over the dreary banks, so that only the gaunt cottonwood trees stood out above the flood, hung with funereal moss. She traveled for hours on hours through muddy sloughs. One day her ambulance wagon broke through the rotten logs that formed a bridge over a slough and pitched her head-first into the mud. Thereupon some "brown, busy, rollicking" Yankee soldiers who were seeking a dry place for an encampment dropped their work of "shebang" building, and rushed to her relief "with rails, and planks, and whoops, and yells sufficient for a whole tribe of Indians." The General himself put in an appearance much concerned, till he found that the lady who was still down in the mud-hole was shaking with laughter at the remarks the boys were making, and then he laughed, too.

Everywhere she found the troops and the hospitals fighting mud and water. In order to figure out what could be done to make men comfortable and healthy under such circumstances, she settled down and lived with the troops, and acted as chief cook for a field hospital. Her principal equipment for the job was a pair of boots reaching to the hips.

When the party that had started from the home town, weeks before, finally reunited and turned homeward, nearly every one of these good legislators and plump citizens was leading by the hand two or three women or children or under-age soldier boys whom they had found in dire distress and were taking back to get some civilized care. Mary Livermore held by one hand a seven-year-old Negro boy who had been "stolen" from a plantation where he was being abused, and by the other hand a fifteen-year-old lad, tall, slender, and pale, named Johnny. His father, a Virginian, had been thrown into Libby Prison because of his denunciations of Virginia's joining the Confederacy. Johnny had fled to a Union regiment who befriended him and made a pet of him till he finally came down with swamp fever. To save his life the chaplain of the regiment had begged Mrs. Livermore to take the boy home with her.

To take Johnny to the North involved no difficulties, but the Negro child was quite another matter. The miserable, low-down whites who congregated at the junction of the rivers were attacking and subjecting to cruel abuse the Negroes who fled from the Southern states. The Illinois legislature had imposed a fine of $1000 and a year in jail on anyone who abetted the coming of a Negro into the state of Illinois. The provost marhal inspected the trains connecting with the river-boats at Cairo to see that the law was obeyed.

Mary Livermore was a law-abiding lady. But laws against Negroes were something that no self-respecting Yankee of her heritage pretended to honor. So, with the help of the stuttering Negro porter, Henry, who was an old friend of hers, she stowed the child away in her suit-case under her berth. "A p-p-p-plantation nig like dis yere ch-ch-chile can sleep anywhar," said Henry.

Then she went to bed in the berth right over the suit-case and did not want to be disturbed.

Next morning, Mrs. Livermore could hear people protesting to Henry. "Why don't you wake that woman up? Is she going to lie abed all day?"

"D-d-d-dat woman's bin down to t-t-t-take keer of de s-s-s-s-sick sojers," stuttered Henry. "S-s-s-she's slep mighty little f-f-f-mos six weeks, and she's done got *monstous* sick. L-l-let her sleep."

Henry, of course, was helping Mrs. Livermore to conceal the Negro child. But the fact was that actually she was "monstous" sick, and could not raise her head, not only that day but for ten days afterwards. But she compelled her will to triumph over her aching, fevered body till she could get the little Negro child cared for. As they moved out of the southern part of the state and came into northern Illinois where some of the most distinguished and prosperous citizens were of the old abolition breed, the child was put into the hands of a railroad conductor who had served a long apprenticeship on the underground railroad. Ultimately the child's mother, a superior colored woman who had escaped, was found, and mother and child were reunited. The woman said she had nearly died worrying about her "chile." But each time the Lord had said to her in her heart, "Dat chile's my chile. I'll take keer of him, and tote him to you bime bye." Mary Livermore remembered her one escapade in law-breaking to her old age, with serene and conscienceless satisfaction, for had she not been an instrument of the Lord in toting that "chile" to his Mammy?

4

It was the great merit of the Sanitary Commission that it could take the ideas which women like Mary Livermore developed in their warm-hearted, personal contacts both with the soldiers and the home-folks, and turn them into large-scale enterprises under expert professional direction, and with the co-operation of the government or of the army. Those convalescent soldiers, for example, who had been so much on Mary Livermore's mind. The idea of a great chain of soldiers' homes or lodges was already being realized. Forty centers were either opened or would soon be opened, where soldiers en route to or from their regiments, or soldiers astray, or in trouble, or sick, or needing care of some sort could be adequately provided for. Agencies were being set up to help the soldiers discharged from the hospitals as unfit for further service, to collect their back pay and put in claims for pensions.

But Mary Livermore had another idea about convalescent soldiers. Everywhere she had seen men who were not well enough for the regular work of the army, and not sick enough to be put to bed. They generally did not want to go home. They wanted to get well and stay on with their units and fight. What these men needed was some kind of mild outdoor occupation plus special care and feeding. Why not set them to planting gardens for the army all through the conquered and devastated parts of the South? That would solve the vegetable problem.

In the spring this plan was carried out on a grand scale as a joint project of the Sanitary Commission and the army, under the immediate direction of Doctor Newberry. The army furnished the land, workmen, tools, farm machinery, and military guards. The Sanitary Commission furnished agricultural experts, seeds, and plants. The army gardens were planted all across the reoccupied area of the South, in the rear of the army, in thirty-, forty-, and one hundred-acre plots, and worked by convalescent soldiers under the leadership of soldiers who had been practical farmers in civil life.

However handsomely her dreams might be realized, Mrs. Livermore never rested content. Something might slip up. So just to make sure that they could lick the scurvy, she had a campaign going among the schools. Each child was to plant a row of onions, to be collected by the teachers. Children's brigades were also enlisted to pick the wild blackberries which grew all through the West in pastures and on the edges of wood lots. Out of these the Ladies' Aids made a blackberry drink popular with ailing, feverish soldiers, and good for the scurvy, too!

Mrs. Livermore was fast becoming a busy woman. Her office was now the western equivalent of the office of Dorothea Dix in Washington. She was charged with the commissioning and transportation of the nurses and other personnel for the western hospitals. She equipped and provisioned hospitals, hospital boats, and ambulance wagon trains. She had 4,000 aid societies under her personal direction. She was more or less concerned in the management of forty soldiers' homes or lodges. She had several hundred thousand persons on her mind, to each one of whom she wanted to give the same careful, loving, half-caressing attention that she gave to Dan, and the children and her old father. But she still had not visualized the position she was beginning to occupy in the public mind. To herself she was not anybody in particular. She was just Dan Livermore's wife, trying to do what she could.

One day Mrs. Livermore was asked to come to Dubuque, Iowa, to tell the Ladies' Aid there about some of the needs of the boys at the front. Expecting to find only a little group of women, to whom she would talk quietly, in her usual fashion, like a hostess at her own tea-table, Mrs. Livermore went. She found the town plastered with posters. *Mrs. Livermore—a Voice from the Front.* The largest hall in the city was full to overflowing. The Governor was to preside. The Governor-elect, home from the army with a gunshot wound, was to be present. The members of both houses of the legislature were all there, and governors, generals, colonels on leave from the army, public characters of all kinds, were coming into town from the surrounding states. The audience was to be almost entirely made up of men, thousands of men, top-flight military men, great political executives.

Mary's courage staged an instant stampede. Trembling all over, she protested to the Ladies' Aid. "I am not a public speaker; I have never made a public speech in my life, and I have never addressed anyone but companies of women. I had something to say to you ladies, but it is not at all worthy to be presented as an address to the great audience that you have unwisely called together. *I cannot do it."*

She was ashamed to be such a coward. But she could not face those people. "No shallop left on the shore by the retreating tide was ever more helpless or inert than I felt myself to be," she said afterwards. "There was no float in me—I could not believe that there ever would be."

Finally, the governor-elect, Colonel Stone, in whose regimental hospital she had worked for several days, said that he would make her speech for her if she would agree to read to them what she had been going to read to the Ladies' Aid. Just appear on the platform with him, and say that. Nothing more! So it was settled. Mary Livermore went on to the stage with Colonel Stone, whispering careful instructions to him: "Let Governor Kirkwood introduce you as the orator of the evening, and say that, before you speak, Mrs. Livermore will just make a small statement to the Ladies' Aid."

When the time came, Mrs. Livermore rose. Not daring to look at that enormous audience, at the generals, colonels, governors, in rows and rows, she talked in utter darkness. It was as if the house were unlighted. She did not hear the sound of her own voice —but only a roaring as if ten thousand mill wheels were thundering about her.

But somewhere in the inner tumult the idea began to stare her in the face that it would be a pity to have wasted her time coming over here. She had come because she felt that the ladies of Iowa weren't doing enough for the soldiers. They just didn't *know* what being a soldier was like. No matter how she hated speaking, she'd have to tell them that. Her voice reaching desperately into the darkness, she began to tell them. Gradually the lights came on in the room. She looked down into one or two faces that she knew. There was utter stillness. Suddenly her eye fell on the clock. She had been talking for an hour and a quarter! In confusion and panic, she sat down. The house rocked with cheers. And the next thing she knew she was staring at checks and bills piling up in her lap. There were eight thousand dollars for the soldiers, sent up to her from the audience, and more money was coming and coming!

11.   *A Lady with a Flask*

The characteristic equipment of the army girl of 1861 was a
flask. She might wear a riding habit, or a strange half military
costume consisting of full tunic and trousers. She might wear
a calico dress and a sunbonnet. She might wear the favorite costume of the girls on the Peninsula, a man's army shirt worn
with collar open, sleeves rolled up, and shirt-tails out over a full
skirt minus hoops. This costume was called an "Agnew"—the
original shirt having been borrowed from Doctor Agnew, a great
physician who was on the Board of the Sanitary Commission. But
whatever she wore, she carried a flask. And to the man parched
with the thirst of bleeding wounds, the lady with a flask was all
the angels of heaven rolled into one.

"Our precious flasks," wrote Katherine Wormeley. "They do
good service at every turn. We wear them slung over our shoulders
by a bit of ribbon or at the end of a rope. If, in the long hereafter
of song, some poet should undertake to immortalize us, he'll do it
thus, if he is an honest man, and sticks to the truth:

> *A lady with a flask shall stand*
> *Beef tea and punch in either hand—*
> *Heroic mass of mud,*
> *And dirt and stains and blood.*"

No matter how the army, the government, and the Sanitary
Commission strove to perfect the arrangements for care of the
soldiers, sick or well, on a large and handsome scale, with the
best professional advice, they could never quite get ahead of some
simple women who continued, to the end of the war, to pioneer
in homely methods of making the boys comfortable.

One of these pioneers was Mrs. Eliza Harris, the pallid, low-

159

voiced invalid from Philadelphia whose sob-stories from the front published in Pennsylvania newspapers kept the money for the army flowing. Wherever the soldiers were worst off, there she was. She would meet a regiment in retreat, tired, ravenous, and, in less than an hour, have ovens turning out fresh bread for the whole outfit. She would assist army surgeons with amputations, while severed arms and legs mounted in a bloody pile beside her, and then spend the evening fastidously washing every stitch of her clothing, "spattered with the mingled blood of Confederate and Union soldiers." She was the inventor of "bully soup" or "ginger panada"—a strange concoction popular with cold and hungry men. It was a hot gruel made of cornmeal, army crackers mashed in boiling water, ginger, and wine. It was believed that many a poor fellow, coming in from his post, after a night in the mud and sleet of a Virginia winter, was saved from pneumonia by Mrs. Harris and her bully soup.

In January, 1863, she wrote to the papers from a canteen which she had set up for pickets in Virginia, describing herself as sitting by her cook-stove in the early morning, amidst soldiers drenched to the skin. Here and there a poor fellow was coiled up on the floor, full of pain and weariness. Seated along the table, as closely as possible, were others, whose expressions told how good they found the fresh baked bread, stewed fruit, and coffee Mrs. Harris had set before them. All were wet and cold, exposed all night to drenching snow and rain. "The vapor from the clothing of the soldiers condenses on my glasses; the eye waters, too; and the lungs are oppressed by the heavy atmosphere. For a moment I am ready to give up, but only for a moment. For suddenly I hear the word 'Halt,' and a chorus of coughs. Seventy-two of our defenders stand there in the raw wind—thoroughly wet, icicles on their blankets, a march of three to five miles ahead of them, every step over their shoe-tops in mud and slush." And so Mrs. Harris came to, and made bully soup for seventy-two men, and whooped up the fire and warmed them, and tried to make them, temporarily at least, a little dry.

Mrs. Harris had a taste for the morbid which led her to tackle, with almost gloating delight, what no one else would touch. One of her enterprises was the care of refugees from the Tennessee mountains, and the attempt to keep typhus fever from spreading there. "Miserable looking women and old men and children of all ages, herding indiscriminately in some dirty warehouse or unfinished, unfurnished tenement, they become an easy prey to typhus fever," she reported. "It comes in the form of a chill, followed by fever, and this is followed by jabbering. The mind of the sick one is filled with old home scenes. Ghastly smiles play over worn and haggard faces. The patient sinks, and in a few days fills a government coffin, and is carried to a nameless grave."

She had also, at one time, 10,000 wounded soldiers, left at various stations behind the battle-lines, under her immediate care, most of them amputations. "By day and by night I see their poor mutilated limbs," she wrote, "red with inflammation, bones protruding, worms rioting, as they were held over the side of the ambulance to catch the cooling breeze."

2

One of the greatest of the ladies with the flask was Clara Barton. Clara Barton was not a nurse. She never was connected with the Sanitary Commission. She was a self-appointed auxiliary to the commissary and the quartermaster, and, as such, she had an uncanny capacity for turning up in emergencies, and making a relatively small amount of supplies perform miracles in the way of sudden comfort. She was a kind of natural multiplier of the loaves and fishes. She had some kind of miraculous capacity for turning water into wine, and making a little basket of bread feed thousands. The legend that surrounded her, and the memory she left behind her were much greater than anything she seems to have actually done or to have had to work with during the Civil War. But though her achievements were probably not great compared with those of women who built up a large machinery, like Mother Bickerdyke or Mary Livermore, and had thrust on them great responsibilities, there was something in her personality that quite justified the legend.

Miss Barton began her career by remembering that soldiers need to eat. It was an obvious fact, but she seems to have been the first to do anything about it when she met the first troops in Washington with a train of Negroes carrying food.

Clara Barton was not on the Peninsula. The great work of the aid societies and the Sanitary Commission during the first year of war developed independently of her. Nevertheless, by September, 1862, Miss Barton was a military institution. She had a large depot in Washington to which people from all over New England steadily sent whatever Miss Barton thought best to provide the army with, and she kept the folks at home informed of all that she did in reports in which there was always a blithe note of adventure. When she proposed to join the army that was trying to push General Lee back from his attempted invasion of Maryland, in September, 1862, the Quartermaster-General sent an army wagon for her and her stores. "I was to ride eighty miles in any army wagon, and straight into battle, and danger, and all," she reported eagerly. "The time was Sunday—the place Seventh St. just off Pennsylvania Avenue, Washington City. I watched the approach of the long and high, white-covered, tortoise-motioned vehicle, with its string of little frisky long-eared animals—with the broad-shouldered driver astride—and the eternal jerk of the single rein by which he navigated his craft up to my door. Then and there my vehicle was loaded with boxes, bags, and parcels, and, last of all, I found a place for myself and four men who were to go with me. I took no Saratoga trunk, but remembered at the last moment to tie up a few articles in my handkerchief.

"Thus equipped and seated, my chain of little uneasy animals commenced to straighten itself, and soon brought us into the center of Pennsylvania Avenue, in full gaze of the whole city in its best attire, and on its way to church. Thus all day we rattled on over the stones and dikes and up and down the hills of Maryland."

In the next few days everything conspired to make Miss Barton look like the rescuing angel of the Battle of Antietam, which turned Lee back from Maryland. This battle was fought on September 17, 1862, under extreme difficulties. The army had suffered a long series of defeats, and the men were tired. The Confederates had captured supplies intended for the army, and had blown up a bridge over which supplies were coming. Miss Barton, starting with one truck, picked up supplies everywhere. One of the officers told her where there was some whisky, which she annexed. She found that her own bottles of wine had been packed in sifted cornmeal, which she carefully saved. She entered a house near the battle line, which had been abandoned by Stonewall Jackson and his men, and, exploring it carefully, found three barrels of flour and a bag of salt.

Miss Barton's original four helpers multiplied to thirty. Meanwhile Mrs. Mary Lee, the cheerful little genius of the Union Refreshment Saloon in Philadelphia, came through with troops from Pennsylvania, bringing an army wagon. She was carrying or acquired on the spot, large supplies of flour, molasses, and apples with which she started a wholesale production of apple dumplings. Mrs. Mary A. Brady soon arrived with another army wagon. And by devious methods, really vast amount of stores from the Sanitary Commission came in by wagon train from Maryland and Pennsylvania—food supplies literally by the ton, bandage materials and clean clothes by the bale.

Clara Barton started fires for exhausted men all along the lines, sent pails of hot cornmeal gruel out through the army, gave clean linen and medicines to hard-pressed army surgeons in a field who were trying to bind wounds with corn-husks, because their bandages had given out, and cased the pain of the most seriously wounded men by making them "measurably drunk" with her liquors till help could be got to them. And all the while she was dashing to and fro, even under fire, her little face black with soot, her sleeve torn, where a bullet had gone through it, overseeing the whole enterprise.

Afterwards she recorded in her diary: "Antietam—eight miles of camping armies face to face, 160,000 men. Miles of artillery shaking the earth. Ten hours of uninterrupted firing. The sharp unflinching order, 'Hold the bridge, boys. Always the bridge.' At length the quiet. The pale moonlight on the cooling guns. The weary men, the dying and the dead."

Among those borne exhausted from the field after the battle was Miss Barton herself. But wounded men, bedded down in leaves and corn-husks by smouldering fires, murmured, "Hang it all! How do the women get their stuff on to the field when the army can't?"

While Miss Barton was recovering from Antietam, she received a note from the Quartermaster General. It read: "The army will fight again. Can you come with us? How much transportation do you want?"

She replied: "I can go. I want three six-mule army-wagons with good drivers."

She was given six wagons and an ambulance, with ten large, rough men, who had driven all through the Peninsula campaign— "drovers, hucksters, butchers, and mule-breakers," strong and experienced but never before exposed to a lady's society. When they saw that they were to work for a woman, said Miss Barton, "they said and looked what they thought, and I understood them."

At four o'clock the first day, the drivers stopped, formed a circle in a field, and prepared to camp for the night. Miss Barton sent for the leader, and asked him why they had stopped. He said they weren't going to drive all night. She said quietly that they were going to drive *till* night and that they would find it to their interest to do so. By some process of reasoning he arrived at the same conclusion, for he called out the teams and they started off again. But when night came, they didn't stop. They went on and on through the darkness, jolting Miss Barton over rocks and stones. "Oh well," thought Miss Barton, "they are going in the right direction, and working off their surplus energy. As long as they can stand it, I can." Finally, unable to make the little lady cry quits, they stopped, and prepared to camp for the night. They had eight days' ration of hardtack and salt horse in their feed-bags, on which they expected to subsist without cooking.

While they were attending to the animals, Miss Barton built a fire, cooked a hot supper, spread a cloth on the ground, poured the coffee, and called the men to supper. Amazed at this unexpected invitation, they came. She took her seat with them and chatted at them. They were silent but respectful. Afterwards, when she had washed the dishes and was sitting by the fire, the whole body of men came toward her, looking very huge in the darkness and very much like brigands.

"It is chilly," she remarked amiably. "Don't you want to gather around the fire here?"

They halted, looking more like brigands than ever. The red glare of the embers lit up their hard brown faces. They were waiting for their chief to speak. His name was George. His "coal black hair and eyes would well befit the chief of banditti," reported Miss Barton afterwards.

George said, "No, thank you, Ma'am. We just came to say that we are ashamed of ourselves."

Miss Barton, who had dealt with many a schoolroom full of big bad boys in her time, reflected that honest confession is good for the soul, and said nothing.

"The truth is," continued George, "that we didn't want to come in the first place. There's fighting ahead, and we've seen enough

164

of that for men who don't carry muskets but only whips. And we'd never seen a train under the charge of a woman before, and we didn't like it. So we thought we'd break it up. But you've been so nice to us. You couldn't have treated us better if we'd been the General and his staff. So we just want to say that whatever you want done, we're going to do it."

That night when Miss Barton went toward the ambulance, in which she was to sleep, George appeared with a lantern, helped her up the steps, and buckled the curtains down carefully. Early next morning she heard the men tiptoeing around and whispering, George came to unbuckle her curtains, bringing her a bucket of warm water for washing. Around the fire were the men, with her tablecloth spread on the ground, and her cups set out, and hot coffee bubbling over the fire. "This morning," they said, beaming, "We've made the breakfast for *you*."

Miss Barton and her men were attached as a regular auxiliary unit to the Ninth Army Corps. Ultimately her train numbered thirty wagons and ambulances. Her original nucleus of men went through battle after battle with her, learning to carry out the wounded, dress their hurts, and bury the dead, and becoming, as she said, "more devoted and gentle every day."

3

Among the many ladies with the flask none was more gratefully remembered than Miss Amy Bradley, another New England school-teacher. Miss Bradley came from Kennebunk County, Maine. For many years she had had a school in San José, Costa Rica, where she had gone to recover from threatened tuberculosis. She was one of those women who were enlisted by state regiments to care for the boys from home, in the early days of the war. When the regiments were formed into brigades, the new brigadier-general, making his rounds, noticed how well the boys of the Fifth Maine were set up with hospital and other welfare services and wanted to know who fixed these fellows up like that. "Miss Bradley," said the boys.

"Miss Bradley, hey? Let me see the lady," said the general.

Thereupon there appeared a stocky little round-faced woman, walking very erect, in a blue stuff gown that was a feminine imitation of an army uniform.

"So," said General Slocum. "You think you're going to keep your Maine boys sitting pretty while the rest of this brigade flounders around in its own filth? We can't have any partiality like that. I've taken two large buildings, the Powell House and the Octagon House, and I'm turning them over to you to be fixed up with whatever you can get from your Ladies' Aids. Henceforth you are in charge of everybody in the brigade who is sick or in trouble."

Miss Bradley was on the Peninsula, where her capacity to make a cheerful, cleanly sort of home comfort for indefinitely large numbers of men out of anything she could lay hands on quickly caught the eye of the various distinguished observers of the United States Sanitary Commission. So when the Commission succeeded in opening the first home and club for soldiers in Washington, Miss Bradley was asked to take charge of it. As mistress of the Soldiers' Home, Miss Bradley set herself up in competition with the various bars, saloons, and sharpers that preyed upon the soldiers. She had good tea, coffee, and chocolate to offer instead of liquor; music, magazines, agreeable little home parties—even the presence of nice young ladies. And for the half-sick, the stragglers, the fellows in some kind of trouble who made up so much of the wandering soldiery—the men who weren't really deserters, but might be shot as such if some one didn't take their affairs in hand —Miss Bradley was Providence itself.

In November, 1862, the Women's Council of Relief met in Washington, and, under the horrified escort of Mary A. Livermore, who, at that moment, couldn't get the poor convalescent soldiers out of her mind, the ladies went over and looked at Camp Misery in Alexandria. And there they found a new job for Miss Bradley.

"Camp Misery" was what was officially called a "Rendezvous of Distribution." To it were sent the soldiers who, at the moment, did not seem to belong anywhere. These were grouped in four camps: 1. A camp for new recruits; 2. A camp for deserters and stragglers recaptured and grouped here until it could be decided what to do with them; 3. Paroled prisoners; 4. Men discharged from the hospitals in and around Washington who were considered unfit for further duty but whose final discharge from the army was yet to be obtained.

These men were sent to the camp, and then nothing whatever was done for them. They generally had no decent clothes when

166

they arrived, and none were given them. Theoretically they could draw hardtack and salt horse as rations, if they could get them. There were some little old mouldy tents available, if somebody else weren't filling them to bursting. The camps were on the side of a slope where the ground was so porous that it absorbed water like a sponge and stayed permanently wet. The lowest of the four camps was devoted to the convalescents. All the drainage from the other camps ran down into that one and stayed there.

Without beds, without adequate blankets even, the sick men slept and lived in foul-smelling mud. They could make no fires because the region around was swept bare of every stick of wood. There was a so-called assistant surgeon, and two assistants to him, but in November, 1862, any surgeon who knew anything was in such demand in the units they were trying to get in readiness for fighting or were actually sending into the field that what was left for Camp Misery in the way of medical talent or knowledge was very little indeed.

The poor wretches at Camp Misery had herded together by states, and had signs over their various settlements—Illinois, Indiana, Ohio, etc. Mary Livermore traversed the whole United States here, from state to state, sick with horror. These bloodless, shivering, dirty, demoralized wretches were Illinois boys, Indiana boys. If their mothers could see them, if their folks only knew! When Mary Livermore reached this point in her cogitations, the mothers and folks soon did know. She and the other women went home, and from all over the country there came an outcry. Camp Misery must go! If the army couldn't find out what to do with all the men it didn't know what to do with, put in someone who did! The result was that, in December, Miss Amy Bradley moved over to Camp Misery as Agent of the Sanitary Commission.

Within a few hours after her arrival, there were the usual signs that Miss Bradley was around. A clean shack was being prepared for a hospital. A distribution of clean, warm army shirts was going on. There was a systematic clean-up campaign in progress. And a line of draymen, with carts bearing the stamp of the U. S. Sanitary Commission, was unloading farina, dried fruits, milk, butter, and other articles that Miss Bradley considered necessary for half-starved, demoralized men. Then she began to sort the men out. Within the next twelve months, Miss Bradley passed under her personal review 111,825 inmates of the camp, relieving the wants of each as needed. Many were desperately ill, some permanently diseased. These were removed in ambulances to hospitals under suitable care. Many men had seven and eight months' pay due them, and were destitute of any means of getting away. Many were presumed to be discharged from the army but did not have discharge papers. Miss Bradley set up a back pay and soldiers' papers agency. Between May 1 and December 1, 1863, she got 150 men who had been unjustly listed as deserters reinstated in their regiments and collected $8,000 in back pay for them.

When Miss Bradley had cleared out the men who should not be in the camp, and had made decency for those who might be temporarily detained there, she made the inmates of the camp a thorn in the flesh of dilatory or careless military officials, by setting them to the job of writing and editing a *Soldier's Journal*. This was the beginning of the military journalism that now flourishes in most national armies. Apart from publishing a few masterpieces written by the soldiers for their own entertainment, the *Journal* gave instructions with regard to the many matters that had caused so many men to be stuck indefinitely in this camp. It explained all about furloughs, told the exact steps to be taken to get an honorable discharge, and like matters. While educating the soldier to take care of himself and not to run afoul of entanglements of red tape, the *Journal* tactfully exposed some of the unnecessary complexities of army procedure to public view. So the inmates of the camp ceased to be a great mass of rotting humanity composed of military pariahs hurled into outer darkness for no reasons that they could understand and kept there for weeks and months after even the good reasons had ceased to be valid. They became, instead, producers of a soldier's paper, self-respecting citizens actively working out their own salvation, or patiently biding their time for reasons that they understood, and meanwhile cheerfully having their say about it all.

The *Soldier's Journal* published its first number on February 17, 1864, and its last, three months after the end of the war, on August 22, 1865. Over and above the value of its printing press and equipment, it made a clear profit of $2,155.75. This money was held for the benefit of orphans of soldiers who had been inmates of the camp.

4

The most famous battle of the Civil War was also the most famous engagement of the ladies with the flask, in their never-ending battle with suffering and decay.

On July 1, 2, and 3, 1863, the armies of the Confederates under Lee were stopped in their great offensive against the North and driven back beyond the Mason and Dixon line by the stand of the Union armies at Gettysburg. Here, all around the sleepy little Pennsylvania market town, amidst beautiful rolling hayfields and orchards, there was fought a battle that was almost exactly parallel in numbers engaged, in cannon employed, and in killed and wounded, with the Battle of Waterloo which, till then, had seemed the great battle of all time. In each battle the total of men on both sides was about 150,000; each side had about 200 cannon; the defeated side lost about 40,000 in killed and wounded; the victors about 20,000. These, at least, were the figures printed at the time of the Battle of Gettysburg in the *Sanitary Commission Bulletin.*

By July 4, the Confederates were retreating southward, and the Union army pursued them, taking almost all their surgeons and medical equipment with them. Behind, on the field, in the broiling sun, lay 22,000 men, still living but unable longer to fight— the badly wounded, the slightly wounded, the exhausted, and the stragglers, including 5000 Confederates left behind by their army. They were spread for twenty miles around Gettysburg, sleeping in haystacks, dying in ditches, refugeeing in private houses. Every one of these men must be located, helped, and sent on to their regiments, to hospitals, or to prison camps.

Fourth of July dawned fair and happy on all the villages of the North. There were no fireworks, for the children had pledged all their firecracker money to buy vegetables for Mary Livermore's scurvy-stricken soldiers in the West. But the flags were flying. The roses were blooming. The scent of mock orange blooms and of hay and clover was sweet on the air, and people were pouring into churches with the news of the victory of Gettysburg bright in their smiling faces.

Then, from every pulpit through the North, east of the Alleghenies, was read the call to the women. "Nurses, matrons, lady superintendents, all females qualified for usefulness in this emergency, are asked to report at once to the headquarters of their aid societies or to the headquarters of the United States Sanitary Commission or the Christian Commission, for service on the battlefield of Gettysburg." At all the main railroad stations women already well known in battlefield relief were stationed, to interview applicants, and organize units of workers. Miss Dorothea Dix was at the railroad station at Baltimore. Mrs. Harris, Mrs. Mary Lee, and Mrs. Mary A. Brady were organizing the units in Pennsylvania. The office of the Women's Central, in New York City, was organizing the women who poured into New York. Some units of Sanitary Commission workers had been on the battlefield or in the town of Gettysburg, all through the fighting. One train of wagons sent by the Sanitary Commission was captured by the Confederates and the surgeons and workers with it were taken to Libby Prison, but there were no women in this group. Some women had got to Gettysburg by wagon train, and were living in the town and going out daily to the battle-field in ambulances to assist the few hard-pressed surgeons, amputating there on long bloody plank tables under trees.

As rapidly as possible a relief train was made up at Baltimore, consisting of freight cars full of bales, boxes, and barrels of Sanitary food and clothing, and tents, stoves, and other equipment. Attached to this were coaches for women sanitary workers, and for Negro contraband workers. The railroad between Baltimore and Gettysburg had been torn up by the Confederates, but army engineers were rapidly repairing it while the women were superintending the packing of the relief cars. They got the train off on Monday afternoon, July 5. With it went Miss Georgiana Woolsey, the merry and ingenious "Georgy" who had been one of Mr. Olmsted's staff in the transport service on the Peninsula, the summer before. Since then she had been working at the Portsmouth Grove General Hospital of which the Surgeon General had appointed her friend, Katherine Wormeley, superintendent. Of the labors and adventures which followed "Georgy" wrote a very interesting account.

Normally it was only four hours' ride from Baltimore to Gettysburg, but they were twenty-four hours on the way. Bridges had been blown up and roads churned up. At every crossing there was the wildest confusion. Miss Woolsey saw a Confederate soldier, "sitting dead" against a barn door. In all that torn and dusty landscape, there was "no food, no rest, no cheer of any kind."

Late Tuesday afternoon, they stopped about two miles short of Gettysburg. They could not go further because the railroad bridge was not yet repaired. It had begun to rain, a murky, warm drizzle, through which the odor of decomposition came foul and heavy from the battlefield. From all directions came tired and slightly wounded soldiers, limping, dragging themselves along, silent, weary, worn, famished for food and drink. Left behind by the army, they had been told that a relief train would come through on the railroad, and had come to meet it. Instantly Georgy and the other women went to work. They pitched two large hospital tents, in one of which they set up a stove, and put two soldiers who had been cooks in hotels to work making vegetable stew. In the other tent they made up seventy-five beds for the most seriously exhausted men. Other men they settled for the night in the coaches and cars. They carried around beef tea and milk punch and cold orangeade. They washed wounds and put splints on broken limbs. They handed out clean shirts, towels, and soap and clean rags doused in cologne to hold to the nose against that ghastly odor from the battlefield. They registered every man and noted where he belonged and what would have to be done with him. Thus through all the night, and the days and nights following, they worked. By Friday afternoon they had provided for 3,000 men.

By that time the engineers had got the railroad repaired, and they moved up to the battlefield, and joined the other units that had come in from Philadelphia and New York. They set up a little village of white tents, with stoves, steam apparatus, and a fine supply of pure fresh spring water. They took over the administration of the tons of ice, lemons, milk, meat, vegetables, sheets, towels, clothes, and medicines now coming in by train from surrounding cities. They also gave care and guidance as needed to the pitiful bands of relatives who came from all sides to seek their wounded and their dead. "Besides our own men at the Lodge," said Miss Woolsey, "we all had soldiers scattered about whom we could help from our supplies; and nice little puddings and jellies, or an occasional chicken were a great treat to men condemned by their wounds to stay in Gettysburg, and obliged to live on what the empty town could provide. There was a colonel in a shoe-shop, a captain just up the street, and a private round the corner whose young sister had possessed herself of him, overcoming the military rules in some way, and carrying him off to a little room, all by himself, where I found her doing her best with a very little. She came afterward to our tent and got for him clean clothes, and good food, and all he wanted, and was perfectly happy in being his cook, washer-woman, medical cadet, and nurse."

Meanwhile, on the field, working directly with the surgeons, there were the army nurses Miss Dix had rapidly interviewed, accepted, and commissioned in the railroad station in Baltimore. One of these was a young and pretty Quakeress, named Cornelia Hancock, who had somehow got past Miss Dix's eagle eye, even though she was well under thirty, and much more good-looking than Miss Dix liked a nurse to be. Cornelia also left a record in which she put Army Nurse, 1863-65 style, completely on paper. Cornelia slept in a tent on the field with three other women. At four o'clock every afternoon all stragglers and strangers were cleared from the field, and a guard set to protect bona fide women workers. The utmost respect to any woman working there was enforced by the Pennsylvania militia who guarded the territory, but Cornelia said no one had to teach the soldiers respect—they were too utterly grateful and reverent. "There is no impropriety in a *young* person being here," said Cornelia, "provided they are more sensible than a sexagenarian. Ladies who work are favored, but the dress-up palavers are passed by on the other side." Still, she said, it would be a capital place to get a husband, if one were interested.

"I am black as an Indian and dirty as a pig and as well as I ever was in my life—have a nice bunk and a tent about twelve feet square," she reported. She greased her shoes, army style, and put on her clothes wringing wet with dew every morning. "I feel like a new person, eat onions, potatoes, cucumbers, anything that comes up, walk as straight as a soldier, and feel life and vigor which I never felt at home. I feel so erect and can go steadily from one thing to another from half past six in the morning until ten o'clock at night, and feel more like work at ten than when I got up in the morning." She concluded that army life was very hardening. "You get so that you don't care about anything except to eat and sleep."

The women worked for three weeks on the field. In that time they sorted out and dispatched some 16,000 men, sending each one off properly rested, cared for, and fed. 4,000 were left in the hospitals on the field. Cornelia decided to stay in the army as a regular nurse, at $12 a month. The ladies at the central Lodge, where Miss Woolsey was, found their work all done. They struck their tents and marched from the field, escorted by two army bands playing *Three Cheers for the Red, White, and Blue.*

5

Following the Battle of Gettysburg, a Sanitary Commission auxiliary relief unit was attached to every army corps, the whole service being under the direction of Frank B. Fay who had organized one of the first battlefield relief units. He was generally known as "the uncle of Helen Gilson," though actually he was a very important relief worker himself. Into these various units were absorbed most of the women who had already become institutions among the soldiers.

Of these ladies with the flask, Dr. Bellows wrote: "The women who did hospital service continuously, or who kept themselves near the base of armies, or who moved among the camps and travelled with the corps, were an exceptional class . . . a class representing no social grade but coming from all, belonging to no rank or age of life in particular; sometimes young and sometimes old; sometimes refined and sometimes rude; now of frail physical aspect and then of extraordinary robustness, but in all cases women with a mighty love and earnestness in their hearts—a love and a pity, and an ability to show it forth and to labor in behalf of it, equal to that which, in other departments of life, distinguishes poets, philosophers, sages and saints, from ordinary or average men. . . . Only the few who had a genius for the work continued in it, and succeeded in elbowing room for themselves through the never-ending obstacles, jealousies, and chagrins that beset the service. Every woman who keeps her place in a general hospital or a corps hospital, has to prove her title to be trusted; her tact, discretion, endurance, and strength of nerve and fibre. . . . They carried into their work their womanly tenderness, their copious sympathies, their great-hearted devotion, and had to face and contend with the cold routine, the semi-savage professional indifference, which ... makes ordinary medical supervision, in time of actual war, impersonal, official, unsympathetic, and abrupt. ... Their position was always critical, equivocal, suspected, and to be justified only by their undeniable and conspicuous merits— their wisdom, patience, and proven efficiency, justified by the love and reverence they exacted from the soldiers themselves."

In this service women—and the men, too, who were in the relief units—suffered as many casualties as any branch of the armed forces. While no woman was killed in battle, many died after each big engagement as the result of overwork, and many were invalided for life. Of this record the women's societies were very proud. They constantly quoted the words of beautiful Margaret Breckinridge who, though a cousin of John Breckinridge, the Confederate leader, was a front-line worker for Grant's armies. She ran a relief boat that went back and forth from St. Louis to Vicksburg. When told that, if she did not give up, she would die, she answered, "Men are dying for their country, why not I?" She died the following winter at the age of thirty-two, of typhoid fever which her body, weakened by army service, could not resist.

When Mary A. Brady, the forty-year-old mother of five children, wore herself out at Gettysburg and died a few months later, she was given a funeral with military honors, and escorted to her grave by bands of women in black, the widows of the men who fell at Gettysburg.

12.   *Glory, Glory, Hallelujah!*

On March 1, 1863, there was such a scene in the halls of Congress as had never before been witnessed there. For a young lady was being married there, with the Senate and House of Representatives in full attendance. 4,000 people jammed the galleries and the hall, and reached in long excited lines around the Capitol Building.

The bride was Miss Elida Rumsey, beloved glamour-girl of the Army of the Potomac.

Elida Rumsey was not a great beauty. She was a slight, graceful girl with long brown curls, and a little scar on one cheek. She had been only twenty when the war broke out, and because she was so young, Miss Dix refused to accept her application to become an army nurse. So Miss Rumsey organized a service of her own for the army. She began by taking flowers, books, and other comforts to the hospitals, on the theory that a wounded man does not live by surgery alone, but wants entertainment for the mind, and even some of the graces of life. It was the habit of the soldiers to ask any lady who crossed their path if she could sing. So hungry were the soldiers for songs that every woman warworker who could sing a note became a warbler. It was not long before the army discovered that Miss Rumsey had a really beautiful voice.

Meanwhile Miss Rumsey had a devoted suitor, a Mr. John Fowle, a clerk at the Washington Navy Yard, who appeared wherever she was, in one of those public and protracted courtships in which so many of the young ladies of that day kept their suitors dangling. Whatever Miss Rumsey suggested, Mr. Fowle did. At her behest he established at the Navy Yard a factory for making crutches to be given to soldiers free of charge. Miss Rumsey used to drive a truck up to the Navy Yard to get the crutches, and come back through the streets of Washington perched on the load. Wherever soldiers recognized her, they would throng the truck and call for a song. Standing on top of the crutches, Miss Rumsey would sing.

Soon no military affair was complete without Miss Rumsey, escorted by the devoted Mr. Fowle. The soldiers liked it best when she sang the *Star-Spangled Banner,* standing on a captured Confederate flag, with the Stars and Stripes waving above her. Pretty soon the soldiers began to suggest themes for songs. Mr. Fowle would immediately scribble some verses on the suggested theme, set to a familiar air, and hand them over to Miss Rumsey, who would sing them on the spot. One song, so composed, was the Civil War favorite, *The Dying Soldier Boy,* set to the tune of *Annie Laurie.*

Miss Rumsey, perceiving the intolerable boredom of a soldier's life, organized a campaign to get books and magazines for the men. At first she distributed these in a wagon, from hospital to hospital and from camp to camp. Then she determined to build a free library for soldiers in Washington. The government gave her the land. To earn the money she and Mr. Fowle went on a concert tour together. She charged the public anything they wished to pay for admission, but the admission price for a soldier was never more than $.25. With the money thus collected, she and Mr. Fowle built a little one-room, one-story club house in Washington, furnished with a melodeon, on which the soldiers could play at any time. Every Wednesday afternoon Miss Rumsey and Mr. Fowle gave singing lessons for the soldiers at the club.

Finally, after two years of courtship, Miss Rumsey announced her forthcoming marriage to Mr. Fowle. Then it was rumored that they had first met in the House of Representatives. And so, in response to public clamor, and the wish of Mr. Lincoln who was one of Miss Rumsey's many admirers, she and Mr. Fowle were married there with an army chaplain officiating. President Lincoln had expected to attend, but he was detained at the last minute. But Mrs. Lincoln herself saw to the making of the bride's bouquet, and just before the ceremony a White House carriage drew up, and attendants brought in baskets and baskets of flowers with the compliments of the President and Mrs. Lincoln.

The bride, said the newspaper account, "was dressed in plain

176

drab poplin, with white linen collars and cuffs, and wore a bonnet of the same color ornamented with red, white, and blue flowers. A bow of red, white, and blue was fastened upon her breast."

At the close of the ceremony, a soldier in the gallery shouted "Won't the bride sing the *Star-Spangled Banner?*" The flag was unfurled over the bridal pair, and standing there with her husband, Mrs. Fowle sang, "with never more fervor in her beautiful voice."

2

As the war went on and on, people began to long more and more for something that would dramatize to them what they were fighting for. Partly because of the compact organization of the women through their aid societies, and a certain articulateness that the constant working and sewing and sharing letters from the front in their society rooms gave them, the "American women," said Doctor Bellows, "were nearer right and more thoroughly united by this means, and by their own healthier instincts, than the American men. The Army whose bayonets were glittering needles advanced with more unbroken ranks, and exerted almost a greater moral force than the army that carried loaded muskets."

So it was natural that the two greatest factors in building national morale in the latter days of the war were both creations of women connected with the Sanitary Commission. One was the *Battle Hymn of the Republic,* by Julia Ward Howe, and the other was the great series of Sanitary Fairs, started by Mary A. Livermore.

One of the hardest working gentlemen of the Sanitary Commission was beloved Doctor Howe. His was the ultimate responsibility and ultimate authority in connection with all matters affecting the health and welfare of New England soldiers.

His varied career made him a man of vast usefulness. As a surgeon in the Greek army he had been forced to improvise surgical care out of the rudest materials. In the care of the deaf, dumb, and blind, he had been a pioneer. Besides, he had been an adviser and friend of Florence Nightingale from her girlhood. In the existing state of the machinery for putting even the most elementary health measures into anything like universal practice, much that a man like Doctor Howe knew and could advise was bound to prove abortive. But he gave himself unstintingly, and during the war the affairs of the Sanitary Commission completely dominated his household life.

Mrs. Howe had been attractive, auburn-haired Julia Ward, a member of the select society of New York and Newport that had created the Women's Central, and devised the hospital transport service for the Peninsula. She looked wistfully on while her friends were working so hard in the hospitals, and studying so devotedly under doctors. As a busy wife and hostess and mother of six children, she had neither time nor energy to spend in acquiring the high professional proficiency that Miss Schuyler and Miss Wormeley and Mrs. Griffith and Mrs. Howland had set as the standard of women's work. Moreover, her education and aptitudes were literary, not practical. But she moved too constantly among people who really knew what adequate welfare and nursing for the army involved, to be interested in any merely amateurish dabbling. She kept asking herself and asking her friends, "What can I do, with my abilities and in my situation, that will really count?"

One day, in the early days of the war, she found her answer. She had driven in a carriage with her husband and some friends to watch the maneuvers of the army of the Potomac near Washington. In the midst of the maneuvers, the Confederates attacked. The army retreated, in good order, but in the retreat the Howes' carriage was pushed to the side of the road. There it had to stay all day and into the evening, while steadily, hour after hour, the lines of men marched back to Washington, singing, as they went, *John Brown's Body Lies a Mouldering in the Grave*. This song of the abolitionists, which had been sung in secret and rebellious conclaves ever since John Brown was hanged, was forbidden in the army. But on occasions like this, when officers were too busy to enforce the rule, it would start rising, in a steady humming that grew and grew from rank to rank, till it burst into a triumphant marching shout that the officers whipping their horses along the lines simply could not silence.

The Howes listened sympathetically. They had one foot in the camps of the radicals, and had attended many meetings where *John Brown's Body* was sung in secret. They were among those who felt that Mr. Lincoln's government could not continue for ever to evade the fact that what all these hundreds of thousands of boys were here to fight for was the freeing of the slaves.

178

"There is a job for you," said one of the gentlemen in the carriage, to Mrs. Howe. "Why don't you write some really worthy words for that stirring tune?"

Mrs. Howe demurred. She did not feel equal to it. But when they finally got back to Washington that night, and she went to bed, she could not sleep because whenever she closed her eyes, she could see those boys in blue endlessly marching, and over and over in her mind there sounded the tune of *John Brown's Body*. Gradually she began to fit words to the tune. Finally she rose and groped her way to a desk, and found a pencil and some paper and in the dark wrote down what she had composed. Then feeling better, she went to sleep.

Next morning she looked at her scribblings, written on a piece of her husband's Sanitary Commission letter paper, and thought, "I think I like this better than anything I have written." So she polished up the piece, borrowed another piece of Sanitary Commission paper, and made a fair copy of it, in ink. This she sent to *The Atlantic Monthly* which published it, in August, 1861.

No one paid much attention to the piece, except a young preacher in the West named McCabe who was a friend of Mary Livermore's. He cut it out and learned it by heart. McCabe became an army chaplain, and was captured and sent to Libby Prison. Libby Prison was one of the horror chambers of the Civil War. It was an old tobacco warehouse in Richmond over which hung the sign, *Libby and Sons*. At a time when old buildings converted into hospitals were sinks of filth and misery, an old building used as an enemy prison camp could not be expected to offer much in the way of cleanliness, toilet facilities, and pure drinking water.

At Libby there was a Negro who was sometimes allowed to sell newspapers to the prisoners. He was called "Old Ben," and, unknown to the Confederates, he had a sneaking sympathy for "Massa Linkum's" cause.

On July 5, 1863, Old Ben brought in Southern newspapers announcing a Confederate victory at Gettysburg. As the Union prisoners pored over these with gloom and cursing, Old Ben contrived to whisper to one man, "That's a lie. The Union men won that battle, and they is chasing 'em." Instantly the word spread from mouth to mouth. The boys cheered and started a wild snake dance around the room to the tune of *John Brown's Body*. Thereupon Chaplain McCabe sprang into the center, and in a rich baritone voice, began to sing the words by Julia Ward Howe.

The men stopped short. "What's that?" they yelled. "Sing it again."

McCabe sang it, stanza by stanza. The men took it up, learning it line by line, right there, and for hours afterwards kept the old prison rocking to the lusty chorus.

Chaplain McCabe was exchanged and was a speaker at a big rally held in Washington, D. C., in behalf of the Christian Commission, which was an association of chaplains and religious workers operating in partnership with the Sanitary Commission. When he told the way the boys at Libby received word of Gettysburg someone shouted, "Sing those words." He sang, and as he went on from stanza to stanza the audience began to take up the refrain, "Glory, glory, Hallelujah, Our God is marching on." When he finished, the voice of Abraham Lincoln was heard above the applause, "Sing it again!"

Next day the papers were full of the story, and every Sanitary Commission and Christian Commission headquarters was besieged for copies of the words. It was sung at the next meeting of every woman's society, and the next service of nearly every church. The bringing out of the old abolition tune, so long interdicted in respectable quarters, with these religious and stirring words, had an extraordinary effect in morally vitalizing the whole North. No more evasion and denial! Behind the Emancipation Proclamation the whole people had risen singing!

3

"As He died to make men holy, let us die to make men free," were noble words, and did much to carry men bravely to their death. But the embarrassments of freeing a long-suppressed, ignorant, and helpless people remained very great. After every battle, the Union army was overwhelmed with slaves who fled to them for shelter. From the first, the greatest women battle-workers had been the mainstays of the army in handling these people, because they provided work for great numbers of them in caring for the wounded, in transporting Sanitary stores, and in laundry work, cleaning, and cooking. The women not only gave them work; they took the trouble to train the Negroes and to see to their welfare. Through nearly every woman's narrative of army service runs the kind, friendly, amusing report on the "contrabands." The brightest passage in the records of the women's service at Gettysburg have to do with the fun the girls had outfitting the contrabands with bright new colored head-kerchiefs, and the Negro prayer meetings at night, in which the Negroes played for "Massa Linkum" whom they seem to have confused with "Massa" Abraham in the Bible.

If the Emancipation Proclamation was not to be a mockery, someone would have to go to bat for these poor Negroes. And more than one of the favorite ladies of the army did so. "Where are the people who have been professing such strong abolition proclivity for the last thirty years," wrote Cornelia Hancock, the pretty young Quaker army nurse, in a letter home to the Society of Friends, who had been the backbone of the abolition movement. "Certainly they are not in Washington laboring for these people whom they have been clamoring to have freed. They are freed now or at least many of them, and herded together in filthy huts, half clothed. And what is worse, guarded over by persons who have not a proper sympathy with them. . . . The situation of their camp is revolting to a degree, 12 or 14 persons occupy a room not 12 feet square, do all their cooking, eating, etc. therein. The camp has but one well of water, and that out of order most of the time. All the water used by nearly 1,000 persons is carted from Washington. So one can judge of the cleanliness of the camp."

Gradually people became aware that one way of dealing with the freedmen was being unobtrusively dramatized for them by a beautiful young woman who had been, from the first, one of the darlings of the soldier's saga. She was Miss Helen Gilson. Miss Gilson was a small, delicately proportioned little girl in her late twenties, with gentle, deliberate speech and motions, and a face "lovely in form and expression." She had got her first experience in service on battlefields under her uncle Frank B. Fay, who had been a pioneer organizer of battlefield relief, and who became the director of all the army auxiliary relief corps. She had attracted such attention by her service in the Transport Service on the Peninsula that thereafter she could get almost anything she wanted from the aid societies for the soldiers, and do what she pleased in relation to the military authorities.

Miss Gilson had a special manner and technique that were carefully studied by observers, and were described again and again. Though most of these studies start by being severely professional and impersonal, they end on a very sentimental note. There was apparently something so moving about Miss Gilson's manner and method that no one could watch her long without becoming lyrical and dewy-eyed. She had an exquisiteness in all her appointments and arrangements for the sick and the suffering equalled only by Miss Florence Nightingale herself. The poorer and more neglected a creature was, the more Miss Gilson would be lavish with perfectly made custards and crisp white linen delicately fragrant with lavender or cologne. She took the forlornest contrabands into service, and turned them out as cleanly, self-respecting maids, cooks, laundresses, and nurses' assistants, all able to work domestic miracles according to her own high ideals. "The management of her kitchen was like the ticking of a clock—regular discipline, gentle firmness, and sweet temper always."

But it was Miss Gilson's manner with the sick, the miserable, and even the recalcitrant that was most often subjected to scrutiny. She had a certain caressing way that was all her own. She would draw the head of a very sick man to her shoulder, and hold him gently, and lovingly. Many a man died on Miss Gilson's shoulder, with an expression of beatific happiness on his face. She sat by men who were undergoing amputations or painful operations and held their hands. As she moved through the hospitals, she would now and then note a patient in pain or utter discouragement, and would step lightly to his bed, and smooth back the hair on his forehead with her soft quiet hand, and catching his eyes, smile into them sweetly.

Miss Gilson was young and personable—younger and more personable than Miss Dix, or even the Sanitary Commission, generally approved of. Naturally these little manners of this lovely lady were subjected to the keenest scrutiny. And no matter how old or judicial the observer was, the verdict was always the same. Though her manner was inimitable—and no other young lady had better try to imitate it—it was worth a dozen doctors and twenty chaplains to the army. She was regarded with an indescribable reverence and with a passionate gratitude. When a man called on her to pray with him, she knelt, and laying her hand quietly and confidingly in his, she prayed, joining her voice with his. Men asked her to sing, and though she had not a remarkable voice, she sang promptly and sweetly anything they asked for. She sang hymns. She sang popular songs. She was surprised at nothing, and shocked by nothing. She had a childlike merriment, and was fertile in devising little amusements which others would consider too childish for soldiers, but which they and she managed to enjoy wonderfully together.

Miss Gilson was, in many people's eyes, something too good for the rough private soldiers on whom she lavished her grace. Her principle was simple: "The less a creature has had in the past, the more it ought to have now." And this principle she proceeded to carry out by asking for the superintendence of the hospital for the colored troops, who first began to be used in large numbers in 1864. In the bloody battles of June, 1864 in Virginia large numbers of these wounded men were brought to City Point, and there dumped. No adequate preparation had been made for them. Many were sick with typhoid and malaria. The weather was hot; the filth and blood indescribable. When Miss Gilson asked if she might take charge of these men, her friends protested. "You cannot live through it. You will die." "I couldn't die in a better cause," she said.

In a little while the hospital for the colored troops at City Point was one of the sights of the army. She had a kitchen which was a marvel of freshness and savory odors. The diet list she made up for her patients has been preserved. It reads: "Roast beef, shad, veal broth, stewed oysters, lemonade, apple jelly, tomatoes, tea, coffee, crackers and sherry cobbler, roast apple." This for the colored troops of an army still clinging to hardtack and salt pork! She stirred up rivalry among the sick soldiers and their convalescent nurses in decorating their hospital tents. Thereupon the tents blossomed out in pictures and streamers, in flower beds and landscape gardening. "Not only was its standard the highest, but it was the most cheerfully picturesque hospital at City Point." She even set the Negro washerwomen, who served in the hospitals, and their families up in style. She had neat little huts built for them, got outfits of clothes for them from her friends in the

North, started thrift clubs and classes in all kinds of liberal and practical knowledge, and pleasantly and naturally joined in their prayer meetings. This became the best of all the freedmen's camps.

Miss Gilson carried among sick Negro soldiers exactly the same tender, caressing manner she had always used with the white soldiers, and aroused in them an even deeper gratitude and an almost religious reverence.

Doctor Reed, who worked with Miss Gilson, later wrote of her: "This colored hospital service was one of those extraordinary tasks, out of the ordinary course of army hospital discipline, that none but a woman could execute. It required more than a man's power of endurance, for men fainted and fell under the burden. It required a woman's discernment, a woman's tenderness, a woman's delicacy and tact; it required such nerve and moral force and such executive power as are rarely united in any woman's character. The simple grace with which she moved about the hospital camps, the gentle dignity with which she ministered to suffering about her, won all hearts. As she passed through the wards, the men would follow her with their eyes, attracted by the grave sweetness of her manner; and when she stopped by some bedside and laid her hand upon the forehead and smoothed the hair of some soldier, speaking some cheering, pleasant word, I have seen the tears gather in his eyes, and his lips quiver, as he tried to speak or to touch the fold of her dress, as if appealing to her to listen, while he opened his heart about mother, wife, or sister far away.

"I have seen her in her sober gray flannel gown, sitting motionless by the dim candle light—which was all our camp could afford —with her eyes open and watchful and her hands ever ready for those endless wants of sickness at night—and I have seen her kneel to pray with a dying soldier, when she seemed, by some special grace of the Spirit, to reach the living Christ and draw a blessing down as the shining way was opened to the tomb. . . . Absorbed in her work, unconscious of the spiritual beauty which invested her daily life—whether in her kitchen, in the heat and overcrowding incident to the issues of a large special diet list, or sitting at the cot of some poor lonely soldier, she was always the same presence of grace and love, peace and benediction. . . . Through scorching heat and pinching cold, in the tent or upon the open field, in the ambulance or in the saddle, through rain and snow, amid unseen perils of the enemy, under fire upon the field, or in the more insidious dangers of contagion, she worked quietly on, doing her simple part, with womanly tact and skill."

4

The dramatizing to the country of the cause for which they were fighting was carried to a magnificent climax in the great series of "Sanitary Fairs," started by Mary A. Livermore. In the autumn of 1863 there were 130,000 wounded and sick soldiers in the hospitals, and no prospect of the end in sight. People were growing very tired of the war. A presidential election was looming, and with it all those tensions and bickerings and whispering campaigns and loud-mouthed criticisms that naturally precede such a national crisis.

Mary Livermore had an idea—one of those simple, homely, tender-hearted, womanish ideas she was always planting somewhere like a little seed, and being herself as astonished as the world when it grew into a big tree. She thought that everyone ought be glad to give the best he had for those poor sick boys. There they lay, blinded, maimed for life, without legs, without arms, dying of typhoid fever, dying of tuberculosis, and for what, for whom? For you and me! For the free farmer who wanted to work his own little land, without suffering competition or social snobbery from the great slave-owner. For the free laborer, who wanted to work for wages, and sell his labor on the best market, and save his money, and some day maybe himself be a capitalist. For the manufacturer who wanted to sell sewing machines and washing machines and harvesting machines to the many, many people who, under a free enterprise, free labor system could accumulate a cash surplus to pay for them. For all of us who want to stop this miserable and degrading blight of human slavery, before it drags the whole country down in poverty and stagnation.

And what ought we to do for the boys who have fought and suffered for us? Give them the best we can make with our labor or our skills! Give them the best crops we have raised, the best workmanship we have produced, our choicest piece of manufactured goods, our finest professional service. Pick out the very best of our personal creations—whatever it is—and make a present of it to the boys!

This simple idea, publicized by Mrs. Livermore, resulted in a colossal performance in Chicago. On the 27th of October, 1863, banks closed, courts adjourned, schools were dismissed, and all Chicago turned out to see and to welcome the people who were bringing Mrs. Livermore the best they had for the soldiers. The performance began with the Lake County delegation—one hundred wagons laden with potatoes in heaps, silver-skinned onions, cabbages, beets, the whole antiscorbutic fraternity; barrels of cider, kegs of beer, and, rolling among the vegetables and the produce, small boys by the cartload! Through jammed crowds they rolled up to the Sanitary Commission rooms, and then, with a wild whoop, the spectators threw up their hats and cheered, and rushed up to help unload the wagons.

For fourteen days, in one steady procession, Mrs. Livermore had stuff coming into Chicago like that. The country people, for hundreds of miles around sent chickens from their barnyards; the bull or the calf from the barn; loads of hay; loads of apples. Every railroad freight office was jammed with material addressed to Mrs. Livermore. On every road leading to the city there were rickety and lumbering wagons, made of poles, loaded with mixed freight—a few cabbages, a bundle of socks, a coop of tame ducks, a pot of butter, a bag of beans. Mechanics and artisans of the villages and towns came marching, came riding on wagons, came on trains, bringing every kind of product of mechanical skill. Manufacturers shipped every kind of article from pianos to threshing machines. Watchmakers sent watches. Lace, cloth, iron, steel—there was no end to the stuff! It took all the business machinery, the banks, and the working personnel of Chicago to handle it. Hay was sold on the haymarket. Cattle on the cattle market. There were auctions and salesrooms all over the city. As fast as one set of persons brought in the stuff as a gift, another set bought it at a high price. Mrs. Livermore had dining-rooms to feed all these people, manned by the town's young ladies, "and everybody was as well served as at a first-class hotel, for $.50 a dinner." While Mrs. Hoge ran the culinary business, Mrs. Livermore herself acted as hostess and chairman of the "department of public amusements." Every professional singer sang. Every professional actor acted. There was a concert of 200 children, dressed in white, wearing wreaths of flowers. A party from Detroit put on tableaux on a revolving stage. Another party managed a promenade concert.

Day after day newspapers printed touching stories about the gifts for the soldiers that were pouring in. There were the six young girls who arrived bringing five barrels of potatoes. They had obtained the use of some ground, spaded it, planted the potatoes, cared for them, and harvested them, all with their own hands, with no help whatever, and here they were riding triumphantly into Chicago. An old Negro woman who had got up the Mississippi River from Montgomery, Alabama, appeared with a sheet, saying to Mrs. Livermore's secretary, "Please, Missis, may this sheet which I got with my own money, and stitched with my own hands, be sold for the Union sogers?" It was sold, and brought a price that would have been high for a shawl.

The net profits of these fourteen days of giving and selling were $72,000. But this was only the beginning, because the whole country was electrified by this demonstration in Chicago. City after city proposed to do likewise. The offerings and the fair programs grew in scope and magnificence from city to city. In the end about $2,500,000 in money was cleared, half of the whole operating budget of the Sanitary Commission for offices, salaries, etc., for all the years of the war. But the money was a very small part of the actual value of these fairs. At a time of great uncertainty, of argument, and recrimination, and profound national discouragement, Mrs. Livermore had appealed to the great warm heart of the people. As one newspaper editor said, "No man is so wealthy or high, and no man so poor or degraded as to refuse the gift of patriotism on the altar of our common country. At the recent fair in Boston the millionaire piled his munificent gifts on a common table with the voluntary handicraft labors of the inmates of the Charlestown state prison."

After seeing the Cleveland Fair, the editor of the Louisville *Sanitary Reporter* wrote: "To promote their comfort, to be able to buy these essentials for the army, is an incalculable good. But this charity is twice blessed. A rich and subtle blessing must lie in the wide sympathies called out, the new relations of acquaintance, friendship, and intimacy formed, and in the surprising revelation of talent and worth in remote and unexplored localities. Neighbors

187

and neighborhoods must come to respect each other more, to depend on each other more, and wonder that they have missed finding out each other for so long. . . . After so complete a flooding of all the field of life with the resistless tide of a sweet and noble enthusiasm, we cannot but look for a new bloom, and unexampled harvests."

13.   *Mother Bickerdyke Marches Through Georgia*

In the spring of 1864, Nashville, Tennessee, was crowded with blue-coated Union troops, guarding every road, patrolling every street. In a steady line, day after day, the army wagons, drawn by strings of mules, rumbled toward the station of the new railroad the army had built through to Chattanooga—the old railroad line having been used up and torn up with all the troop movements and fighting of the summer before. General William Tecumseh Sherman was assembling at Chattanooga his stores and supplies for the last great movement of the war, the march that would end all soldiers' marching, it was hoped, for ever on this continent. Southeastward from Chattanooga in Tennessee to Atlanta in Georgia, his tough, tired men, still nursing the last pains and bruises of the winter's frostbite, were going to march and fight their way, mile by mile, mountain valley by mountain valley, down into the rich plantation country, the warm and still unharried lands that were feeding the armies of the South.

No civilian of any sort could approach the railroad station, except an official from Washington, accompanied by an officer. Even the Sanitary Commission agents were fuming and fussing beyond the military lines, unable to get transport for their stores, unable to get recognition even on the strength of a letter from the Secretary of War himself. But from one of the army trains a large woman in a shawl and a Shaker bonnet was serenely alighting, carrying a lot of bags and bundles. She had a comely, weatherbeaten, well-featured face, and large, flashing blue eyes, and moved with a kind of powerful agility. At the sight of her, an army band instantly struck up "Hail to the Chief." There was a rush of soldiers to take her parcels. A soldier whipped up an army wagon

189

which came careering to a dead stop before her. Several soldiers moved as if to help her in, but, with a cheerful grin, she lightly pushed them aside and leaped in on her own power. As she rode away, every soldier saluted her. An officer remarked to the visitor from Washington he was showing around, "There goes the woman who is to this army what the Virgin Mary is to a Catholic!"

Steadily, month by month, Mother Bickerdyke had become the power in the western army in all matters affecting the personal welfare of soldiers. About the time Grant first came to Cairo as colonel of a newly formed regiment of three-year volunteers from Illinois, Mrs. Bickerdyke had arrived there with $500 her towns-women of Galesburg, Illinois, had given her to use in helping Miss Safford equip hospitals for the boys. Since then she had come along up the ladder of military rank, first with Grant, then with Grant and Sherman, and finally by Sherman's request, with him in particular, as partner in all military adventures, and apparently their confidante in most military secrets. She and Sherman had become bound together in a fast partnership. To Mother Bickerdyke Sherman was the great soldier—gallant, audacious, swift, decisive, impatient of red tape. To Sherman Mother Bickerdyke was the great soldier, gallant, audacious, swift, decisive, impatient of red tape. They understood each other perfectly.

Just what Mother Bickerdyke's military status was it was difficult to tell. Sherman said she ranked him, and in a certain sense this was actually true, because she had a pass from Grant which in one or two instances she used to override Sherman's orders. After Vicksburg Sherman had asked Grant to let him have Mrs. Bickerdyke as mother and nurse of the Fifteenth Army Corps, which was destined to do the hardest fighting in the West. And then he had left the interpretation of her rank and authority to the lady herself, only laughing uproariously when she had a set-to with some of his officers, and sustaining her with formal orders in whatever she thought fit to do.

Mother Bickerdyke's own interpretation of the source of her authority varied with circumstances. At the Battle of Donelson, for example, an army surgeon, accompanying a wounded officer to the rear, found a woman wrapped in the great-coat of a Confederate officer, with an army slouch hat drawn down over her brow, cooking soup and hot coffee on a series of field kettles, assisted by what appeared to be a well-drilled little army of Negroes.

The Negroes were passing out hot soup, tea, crackers, ginger panada, whisky and hot water, and other refreshments to shivering, exhausted, or wounded men, reclining in their blankets against every nearby rock and stone.

"Where did you get those articles? And under what authority do you work?" asked the surgeon.

Mother Bickerdyke did not deign to reply. "Here, Andy," she merely said to a large negro. "That man coming down the slope is going to fall. Go help him, and lay him by the rock there, and put this blanket over him, and give him some hot whisky and water till I can see to him."

The surgeon, curious, walked around among the men, sampled the various doses that were being given them, and then came back to the strange woman, and addressed her courteously, in a tone of genuine respect, "Madam, you seem to combine in yourself a first-rate diet-kitchen and a medical staff. May I ask under whose authority you are operating?"

Slightly mollified by his tone, Mrs. Bickerdyke paused briefly. "My authority comes from God Almighty," she said. "Have you got anything that ranks *that?*"

At another time, when an officer, not knowing who she was, ordered her out of a building, she replied. "It's no use your putting me out of the door, because I'll come in by the window, and the whole army *will help me in.*"

In a set-to with a surgeon she respected, she deigned to explain herself. "I've come to the army to stay. I mean to stay till this thing is played out. I've enlisted for the war, as the boys have, and they want me and need me and can't get on without me. So there's no use in you or anybody else trying to tie me up in red tape, because I'm too busy for that. And there's no use getting mad if I don't play second fiddle to you, because I tell you there isn't time for that, either. And let me tell you," she concluded, turning a thunderous blue eye on him, "you'd better not get into a row with me, because when any man tries that, one of us goes to the wall, and that *one ain't never me.*"

When remarks like this were repeated to Sherman, he just roared, and gave all the necessary military orders.

Mother Bickerdyke was as tender to the weak and suffering and downtrodden as she was rough with the healthy, conceited, and officious. Once when she was taking a lot of trouble for a miserable, worthless fellow, someone said to her, "Why do you waste your time on trash like that?"

"Because," said Mother Bickerdyke, "when there's any creature around here so low down and miserable that there's nobody to care for him, he's still got two friends in this army. One's God, and the other is *me.*"

She had, in particular, a stormy, maternal tenderness for the poor fellows decaying with scurvy. Sometimes when these men had been got to bed under her care, they had become quite babyish. When she assured them that they were going to have the right food now, they would insist on seeing the food, and would want to keep it right under their eye, sometimes breaking down and sobbing piteously if it were taken out of their sight. So, in one hospital she had several patients, in the last stages of decay, who could take only liquid food, but who were hopefully cherishing a potato or a hard-boiled egg which Mother Bickerdyke said they might eat just as soon as they were a little better. A newly appointed surgeon was scandalized to find one man with some hard-boiled eggs under his pillow. "Take that hen's nest out of here," he ordered.

The poor boy began to weep. Mother Bickerdyke came swooping down. "Look here, doctor, when we've let boys get to this state, because we didn't feed 'em right—*because we didn't feed 'em right,*" she repeated darkly, "the least we can do is to humor them a little. You know it isn't doing a mite of harm to let him have his eggs, and he's going to have 'em." With a kind, maternal hand, she tucked the eggs back under the pillow, and said gently, "There you are, my dear. You just take your eggs, and set on them till they *hatch.*"

It particularly infuriated her to have assistant surgeons, ward masters, hospital attendants, and rascally young officers try to make off with any of the delicacies sent by the Sanitary Commission for the scorbutic patients. There were many half-educated men from what presumed to be the "better walks of life" who thought that these luxuries the women of the nation were pouring out on the common soldier were sheer waste. Whether a common soldier was sick or well, there were some degrees of refinement to which only a gentleman was entitled. Most snobs of this sort were ready to grant the scorbutic men the potatoes and onions, but when it came to the fruits and cordials—those fellows were too far gone to appreciate them anyway! One day Mother Bickerdyke settled this sort of talk, at least in one hospital. She left a large kettle of peaches stewing fragrantly on the hospital stove. Into the kettle she had poured a strong emetic. Shortly after supper, she went on a little stroll through the parts of the hospital occupied by the staff. Sure enough, several of the staff were retching and vomiting. Stalking among the sufferers with a sardonic grin on her face, she said, "I could have told you not to eat those peaches. Peaches aren't good for you unless you've had *scurvy.*"

Sometimes when particularly handsome bathrobes, nightshirts and night-drawers, or slippers came in among the Sanitary Commission stores, the assistant surgeons, stewards, or other workers around the hospital would take possession of them, on the theory that goods of this sort were wasted on common soldiers who were nearly dead anyway. One day Mother Bickerdyke routed out a hospital official early in the morning. Sure enough, he appeared in a fine bathrobe, pajamas, slippers, and socks. Her keen eye immediately detected where this outfit had come from. She seized the fellow by the ear, between her strong thumb and forefinger, and dragged him into the ward. "Boys," she said, to the men on the beds. "See this walking clotheshorse! See what he's got on? Every stitch of it belongs to you. Kind women, good women made them for you. Women made them for men who have *fought* for their country, who have *bled* for it, and who are *sick for it now.* Here, boys, take your clothes!"

And grasping the poor gentleman firmly in her iron grip, she took off one garment after another, tossing it to the boys on the beds. When she had stripped him naked, she walked out, leaving him standing there.

The resources Mrs. Bickerdyke controlled in behalf of the common soldiers and the sick were practically unlimited. Grant had given her the right to draw as she thought best on army stores and transport. In addition she had carte blanche to draw on the Sanitary stores and depots of Cairo, Chicago, Cincinnati, Louisville, and other points. She could also draw money against the Chicago

193

office of the Northwest Sanitary Commission. Several times when the careful gentlemen who handled the funds for the Commission questioned some of her drafts, or thought they were more than the Commission could afford, Mary A. Livermore and Mrs. Hoge went out and personally raised the money to cover Mrs. Bickerdyke's obligations.

Mary A. Livermore had been drawn to her in the early days at Cairo because the poor woman seemed to be doing so much so heroically, and needed someone to back her up. Mrs. Bickerdyke's enterprises, and Mrs. Livermore's control of the sources of money and supply grew together in a partnership that put practically everything anyone possessed west of the Alleghenies, at their joint disposal. When Mrs. Bickerdyke needed something, she used to say to Mary Livermore, "I guess you girls will have to hump yourself and stir the aid societies up with a spoon."

As Mother Bickerdyke's fame grew, Mary Livermore was besieged by requests to have her appear in person at this or that public rally in behalf of the soldiers. Mrs. Livermore could have raised literally millions of dollars in this way. But on this subject Mother Bickerdyke was adamant. "There's a big war on," she said, "and I have too much to do to be gallivanting around, and so has everybody else that is doing what he should. What's the matter with those folks? Can't they give the boys what they need without having to have a fancy show put on for them?"

But on one occasion she was finally persuaded to thank in person the gentlemen of the Milwaukee Chamber of Commerce who pledged $1,200 a month to her for hospital relief. Her speech on that occasion has been preserved. This is what she said: "I am much obliged to you gentlemen for the kind things you have said. I haven't done much, no more than I ought; neither have you. I am glad that you are going to give $1,200 a month for the poor fellows in the hospitals; for it's no more than you ought to do, and it isn't half as much as the soldiers in the hospitals have given for you. Suppose, gentlemen, you had got to give one thousand dollars or your right leg. Would it take long to decide which to surrender? Two thousand dollars or your right arm; five thousand dollars or both your eyes; all that you are worth or your life?

"But I have eighteen hundred boys in my hospital at Chattanooga who have given one arm and one leg, and some have given both; and yet they don't seem to think that they have done a great deal for their country. And the graveyard behind the hospital, and the battlefield a little farther off, contain the bodies of thousands who have freely given their lives to save you and your homes and your country from ruin.

"Oh, gentlemen of Milwaukee, don't let us be telling of what *we* have given, and what *we* have done. *We* have done nothing and given nothing in comparison with *them*. And it's our duty to keep on giving and doing just as long as there's a soldier down South, fighting or suffering for us."

3

The winter Mrs. Bickerdyke spent with the Fifteenth Army Corps under General Sherman, after the battle of Chattanooga, was one of the most terrible in the annals of the Civil War. They were in the enemy's country which had been "stripped and peeled" for the sustenance of the Confederate troops. Adequate stores could not be got to them from the outside until the railroad from Nashville was rebuilt. The men had no warm clothes and almost no food. They had come when the weather was still hot, in thin cotton shirts, with only one light blanket apiece. They had so little to eat that they had to be content for days on end with three ears of hard corn as their daily ration. Ten thousand army mules starved to death that winter. Men who themselves were slowly starving to death, too, lay under thin, light blankets on piles of leaves, in shelters made of spruce boughs, and listened with aching hearts to the whinnying of the dying animals.

On the edge of the forest, five miles from Chattanooga, Mrs. Bickerdyke set up her field hospital. Men were detailed to cut wood and pile log heaps which were kept continually burning, under Mrs. Bickerdyke's superintendence, to warm the camps and hospitals. The hospitals were made out of some of the storehouses. With bricks from demolished chimneys the soldiers built ovens according to a design of Mother Bickerdyke's own. With the help of her best contrabands, she foraged through the countryside. The Negroes had ways of knowing where supplies could be found, and the fame of the good Mother who had done so much for so many of the race had gone from mouth to mouth among the slaves far down into the plantation country. So she discovered a store of huge potash kettles and came across an abandoned mill where there was plenty of flour, and cattle and sheep that had belonged to the Confederate army. She set up her great kettles alongside her brick ovens, and there in a circle of great fires against the wintry background of the forest and the mountain, Mrs. Bickerdyke, assisted by details of soldiers, cooked and cared for the sick and spread such comfort as she could, to fight off the starvation and the cold of that bitter place. The sparks from the fire would light on her dress and catch in her hair. She was always ablaze somewhere. "The boys were all the time putting me out," she said, "and a dozen of 'em were grabbing me whenever I was cooking by the log-fires, for the fire would snap, and my clothes would catch, but I couldn't tell where." Mary Livermore afterwards had on display in her office in Chicago a dress worn by Mrs. Bickerdyke that winter, so burned that it would hardly hold together.

On the memory of the soldiers, the large, strong figure of this woman, cooking amidst a circle of fires that leaped crackling to the skies, against the somber background of snowy forest and bleak mountains, was indelibly etched. There was something heroic and primeval about her in that background, and something grandly beautiful, too, for her large, strong body was well made, and had a kind of powerful grace, and her weatherbeaten face was well modeled and regularly featured, and dominated by wonderful eyes. Her eyes had as many colors and as many aspects as the winter skies. When all was going well, and she could relax, and be kind and motherly, they were a clear, sunny blue. But when she had to go into battle against men or the elements or against Fate itself— as she had to do so often that winter—the pupils would expand, and the eyes would become a stormy dark purple-gray, and flash fire like a thunder cloud. To starving, freezing boys, whom she bedded down on spruce boughs, bringing them hot soup from her great kettles, and putting stones, heated in her fires, at their feet, she was the Everlasting Mother—the power and the tenderness that would still be there when all else was gone.

The last day of the year, 1863, was so bitterly cold in the West that almost all business in Chicago stopped. In the mountains where Sherman was encamped, the cold had been preceded by a furious gale, which swooped down Lookout Mountain and roared through the valleys of Mission Ridge. With it came a downpour of icy rain plunging down the sides of the mountains in wild torrents. The hospital tents which housed the most seriously ill were overturned by the wind. Many sick men were swept out by the roaring waters and drowned.

Then came the cold, settling toward night in deeper and deeper ice. Hour after hour Mother Bickerdyke battled to keep the sick from being frozen to death. She had the fires piled higher and higher with logs till they roared in a great circle, even above the tops of the trees. Before midnight the last stick on the great army woodpile was hurled into the flames.

The surgeons gave up. "We can do no more," they said. "Nobody can order soldiers out in the darkness and the bitter cold to cut more wood in the forests. They couldn't get wood no matter how they tried. As well try to cut iron with a butter knife, as to try to get wood that will burn after the way everything's been first flooded and then frozen. We'll have to tuck the men in as best we can, and wait till morning. Go to bed, Mrs. Bickerdyke."

"Go to bed yourselves," she said.

They went to bed. But she couldn't. Huddled in an officer's greatcoat, she determined to make the rounds once more, to see if anything could still be done to snug the sick boys in. She soon saw that it was no use—1,500 boys would be frozen to death by tomorrow morning. She stepped a little way into the forests. The surgeons were right. The wood couldn't be cut. But suddenly, against the cold sky now glittering with stars, she saw the line of the old breastworks which had been built for defense last summer, but which had now served their purpose—vast and solid, with foundations and inner structures of wood covered with earth. There was a lot of wood in under there, and it wasn't wet or frozen solid!

Mrs. Bickerdyke knew as well as anyone that even her authority could not cover an order to demolish military fortifications. They might be of no use now, but she wasn't the one to say so. But there was no time now to wake up the General and argue with him or anyone else about it. She tramped around to the encampment of the Pioneer Corps of the army, whose job it was to handle tough jobs in wild country. "Come, boys," she said. "Get out your mules, axes, hooks, and chains. We're going to take down the breastworks."

When the men appeared shivering, driving out their balking, half-starved mules, shaking with cold, Mrs. Bickerdyke had already ripped out with her own hands enough wood to start the fire up again. She had taken the heads off six barrels of meal which she had been saving for emergencies, and mixing the meal with hot water, was ready to serve it to the mules. And she had ginger panada, ready in quantity for the men. So, between twelve and two o'clock on that bitter morning, the men and the mules ripped out the breastworks. As fast as logs could be torn out, they were thrown on the fires, which mounted higher and higher in vast, crackling pyramids of flame. All night Mother Bickerdyke kept immense cauldrons steaming with coffee, ginger panada, and soup. She put layers of hot bricks around every one of 1,500 men, herself running from tent to tent in the icy gale, carrying bricks, and she changed the bricks when they cooled. When one of the surgeons discovered what was happening, he called out every other surgeon, and together they worked with Mrs. Bickerdyke till morning.

Morning brought out the Major, very much embarrassed, for naturally an unauthorized demolition of the breastworks—even if they were old ones and no longer used—was a breach of military discipline.

"Madam, consider yourself under arrest," he said.

"All right, Major, I'm arrested," answered Mrs. Bickerdyke, flying past him with a hot brick in one hand and a hot drink in the other, "only don't meddle with me till the weather moderates, because I've got too many boys on my hands that will freeze to death if you do."

They had quite a discussion about it afterwards, Mrs. Bickerdyke going through the form of explaining herself to a military conclave while they concealed smiles in their beards.

"I know well enough the predicament you're in, and I'm sorry to put you to the trouble of getting me up before you like this," she said. "I respect military discipline as well as any one, and enforce it, too, and you know it. But in the situation we're in here, we can't be red-taping all over the place while our men die. We have to do what we have to when it has to be done. Those 1,500 men who had already got thrown out in the wet and chilled to the bone would have frozen to death if I hadn't done what I did. Quite apart from the value of those poor boys' lives to us and their families and their country, you know that sooner or later the fact that they'd frozen to death under you, as officers, would have been known in the North, and then just imagine—the newspaper talk, and the Congressional investigation—and how much good in a military way do you think that would do you? I guess the best thing you can do with this little breach of mine is to forget about it. What nobody knows won't hurt 'em."

4

As the winter wore on, Mother Bickerdyke was put to still harder shifts. Ragged as they were, in the remnants of last summer's clothes with barely enough food to hold body and soul together, Sherman's men nevertheless managed to relieve 15,000 men under Burnside, whom the Confederates had shut up in Knoxville, and to drive off the almost equally ragged Confederates. In squads of twenty, thirty, sometimes fifty, the weary, famished, shivering victors made their way back to such care as Mother Bickerdyke could still give them. She was on short rations herself, along with them, but she still concocted wonderful soups—out of what they hardly dared to ask; and she could still produce endless warm water to wash swollen, bleeding feet. She could still make beds out of dried leaves, and old grass, and pine needles, heated with warm stones, into which a near-naked, shivering man could snuggle down and be blessedly at rest. And withal, she kept them clean. She was a great hand with the laundry tubs and the scrubbing brush. Water was not scarce in the Tennessee mountains, though nearly everything else was. And whatever else happened to them, they weren't going to be one of those encampments that have filth diseases!

One day when it seemed that they could survive no longer, they heard far off the distinct sound of a steam whistle. The railroad! They were getting the railroad through to them! When lookouts on the mountains reported the first long train actually arriving, Mother Bickerdyke let the beds and hospitals be emptied so that the sick men could see it, rightly surmising that the sight would be better for them than medicine. The stronger soldiers led and supported the weak. Willing comrades carried the sick men out on litters. Some hoisted those too feeble to walk on their backs or their shoulders, but all were out to see that blessed sight. Food was coming, clothes were coming, comforts of every kind were coming. As Mary Livermore said, "They were not forgotten—the long-silent North was reaching down to them with a hundred-handed bounty."

Sherman immediately began to pile up stores and ammunition in Chattanooga against his projected march down into Georgia. Over the new railroad the trains rumbled continually carrying military materials. Meanwhile, though adequate food, clothing, and vitally essential medicines were supplied through the army stores, and the troops were, to that extent, well off, a great bulk of Sanitary stores was jammed at Nashville. Sherman didn't see how he could transport them unless and until he could get vitally necessary military materials through. Mother Bickerdyke went down to Nashville and saw to it that these Sanitary goods were dispatched to other points whence she knew that they could be got through to them later. How Mother Bickerdyke knew where to send the Sanitary goods, no one knew. She never confessed to being in the secrets of the military High Command. But the fact was that Sanitary stores dispatched from Nashville before the march into Georgia began, according to Mother Bickerdyke's directions, arrived, by various and devious routes, at points where the soldiers under Sherman later turned up.

Mother Bickerdyke had not consulted Sherman about this trip to Nashville. To get down there she used her pass from Grant, which on the military railroad ranked Sherman's orders, and to get back she used the same means. She went straight from the railroad train to Sherman's tent. The guard there said, in the rather feeble way in which military instructions were applied to Mother Bickerdyke.

"The General is very busy this morning. He won't see you."

"Oh, won't he?" said Mother Bickerdyke, walking in.

Sherman was writing, and did not look up. Mrs. Bickerdyke sat down and waited. Finally Sherman said, "So you've come back."

"Yes," said Mother Bickerdyke, "and I won't bother you. All you've got to do is sign this order so's I can get what I'm going to need out of the Sanitary stores up here on the railroad."

Sherman laid down his pen, and tossed back his red head. "Do you know what this army's going to do? It's going to *fight*. And do you know what one fights with? One fights with guns."

"Nonsense," said Mother Bickerdyke. "What you fight with is *men*. A man without a gun can still fight some, but if all you've got is a gun without a man, where are you?"

Then she began to coax, in that warm, soft, Come-be-a-good-boy-

and-do-what-Mamma-says way that she could use sometimes. "You've given me the job of keeping your men fit to fight. And I know what I need for that better than you do. I've fixed it up for most of the Sanitary stores to be picked up as we go along."

"Oh, you have, have you?" said Sherman looking at her sharply.

"Don't look at me like that," she said. "I've got some sense the same as you have. And all I want is for you to sign this order now, for two train-loads of stores to come up here. That's all, and you won't be bothered again."

He took the paper, and, as he signed his name, he said, "What's this I heard you telling the boys one night about your husband, Mrs. Bickerdyke?"

"I said that he was a mild, good man, and we lived happily together for twenty-five years, and I said he'd be living yet, except for one thing."

"What was that?"

"He wore himself out trying to boss me."

She picked up the paper, and, as his twinkling eyes met the sweet azure that would be in her eyes when she was content, she added. "I said to the boys, 'Let that be a lesson to you. *Never try to boss a woman.*'"

5

Practically nothing that had hitherto been wrong with the care and preservation of military man-power was wrong with that extraordinary march of Sherman from the mountains to the sea. No dropping off of the tired or the sick or the discouraged here. The men were reviewed by the surgeons every day. Tired or ailing men were picked up and rode along on wheeled carts for a day or two till they felt strong enough to join the march again. Under Mrs. Bickerdyke's direction, 300 rude hospitals were built, staffed, and equipped all along the way, with the help of Sanitary Commission agents who, by devious trails joined the army, from time to time with extra hospital stores. Wounded men were promptly rescued and well nursed. The foresight of the commander, the excellence of the army ambulance and field service, organized according to the plan worked out on the Peninsula and functioning well under good army surgeons, and the skill and ingenuity of the many United States Sanitary Commission agents who brought their stores and workers to the relief of the army at various points—all these deserved much credit.

But the soldiers thought they knew who had seen them so victoriously through Georgia and on to the end of the war. For when all was ended, and Lee had surrendered, and the Fifteenth Army Corps staged its "Victory March" back to Washington to join the Grand Review, on May 23, 1865, they had Mrs. Bickerdyke, riding on a magnificent charger, at the head of the parade, dressed in a calico dress and sunbonnet, such as she had worn in Georgia, with a string of the medals with which she had been decorated across her ample bosom.

With fife and drum the army marched riotously through Alexandria and crossed the Long Bridge between that town and Washington, led by Mother Bickerdyke. At the Washington end of the bridge Mother Bickerdyke was met by Dorothea Dix, riding out at the head of a troop of army nurses, and followed by marching soldiers, and there she was welcomed home with her boys in the name of the American people.

A Committee which had been appointed to collect and preserve the most cherished relics of the war then asked Mrs. Bickerdyke if she would sell her calico dress and bonnet. She sold them the costume for $100 which she immediately distributed in little gifts to the boys "where it will do most good." Asked to write her own record, she wrote simply: "I served in our Civil War from June 9, 1861, to March 20, 1865. I was in nineteen hard-fought battles in the departments of the Ohio, Tennessee, and Cumberland armies. I did the work of one, and I tried to do it well."

EPILOGUE

Happily Ever Afterward

And what happened to them all after the war was over? The answer is pleasant and heartening.

Because, as Doctor Bellows said, the women kept their men "half civilians" by making themselves through four years of war and lonely separation "half soldiers," the war ended in a "homogeneousness of feeling" very much greater than that with which it had begun. And this great army of 2,500,000 men, many times the size of any military force that had ever been assembled in the world before, laid down its arms, and demobilized into communities wonderfully well organized to receive them and put them again to peacetime work.

Because of the "immense correspondence between the army and the homes, prodigious beyond belief, some regiments sending home 1,000 letters a week, and receiving as many back," said Doctor Bellows, the soldiers through four years had felt "all the impulses of home strengthening their arms and encouraging their hearts. The influence on the tone of their correspondence exerted by the fact that the women were always working for the army, and that the soldiers always knew that they were working, and were always receiving evidence of their care, may be better imagined than described. It largely ministered to that sympathetic unity between the soldier and the country, which made our army always a corrective and an inspiration to our governmental policy, and kept up that fine reciprocal influence between civil and military life, which gave an heroic fibre to all souls at home, and finally restored to us our soldiers with their citizen hearts beating regularly under their uniforms as they dropped them off on the last drum-tap."

Most of the groups and the individuals involved in this work for the army continued their public ministrations in ways that bless our country to this day. The aid societies were busy for many years in helping the soldiers re-establish themselves in civil life and in caring for the widows and the orphans. Mrs. Bickerdyke devoted her great talents to this for a decade following the war. Having earned the admiration of the medical profession by the way she mastered medicine during the war, at fifty she was admitted to the legal profession, as a pension attorney for the soldiers. When she pleaded one of her first cases, she was introduced by General Logan, who said, "This is Mrs. Bickerdyke. What she wants is always right. And what she says is always the truth." Mother Bickerdyke also organized a scheme for settling Civil War soldiers on new lands in Kansas. After a long and valuable career, she finally settled down, in her very old age, at the home of her son, who was a professor at the University of Kansas, and died at 83, her finely modeled face more beautiful even in extreme old age than it had been in her magnificent prime.

Mary Livermore and Julia Ward Howe became the leaders for twenty-five years of the woman's suffrage and women's club movements, which opened the way for practically all the public and social activities of women in the world to-day. For several years after the war Louisa Lee Schuyler, like many of those Civil War heroines, was an invalid, as a result of her great exertions during the conflict. But in 1872 she had recovered sufficiently to carry the old work of the Women's Central forward in a magnificent new attack on suffering and disease. In a meeting of men and women at her father's house, she organized the State Charities Aid Association of New York State, of which she remained the guiding spirit for the next fifty years, and thus became the creator of modern social work. In 1874 she participated in founding the first training school in America for nurses, at Bellevue Hospital in New York City. In 1923 she was awarded the Roosevelt medal, as the woman who had virtually founded and had led for fifty years the two great professions of nursing and social work. "The principles she promulgated fifty years ago have become the commonplace of modern philanthropy."

Others among the famous young women of the Union soldiers' saga had also great pioneer careers. Miss Mary Safford, the little

Angel of Cairo, who so sadly disappeared from public notice after the Battle of Shiloh, where she had injured her spine, ultimately recovered. She studied medicine, and became a pioneer woman physician in Boston, with a delightful home which she made a social center for children whom she had adopted. Katherine Wormeley, who had had a factory where wives and mothers of soldiers made army shirts, later established the Girls' Industrial School of Newport, Rhode Island. And meanwhile she had a long and quietly distinguished literary career as translator and interpreter of French literature.

The gentlemen whom the ladies had associated with them in their work also carried on. The various devoted and able men who formed the Branch Sanitary Commissions and board of managers for the Ladies' Aid societies were absorbed into the Union League Clubs, founded by Doctor Bellows and Frederick Olmsted in 1863, which did a great and effective work in socially implementing the military victory of the Union armies. Of the work of Doctor Bellows as one of the founders of Antioch College in Yellow Springs, Ohio, it is hardly necessary to speak, nor of the great career of Frederick Olmsted as founder of the art of landscape gardening in the United States, and creator of city and national park systems and college campuses. The campus of the University of California at Berkeley, the National Park at Yosemite, the Riverside Drive and Morningside Drive in New York City, parks in Boston, Chicago, Hartford—all over the country—are a legacy to us from the man who spent the Civil War years in helping the ladies see that military camps had decent drains.

Meanwhile various philanthropic gentlemen whose pocketbooks the Ladies' Aids had expertly and systematically tapped for the soldiers during the war acquired such an admiration for female ability that, when the soldiers no longer needed the money, they were ready to devote their fortunes to the ladies themselves. There was, for example, a brewer in Poughkeepsie, New York, who was induced to set up for the Ladies' Aid the "Vassar Sanitary Emporium." To it, in one of those great sanitary fairs started by Mary Livermore, all the good people up and down the Hudson River brought their gifts and produce to be sold for the soldiers. This was such an education for Matthew Vassar that he proceeded to establish Vassar College to give the female mentality, whose worth he had discovered, a chance for training equal to that of men. Up in Ithaca, New York, Ezra Cornell was similarly impressed, and founded Sage College for Women as part of Cornell University.

One thing that universally impressed the many gentlemen whose time or money the Ladies' Aid societies commandeered was the "perfect aptitude of women for business." By the end of the Civil War this Sanitary Commission enterprise which the ladies had started, and of which they remained to the end the backbone, was worth about $50,000,000. And in those days that was a very large business enterprise, indeed. They had the co-operation of all railroads and express companies in transporting their stores free, and of the telegraph companies in sending their messages free. They had many and intricate arrangements for co-operation with the army. They had, in all, about 32,000 groups of women, large and small, organized as co-operating Ladies' Aid societies.

To keep this vast network of business in any kind of order was a test of efficiency in detail and in over-all organization to which the housewives of the land had risen nobly. As Doctor Bellows said, in a message quoted, with endorsement by Limus P. Brockett, a merchant of New York, "A generous emulation among the branches of the United States Sanitary Commission, managed generally by women, usually, however, with some aid from men, brought their business habits and methods to an almost perfect finish. . . . They acknowledged and answered, endorsed and filed their letters; they sorted their stores and kept an accurate account of stock; they had their books and reports kept in the most approved forms; they balanced their cash accounts with the most painstaking precision; they exacted of each other regularity of attendance and punctiliousness of official etiquette."

They did even more than this. They created and introduced into the government records the first complete clerical system any army had ever had. It was their careful registering of the soldiers that formed the basis of the pension system for Civil War veterans.

Because of this aptitude for business the women had displayed, Silas Sadler Packard, the great pioneer in business education, announced that the school of business which he was founding in New York City, and which still carries on under the name of The Packard Commercial School, was prepared to train "female amanuenses." No large number of applicants at first appeared, perhaps because the businesslike housewives of the aid societies were

206

at that moment too busy trying to find jobs for husbands and sons demobilized from the army. But slowly, at first, and finally in great resistless numbers, women found their way into the business and clerical positions that, in this war, have become practically a monopoly of women.

Withal, the greatest modern representative of the old U. S. Sanitary Commission and the affiliated Ladies' Aid societies is the American Red Cross, founded by the plucky little individualist from Massachusetts, Clara Barton.

Throughout the Civil War the work of the United States Sanitary Commission had been carefully watched in Europe, and publicized by an international committee, headed by a Swiss, Henri Dunant, with headquarters in Geneva, Switzerland. With this Committee the United States Sanitary Commission had a co-operating agent, Mr. Charles Bowles. Mr. Bowles explained the workings of the Commission in detail to a meeting of the diplomatic representatives of several nations called at Geneva in 1863. At this meeting a committee was appointed to secure the agreement of all national governments to the formation of an international relief organization to be called The Red Cross. Doctor Bellows, as chairman of the United States Sanitary Commission, was asked to found a Red Cross society in America and to secure the co-operation of the American government.

The American society was founded in 1866, but it had a short life. Doctor Bellows was unable to interest either the American government or the American people in it. Our officials took the position that we were never going to have another war, and that we should not join a society that concerned itself with Europeans who made war.

There the matter rested until 1869, when Clara Barton went to Geneva in an effort to recover her health. She was one of the many Civil War heroines who had been invalided by her excessive work during the war and immediately after it. In Geneva a delegation from the International Red Cross called on her. They had come to ask the great American heroine why, when thirty-one nations had ratified an agreement largely inspired by the magnificent creation of the American people—the United States Sanitary Commission—the Americans would still have nothing to do with it. Miss Barton had never heard of the Red Cross. But she listened attentively and made friends of the Red Cross representatives.

The following year, while she was still in Europe, the Franco-Prussian War broke out. This was the first chance for the Red Cross societies to go into action. Miss Barton joined them, went to the front, and took the lead in organizing relief on the patterns of the Sanitary Commission, but with many improvements. In four months, she said, "we had a whole continent marshalled under the flag of the Red Cross, working instead of weeping, nursing instead of waiting." She served through the war, and through the cruel days that followed in France, and returned to the United States utterly broken and ill, to years of helplessness, in which, as she said, "I forgot how to walk."

When she began to recover, her Red Cross friends again importuned her to renew the agitation for ratification of the Geneva Convention by the American government. In 1880, she carried her plea to Robert Todd Lincoln, son of Abraham Lincoln, and then Secretary of War. He introduced the idea to the State Department and later to the Senate and House of Representatives. After some further ups and downs, the Convention was ratified on March 1, 1882, and the American Red Cross was founded, with Clara Barton as its first president.

Over the white national headquarters of the American Red Cross in Washington stands this inscription: "Erected to the Memory of the Women of the Civil War." Their work, says one of the old historians of the Commission, "shines with ever fresh beauty in the dark background of civil strife. It is the true glory of our age and of our country. May it ever prove a beacon, to warn, to guide, and to encourage those who, in future ages, and in other countries, may be afflicted with the dire calamity of war."

BIBLIOGRAPHICAL NOTE

The documentation for this story is immense, most of it covered with the dust of oblivion which fell on it at the end of the Civil War and which has not been disturbed by the curious hand of any scholar to this day.

The fundamental source is the Archives of the United States Sanitary Commission, consisting of nearly a thousand large boxes of documents, invoices, receipts, letters, circulars, and miscellaneous items. These were deposited in the Astor Library, on January 7, 1879, by Doctor Henry Bellows, together with $4,000 to provide for their proper housing on suitable shelves, under expert guardianship. In making the transfer, Dr. Bellows wrote:

"It is a great relief to deposit our archives in the care of such experienced trustees, and we may lay down the burdens and cares of eighteen years of oversight and direction with a sense of great relief and of gratitude to those whose Hospitality shelters our record of our work.

"With this act and with my signature as President of the United States Sanitary Commission—the last official act of my service— the United States Sanitary Commission expires. You receive its ashes in which, I hope, some fragrance may linger, and at least a spark survive to kindle in time of need a flame equal to its own."

Besides the Archives, the Astor Library has a large number of individual documents and circulars of the United States Sanitary Commission which had come into its hands from time to time during the Civil War and which are listed in the catalogue in the American History room.

However, the well-trained professional persons who formed the backbone of the Commission did not trust their great story exclusively to the dusty incarceration of Archives. Among the leaders of the Commission were several excellent writers, each of whom put the story on paper. Among these records are:

My Story of the War by Mary Ashton Rice Livermore (Hartford, 1889); *The U. S. Sanitary Commission in the Valley of the Mississippi, 1861-1866.* Final report by Doctor J. S. Newberry, Secretary of the Western Department (Cleveland, 1871); *Hospital Transports, a Memoir of the Embarkation of the Sick and Wounded from the Peninsula of Virginia in the summer of 1862, Compiled and published at the request of the Sanitary Commission* by Frederick Law Olmsted (Boston, 1863); *Soldiers' letters from Camp, Battlefield, and Prison, edited and published for the United States Sanitary Commission* by Lydia Minturn Post (New York, 1865); *The History of the United States Sanitary Commission, being the General Report of its Work During the War of the Rebellion,* by Charles Janeway Still, one of the members of the Commission (Philadelphia, 1866); *The United States Sanitary Commission, a Sketch of Its Purposes and Its Work* by Katherine P. Wormeley (Boston, 1863); *The Cruel Side of War with the Army of the Potomac, Letters from the Headquarters of the U. S. Sanitary Commission during the Peninsular Campaign in Virginia in 1862* (Boston, 1863); *The Other Side of War,* a reprint of *The Cruel Side of War* by Katherine P. Wormeley (Boston, 1889).

Other contemporary publications of the United States Sanitary Commission include: *Documents of the United States Sanitary Commission,* 2 vols. (New York, 1866); *The United States Sanitary Commission Bulletin,* 3 vols. (New York, 1866); *The Sanitary Reporter,* May 15, 1863-August 15, 1865, published bi-monthly for the Western Department of the United States Sanitary Commission and *Surgical Memoirs of the War of the Rebellion, Collected and Published by the United States Sanitary Commission,* Cambridge, 1870-71.

The work of the local women's societies and of individual women was described in *Women, or Chronicles of the Late War* by Mary Tucker Magill (Baltimore, 1871); *The Women of the War, Their Heroism and Self-Sacrifice* by Frank Moore (Hartford, 1867); and *Woman's Work in the Civil War* by Mrs. M. C. Vaughn and Linus P. Brockett (Philadelphia, 1868).

An interesting book full of current newspaper reports and cartoons is *The Tribute Book, a Record of the Munificence, Self-Sacrifice, and Patriotism of the American People During the War for the Union* by Frank B. Goodrich (New York, 1865).

The interest abroad, among Europeans in general, and the Geneva Committee of Henri Dunant in particular, was ministered to by at least two reports in French on the United States Sanitary Commission. One was *La Commission Sanitaire des Etats Unis* (Paris, 1865) and the other was *L'Oeuvre d'un Grand Peuple* by J. Proeschel (Paris, 1864). An English report on the Sanitary Commission was entitled *A Woman's Example and a Nation's Work. A Tribute to Florence Nightingale* by Frederick Milnes Edge (London, 1864).

Unfortunately I did not have space in which to deal adequately with the Western Sanitary Commission of St. Louis, which was distinct from the Western Branch of the U. S. Sanitary Commission, under Doctor Newberry, with headquarters in Cleveland, and the

Northwest Sanitary Commission, under Mary A. Livermore, with headquarters at Chicago. The Western Sanitary Commission operated in territory that was either Southern in sympathy or had recently been reconquered from the South. It could not be organized in the same way as the Commission in loyal territory as an advisory board of professional managers for fairly independent and self-directing women's societies. Organized by Miss Dorothea Dix and General Frémont, it functioned practically as a branch of the army. Any one interested in its noble and heroic story will find it in *The Western Sanitary Commission. A Sketch of Its Origin, History, Labors for the Sick and Wounded of the Western Armies, and Aid Given to Freed Men and Union Refugees, with Incidents of Hospital Life* (St. Louis, 1864).